CPAG'S

Housing Benefit and

Council Tax Benefit

Legislation

20th Edition

2007/2008

Supplement

Commentary by
Carolyn George *MA*
Stewart Wright *MA, Dip. Law, Barrister*

Statutory instruments up to date to 19 May 2008

Published by CPAG, 94 White Lion Street, London N1 9PF

CPAG promotes action for the prevention and relief of poverty among children and families with children. To achieve this, CPAG aims to raise awareness of the causes, extent, nature and impact of poverty, and strategies for its eradication and prevention; bring about positive policy changes for families with children in poverty; and enable those eligible for income maintenance to have access to their full entitlement. If you are not already supporting us, please consider making a donation, or ask for details of our membership schemes, training courses and publications.

Published by Child Poverty Action Group
94 White Lion Street, London N1 9PF
020 7837 7979

Child Poverty Action Group is a charity registered in England and Wales (registration number 294841) and in Scotland (registration number SC039339). Company limited by guarantee registered in England (registration number 1993854).

This book is sold subject to the condition that it shall not, by way of trade or otherwise, be lent, resold, hired out or otherwise circulated without the publisher's prior consent in any form of binding or cover other than that in which it is published and without a similar condition including this condition being imposed on the subsequent purchaser.

A CIP record for this book is available from the British Library

Main work: ISBN 978 1 906076 07 8

Supplement: ISBN 978 1 906076 08 5

Design by Devious Designs
Typeset by David Lewis XML Associates Limited
Printed in the UK by CPI William Clowes Beccles NR34 7TL

Contents

Introduction

A major change since the twentieth edition of the main work has been the introduction of new housing benefit rent restriction rules – the 'local housing allowance' (LHA) rules from 7 April 2008. These follow from a pilot of the rules in 18 Pathfinder areas from late 2003, although the national scheme differs from the pilot scheme in a number of respects.

From 7 April 2008, there will be three schemes for rent restriction: the 'local housing allowance' rules, the 'local reference rent' rules and the 'pre-January 1996' rules (the latter applying to 'exempt tenants' and those living in 'exempt accommodation'). The rules are complex; the challenge for local authorities, claimants and their advisers will be to ensure that the correct scheme is applied in any particular case. An added difficulty is that until 6 April 2009, there will be two versions of some of the Housing Benefit Regulations 2006 and the Housing Benefit (Persons who have attained the qualifying age for state pension credit) Regulations 2006. It should be noted that the amending regulations (and amending order) were themselves amended prior to them taking effect. The amendments are shown in the affected Statutory Instruments in this Supplement.

Included in the Supplement is a table of comparative housing benefit and council tax benefit provisions. It is hoped this will enable readers to locate relevant commentary more easily.

Many thanks go to Richard Poynter for his support and helpful suggestions. Thanks are also due to Nicola Johnston for her efficient help and careful editing of this work.

Comments on this supplement and the main work are welcomed, and can be sent to the authors via CPAG.

Carolyn George and Stewart Wright

Table of cases

Table of commissioners' decisions

Table of comparative provisions

HB Regs	CTB Regs	HB Regs	CTB Regs
1	1	52	42
2(1)	2(1)	53	43
2(2)		54	44
	2(2) – (3)	55-58	
2(3)	2(4)		45
2(4)		59	46
	2(5)-(6)	60	47
3	3	61	48
4	4	62	49
5	5	63	50
6	6	64	51
7	8	64A	51A
8-9		65	52
10	7	66	53
10A	7A	67	54
11-18A		68	55
19	9	69	56
20	10	70-71	
21	11		57
22	12	72	60
23	13	73	61
25	15	74	58
26	16	75	
27	17		59
28	18		62-63
29	19	76	64
30	20	77	65
31	21	78	66
32	22	79	67
33	23	80-81	
34	24	82	68
35	25	83	69
36	26	84	70
37	27	85	71
38	28	86	72
39	29	87	73
40	30	88	74
41	11	89	75
42	12	90	76
43	13	91-96	
44	34		77-79
45	35	97	80
46	36	98	81
47	37	99-102	
48	38		82-87
49	39	103	88
50	40	104	89
51	41	105	90

HB Regs	CTB Regs	HB Regs	CTB Regs
107		Sch 5/6-17	Sch 4/7-18
108	91	Sch 5/18	Sch 4/64
109	92	Sch 5/19-22	Sch 4/19-22
110	93	Sch 5/23-35	Sch 4/24-36
111	94		Sch 4/37
112	95	Sch 5/36-41	Sch 4/38-43
113-114		Sch 5/42	Sch 4/23
115	96	Sch 5/43-50	Sch 4/44-51
116	97	Sch 5/51	
117-122		Sch 5/52-63	Sch 4/52-63
		Sch 6/1-28	Sch 5/1-28
Sch A1	Sch A1	Sch 6/29	Sch 5/30
Sch 1		Sch 6/30	Sch 5/29
Sch 2		Sch 6/43	Sch 5/31-43
Sch 3	Sch 1		Sch 5/44
	Sch 2	Sch 6/44	Sch 5/45
Sch 4/1-15	Sch 3/1-15		Sch 5/46
Sch 4/16	Sch 3/17	Sch 6/45-60	Sch 5/47-62
Sch 4/17	Sch 3/16	Sch 7	Sch 6
Sch 5/1-5	Sch 4/1-5	Sch 8	Sch 7
	Sch 4/6	Sch 9	Sch 8

How to use this supplement

Use the Noter-up to find out about changes to the main volume. The page numbers on the left refer to pages in the main volume. The entry opposite either states what the change is or refers to another part of this supplement where the amending legislation is set out.

For abbreviations, see the table on pxxxv of the main volume.

PART I: NOTER UP

General
Note

The amounts for, for example, personal allowances, premiums, non-dependant deductions and deductions from rent are confirmed/uprated by the Social Security Benefits Up-rating Order 2008 SI No.632 as from 1 April 2008 (7 April 2008 if rent is payable weekly or in multiples of a week).

pp10-11   SSCBA 1992 s130

Subsection (4) ceases to have effect by s30(1) of the Welfare Reform Act 2007 as from 7 April 2008, save for the transitional and savings provisions in the Welfare Reform Act 2007 (Commencement No.4, and Savings and Transitional Provisions) Order 2007 SI No.2872.

p11   SSCBA 1992 new s130A

New s130A inserted by s30(2) of the Welfare Reform Act 2007 as from 7 April 2008.

pp35-36   SSAA 1992 s5

Subsections (2A), (2B) and (2C) inserted and subsection (3) ceases to have effect by s35 of the Welfare Reform Act 2007 as from 7 April 2008, save for the transitional and savings provisions in the Welfare Reform Act 2007 (Commencement No.4, and Savings and Transitional Provisions) Order 2007 SI No.2872.

pp42-45   SSAA 1992 s75

[p45: after the first paragraph of the analysis of Subsection (3) add a new paragraph:]

In *CH 3622/2006* the claimant had been overpaid HB and CTB when his wife failed to disclose her entitlement to an occupational pension. The local authority contended that the liability to repay the overpayment lay with the claimant's wife as well as the claimant because 'the claim has always been a joint claim'. Agreeing with *CH 3817/2004*, Commissioner Howell said that there cannot be a 'joint claim' by a couple, as the regulations clearly require any claim for HB or CTB to be made by just one of them. The overpayment was only recoverable from the claimant, and not from his wife, since she was not the claimant or recipient of any of the awards in question and the decision was not addressed to her, nor did it purport to make any overpaid or excess benefit recoverable from her so as to give rise to any such liability, or any separate right of appeal for her under paragraph 6(6) of Sch 7 CSPSSA or reg 3 of the D&A Regs.

pp54-55   SSAA 1992 s110A

Subsections (1), (2) and (8) amended and subsections (1A) to (1C) inserted by s46 of the Welfare Reform Act 2007 as from 19 February 2008 (for making regulations) and 7 April 2008.

pp54-55   SSAA 1992 new s116A

New s116A inserted by s47 of the Welfare Reform Act 2007 as from 19 February 2008 (for making regulations) and 7 April 2008.

pp76-79   SSAA 1992 s123

Subsection (8)(ja) amended by s146 and Sch 9 of the Local Government and Public Involvement in Health Act 2007 as from 1 April 2008.

p86   SSAA 1992 new s139BA

New s139BA inserted by s150 of the Local Government and Public Involvement in Health Act 2007 as from 1 April 2008.

pp87-88   SSAA 1992 s139D
Subsections (1), (2) and (4) amended, subsections (2A) to (2C), (3A) to (3C) and (4A) to (4E) inserted and subsection (3) substituted by s39(1) to (8) of the Welfare Reform Act 2007 as from 1 April 2008.

Subsection (1)(bb) inserted by s147(2) of the Local Government and Public Involvement in Health Act 2007 as from 1 April 2008.

p88   SSAA 1992 new s139DA
New s139DA inserted by s39(9) of the Welfare Reform Act 2007 as from 1 April 2008.

p88   SSAA 1992 s139E
Subsection (1) amended by s40 and Sch 5 para 5 of the Welfare Reform Act 2007 as from 1 April 2008.

pp88-89   SSAA 1992 s139F
Subsections (1), (2) and (4) amended and subsection (4A) inserted by s40 and Sch 5 para 6 of the Welfare Reform Act 2007 as from 1 April 2008.

pp89-90   SSAA 1992 s139G
Subsections (1), (3) and (5) amended by s40 and Sch 5 para 7 of the Welfare Reform Act 2007 as from 1 April 2008.

pp91-92   SSAA 1992 s140B
Subsection (5A) amended by s40 and Sch 5 para 9 of the Welfare Reform Act 2007 as from 1 April 2008.

pp139-141   HRA 1998 Schedule 1. First Protocol, Art 1

[p140: within the first paragraph of the analysis on p140, replace 'In R (Couronne) . . . the High Court' in the sentence beginning with that phrase, with:]

In *Couronne and Others v Crawley Borough Council, the Secretary of State for Work and Pensions and the First Secretary of State* [2007] EWCA Civ 1086, 2 November 2007, unreported, the Court of Appeal...

[p140: at the end of the first paragraph of analysis on p140, delete the final sentence beginning 'Moreover, although in R(RJM) . . . .', and replace with:]

Whether of not *Stec* applies in the UK should be resolved by the House of Lords in June 2008 when it hears the appeal of the claimant from the Court of Appeal's decision in *R(RJM) v Secretary of State for Work and Pensions* [2007] EWCA Civ 614.

pp147-176   CSPSSA 2000 Sch 7
Para 4 amended by s30(3) of the Welfare Reform Act 2007 as from 7 April 2008.

[p162: in the analysis to paragraph 7, after the second paragraph under: 'Scope of the right of appeal: failure to exercise inquisitorial jurisdiction' add a new paragraph:]

An appeal by the claimant in *CH 1220/2005* was unsuccessful: *Mote v Secretary of State for Work and Pensions and Chichester District Council* [2007], unreported, EWCA Civ 1324 14 December 2007. The Court rejected an argument that under the Human Rights Act 1998, the civil court or tribunal had a duty to safeguard the claimant's rights in criminal proceedings and must not proceed if to do so would breach those rights. It also rejected the contention that proceeding with the tribunal before the criminal proceedings would provide the DWP or local authority with an unfair opportunity to rehearse the criminal trial and also the contention that proceeding was a breach of the claimant's right to silence. The claimant had been obliged to make early disclosure in the criminal proceedings, and there was not one example of how at the criminal trial it would have been damaging for the claimant to have participated in the appeal tribunal hearing.

pp185-194   HB Regs reg 2

Definitions of 'eligible rent', 'housing association', 'maximum rent', 'non-dependant deduction', 'Rent Officers Order' and 'young individual' substituted and definitions of 'amended determination', 'broad rental market area', 'broad rental market area determination', 'linked person', 'local housing allowance', 'maximum rent (LHA)', 'reckonable rent', 'registered housing association', 'relevant information', and 'single room rent' inserted by reg 4(1) of the Housing Benefit (Local Housing Allowance and Information Sharing) Amendment Regulations 2007 SI No.2868, as amended by reg 4(3) of the Housing Benefit (Local Housing Allowance, Information Sharing and Miscellaneous) Amendment Regulations 2008 SI No. 586, as from 7 April 2008, save that for someone to whom reg 1(5) of those regulations apply, the amendments come into force on the day on or after 7 April 2008 when the first of the events specified in reg 1(6) applies to her/him, or on 6 April 2009 if none have before that date.

Definition of 'Intensive Activity Period for 50 plus' omitted by reg 6(2) of the Social Security (Miscellaneous Amendments) Regulations 2008 SI No. 698 as from 14 April 2008.

Definition of 'concessionary payment' amended and definition of 'person on state pension credit' omitted by reg 3(2) of the Social Security (Miscellaneous Amendments)(No.2) Regulations 2008 SI No.1042 as from 19 May 2008.

pp199-200   HB Regs reg 3

Para (4) amended by reg 4(2) of the Housing Benefit (Local Housing Allowance and Information Sharing) Amendment Regulations 2007 SI No.2868 as from 7 April 2008, save that for someone to whom reg 1(5) of those regulations apply, the amendments come into force on the day on or after 7 April 2008 when the first of the events specified in reg 1(6) applies to her/him, or on 6 April 2009 if none have before that date.

pp206-210   HB Regs reg 7

Para (8)(c)(ii) amended by reg 3(3) of the Social Security (Miscellaneous Amendments)(No.2) Regulations 2008 SI No.1042 as from 19 May 2008.

pp223-239   HB Regs reg 9

[p234: in the analysis to paragraph (1)(h): Former owners, at the end of the first complete paragraph on p234 ending '...unamended form of regulation 7(1)(h).' add:]

Commissioner Angus agreed with this interpretation in *CH 3220/2005*. He said that there is no ambiguity in the wording of either the old or the new version of sub-paragraph (h) which would warrant reading into them a proviso or a precondition of continual occupation: paragraph 10.

pp223-239   HB Regs reg 9

[p235: in the analysis to paragraph 9(1)(l): Contrived agreements, after the paragraph beginning 'l. General Principles' add a new paragraph:]

Commissioner Jacobs dealt with the meaning of 'to take advantage of the scheme' in *CH 39/ 2007*. He said that it means something akin to abuse of the scheme or taking improper advantage of it. It did not mean merely using the scheme, nor did it mean 'make the most of the opportunities that it presents'. If it did, there would be no market for tenants requiring financial support for their rent. He said at paragraph 19: 'Many landlords use the housing benefit scheme as a way of financing the purchase of property as an investment or of financing a business, but it is not the function of regulation 9(1)(l) to impede the proper operation of the private rented housing sector.' The provision had to be interpreted in the context of other control mechanisms provided for in the legislation – eg, the various rules for restricting 'eligible rent', now in regs 12C to 14 of both the HB and the HB(SPC) Regs.

pp239-251   HB Regs reg 10

[p246: at the end of the first paragraph under EC Directive 2004/38, add:]

The Directive does not, however, codify all rights of residence for EU nationals. For example, it plainly does not address the right to reside of EU workseekers, who can qualify for JSA by 'signing-on' and seeking work; a right which arises directly under Article 39 of the EC Treaty (see *Antonissen* [1991] ECR I-745). Where other gaps (if any) lie in the Directive has been the subject of a number of commissioners' and court decisions. At the forefront of these has been whether the Directive replaces (and then cuts down on) the rights of EU national parents to remain in the UK while their children complete their school education where the children had been installed in education when the parent(s) was in work. This right was said to derive from Article 12 of EC Regulation 1612/68 (which has *not* been) revoked by Directive 2004/38 and the ECJ's decision in *Baumbast* [2002] ECR I-7091. Different commissioners have arrived at different conclusions as to whether *Baumbast* remains effective and what its precise scope is (contrast *CIS 1685/2007* with *CIS 3444/2006*), thus leaving it open to decision makers and tribunals to choose which approach they prefer. However, in *Harrow LBC v Ibrahim* (a housing case) the Court of Appeal has referred to the ECJ certain questions as to the scope and application of *Baumbast* in a right to reside context. For whether Art 18(1) of the EC Treaty may, exceptionally, be used to fill gaps left by Directive 2004/38 see *CIS 408/2006*.

[p247: after the penultimate sentence in Analysis under (1)(c), beginning 'The commissioner was not, however...' add:]

Commissioner Jacobs declined to follow Commissioner Rowland's approach in *CIS 4144/2007* (para 24).

[p250: at the end of the paragraph beginning 'Note that although Zalewska..' add the following sentence and then a new paragraph, as follows]

Zalewska is under appeal to the House of Lords.

In *CIS 3232/2006* (and others), Commissioner Rowland followed *Zalewska* in rejecting arguments by A8 nationals that it was unnecessary for them to have been in registered employment for 12 months and that all that was required was that they had been lawfully in employment in the UK for 12 months. In the commissioner's view the requirement that for the work to count it had to be registered was both lawful and proportionate.

[p251: before the last sentence in the last paragraph under the Analysis to Paragraph (3B)(k) insert:]

The same Deputy Commissioner has now accepted these criticisms in *CIS 34/2006* and others (paragraph 47), and has recanted from what he said in paragraph 39 of *R(H) 9/04*. However, he went on to rule in *CIS 34/2006* that a person is not 'in receipt' of income support for a period where it has later been established that they were not entitled to that benefit.

[p252: delete the final two paragraphs of the General Note on Part 3 and add:]

From 7 April 2008, regs 12 to 12D set out what is 'eligible rent' for HB purposes, and regs 13 to 14 set out the schemes for restricting this. It is important to note the transitional protection and modifications that exist in relation to these regulations.

New HB rent restriction rules – the 'local housing allowance' (LHA) rules – are being introduced nationwide from 7 April 2008, adding a new layer of complexity. An added difficulty for local authorities, claimants and their advisors is that until 6 April 2009, there will be two versions of some of the HB Regs and the HB(SPC) Regs.

There will now be three schemes for rent restriction: the 'local housing allowance' rules, the 'local reference rent' rules and the 'pre-January 1996' rules (the latter applying to 'exempt tenants' and those living in 'exempt accommodation').

The Government's intention is that if a claimant's HB was being restricted under any of the rules that applied before 7 April 2008, it will continue to be restricted under the same rules, until there is a break in her/his claim or s/he moves to a new home while entitled to HB. From that point, HB will be restricted (if relevant) under whichever rules then apply.

The LHA rules were piloted in 18 Pathfinder areas from late 2003. The new LHA rules will apply to those living in a former Pathfinder area to whom the pilot rules applied before 7 April 2008. The pilot rules were more generous in some respects than the new LHA rules. Some transitional protection is provided. For a summary of the new LHA rules, see the article *'The 'local housing allowance' rules'* in CPAG's *Welfare Rights Bulletin* 202.

p252   HB Regs reg 11
Para (1) substituted and para (3) amended by reg 4(3) of the Housing Benefit (Local Housing Allowance and Information Sharing) Amendment Regulations 2007 SI No.2868 as from 7 April 2008, save that for someone to whom reg 1(5) of those regulations apply, the amendments come into force on the day on or after 7 April 2008 when the first of the events specified in reg 1(6) applies to her/him, or on 6 April 2009 if none have before that date.

pp253-259   HB Regs reg 12
Paras (3) to (7) omitted and para (8) amended by reg 4(3) of the Housing Benefit (Local Housing Allowance and Information Sharing) Amendment Regulations 2007 SI No.2868 as from 7 April 2008, save that for someone to whom reg 1(5) of those regulations apply, the amendments come into force on the day on or after 7 April 2008 when the first of the events specified in reg 1(6) applies to her/him, or on 6 April 2009 if none have before that date.

[p257: in the analysis to Subpara (f) delete 'but the following definitions ... Tax Act 1994)'. Before the final paragraph add a new paragraph:]

In *CH 4250/2006*, Commissioner Levenson pointed out that the legislation could have defined the term but did not. He said at paragraph 19 that for HB purposes 'houseboat' is an ordinary English word without a technical meaning and that it is a matter of fact in any particular case whether a boat is a 'houseboat' in this sense. He found it difficult to imagine a case in which a reasonable tribunal would conclude that a boat which is fitted out as a dwelling suitable for permanent residence is not a houseboat. Definitions in other legislation or regulations for different purposes (eg, tax liability) are not relevant. These might reflect or inform common usage but cannot define 'houseboat' for HB purposes. Neither can the classification for the purposes of licensing, or the operation of other schemes, such as the definition of a houseboat used in paragraph 38 of the British Waterways Boat Licence and Permit Conditions.

[p258: in the third paragraph under Paragraph (5) of the analysis substitute 'CH 3376/2002' for 'CH 3776/2002'.]

p259   HB Regs new regs 12B, 12C and 12D
New regs 12B, 12C and 12D inserted by reg 5 of the Housing Benefit (Local Housing Allowance and Information Sharing) Amendment Regulations 2007 SI No.2868 as from 7 April 2008, save that for someone to whom reg 1(5) of those regulations apply, the amendments come into force on the day on or after 7 April 2008 when the first of the events specified in reg 1(6) applies to her/him, or on 6 April 2009 if none have before that date.

pp259-262   HB Regs reg 13
Reg 13 substituted by reg 6 of the Housing Benefit (Local Housing Allowance and Information Sharing) Amendment Regulations 2007 SI No.2868 as from 7 April 2008, save that for someone to whom reg 1(5) of those regulations apply, the amendments come into force on

the day on or after 7 April 2008 when the first of the events specified in reg 1(6) applies to her/him, or on 6 April 2009 if none have before that date.

p265   HB Regs new regs 13ZA and 13ZB
New regs 13ZA and 13ZB inserted by reg 6 of the Housing Benefit (Local Housing Allowance and Information Sharing) Amendment Regulations 2007 SI No.2868 as from 7 April 2008, save that for someone to whom reg 1(5) of those regulations apply, the amendments come into force on the day on or after 7 April 2008 when the first of the events specified in reg 1(6) applies to her/him, or on 6 April 2009 if none have before that date.

p265   HB Regs new regs 13C, 13D and 13E
New regs 13C, 13D and 13E inserted by reg 7 of the Housing Benefit (Local Housing Allowance and Information Sharing) Amendment Regulations 2007 SI No.2868, as amended by reg 4(4) of the Housing Benefit (Local Housing Allowance, Information Sharing and Miscellaneous) Amendment Regulations 2008 SI No.586, as from 7 April 2008, save that for someone to whom reg 1(5) of those regulations apply, the amendments come into force on the day on or after 7 April 2008 when the first of the events specified in reg 1(6) applies to her/him, or on 6 April 2009 if none have before that date.

pp265-267   HB Regs reg 14
Paras (1), (3) and (9) omitted and para (4A) inserted by reg 3(1) of the Housing Benefit (Local Housing Allowance and Information Sharing) Amendment Regulations 2007 SI No.2868, as amended by reg 4(2)(a) of the Housing Benefit (Local Housing Allowance, Information Sharing and Miscellaneous) Amendment Regulations 2008 SI No.586, as from 7 April 2008.

Reg 14 substituted by reg 8 of the Housing Benefit (Local Housing Allowance and Information Sharing) Amendment Regulations 2007 SI No.2868, as amended by reg 4(5) of the Housing Benefit (Local Housing Allowance, Information Sharing and Miscellaneous) Amendment Regulations 2008 SI No.586, as from 7 April 2008, save that for someone to whom reg 1(5) of those regulations apply, the amendments come into force on the day on or after 7 April 2008 when the first of the events specified in reg 1(6) applies to her/him, or on 6 April 2009 if none have before that date.

pp269-271   HB Regs regs 15 to 18
Regs 15 to 18 substituted by reg 9 of the Housing Benefit (Local Housing Allowance and Information Sharing) Amendment Regulations 2007 SI No.2868 as from 7 April 2008, save that for someone to whom reg 1(5) of those regulations apply, the amendments come into force on the day on or after 7 April 2008 when the first of the events specified in reg 1(6) applies to her/him, or on 6 April 2009 if none have before that date.

p271   HB Regs new reg 18A
New reg 18A inserted by reg 10 of the Housing Benefit (Local Housing Allowance and Information Sharing) Amendment Regulations 2007 SI No.2868 as from 7 April 2008, save that for someone to whom reg 1(5) of those regulations apply, the amendments come into force on the day on or after 7 April 2008 when the first of the events specified in reg 1(6) applies to her/him, or on 6 April 2009 if none have before that date.

pp285-288   HB Regs reg 28
Paras (11)(a), (b) and (g) amended by reg 3(4) of the Social Security (Miscellaneous Amendments)(No.2) Regulations 2008 SI No.1042 as from 19 May 2008.

p301   HB Regs reg 37
Paras (3) and (4) inserted by reg 6(3) of the Social Security (Miscellaneous Amendments) Regulations 2008 SI No.698 as from, as they relate to a particular beneficiary, the first day of the benefit week on or after 7 April 2008.

pp301-305   HB Regs reg 38

[p304: in the analysis to Paragraph 5, sub-para (d), substitute 'R(H) 5/08' for 'CH 1009/2007' (which should have read CH 1099/2007 in any event).]

pp309-312   HB Regs reg 42

Paras (7)(c)(iii) and (10(b)(i) amended by reg 6(4)(a) of the Social Security (Miscellaneous Amendments) Regulations 2008 SI No.698 as from 14 April 2008.

Paras (3) to (5) omitted by reg 3(5) of the Social Security (Miscellaneous Amendments)(No.2) Regulations 2008 SI No.1042 as from 19 May 2008.

pp320-321   HB Regs reg 49

Para (4)(b)(iii) amended by reg 6(4)(b) of the Social Security (Miscellaneous Amendments) Regulations 2008 SI No.698 as from 14 April 2008.

pp325-327   HB Regs reg 50

Para (4)(a) amended by reg 11 of the Housing Benefit (Local Housing Allowance and Information Sharing) Amendment Regulations 2007 SI No.2868 as from 7 April 2008, save that for someone to whom reg 1(5) of those regulations apply, the amendments come into force on the day on or after 7 April 2008 when the first of the events specified in reg 1(6) applies to her/him, or on 6 April 2009 if none have before that date.

pp332-335   HB Regs reg 53

Definitions of 'grant' and 'student loan' amended and definition of 'sandwich course' substituted by reg 3(6) of the Social Security (Miscellaneous Amendments)(No.2) Regulations 2008 SI No.1042 as from 19 May 2008.

pp339-340   HB Regs reg 56

Paras (2) and (4) amended by reg 3(7) of the Social Security (Miscellaneous Amendments)(No.2) Regulations 2008 SI No.1042 as from 19 May 2008.

pp350-351   HB Regs reg 63

Para (2) amended by reg 3(8) of the Social Security (Miscellaneous Amendments)(No.2) Regulations 2008 SI No.1042 as from 19 May 2008.

pp356-357   HB Regs reg 70

Reg 70 substituted by reg 12 of the Housing Benefit (Local Housing Allowance and Information Sharing) Amendment Regulations 2007 SI No.2868 as from 7 April 2008, save that for someone to whom reg 1(5) of those regulations apply, the amendments come into force on the day on or after 7 April 2008 when the first of the events specified in reg 1(6) applies to her/him, or on 6 April 2009 if none have before that date.

pp357-358   HB Regs reg 72

Para (4) amended by reg 13 of the Housing Benefit (Local Housing Allowance and Information Sharing) Amendment Regulations 2007 SI No.2868 as from 7 April 2008, save that for someone to whom reg 1(5) of those regulations apply, the amendments come into force on the day on or after 7 April 2008 when the first of the events specified in reg 1(6) applies to her/him, or on 6 April 2009 if none have before that date.

pp359-360   HB Regs reg 73

Para (4) amended by reg 13 of the Housing Benefit (Local Housing Allowance and Information Sharing) Amendment Regulations 2007 SI No.2868 as from 7 April 2008, save that for someone to whom reg 1(5) of those regulations apply, the amendments come into force on the day on or after 7 April 2008 when the first of the events specified in reg 1(6) applies to her/him, or on 6 April 2009 if none have before that date.

pp361-362 HB Regs reg 74

Reg 74 substituted by reg 14 of the Housing Benefit (Local Housing Allowance and Information Sharing) Amendment Regulations 2007 SI No.2868 as from 7 April 2008, save that for someone to whom reg 1(5) of those regulations apply, the amendments come into force on the day on or after 7 April 2008 when the first of the events specified in reg 1(6) applies to her/ him, or on 6 April 2009 if none have before that date.

pp369-370 HB Regs reg 79

Paras (1) and (3) amended by reg 15 of the Housing Benefit (Local Housing Allowance and Information Sharing) Amendment Regulations 2007 SI No.2868 as from 7 April 2008, save that for someone to whom reg 1(5) of those regulations apply, the amendments come into force on the day on or after 7 April 2008 when the first of the events specified in reg 1(6) applies to her/him, or on 6 April 2009 if none have before that date.

pp372-375 HB Regs regs 80 and 81

Regs 80 and 81 substituted by reg 16 of the Housing Benefit (Local Housing Allowance and Information Sharing) Amendment Regulations 2007 SI No.2868 as from 7 April 2008, save that for someone to whom reg 1(5) of those regulations apply, the amendments come into force on the day on or after 7 April 2008 when the first of the events specified in reg 1(6) applies to her/him, or on 6 April 2009 if none have before that date.

pp387-390 HB Regs reg 86

[p389: immediately aboveParagraph (3): The authority's obligations, add:]

The decision to seek certain information or seek it in certain ways (eg, a home visit) is not itself appealable. However, *CH 2555/2007* reminds appeal tribunals that when an appeal has been made against a decision altering or stopping an award of benefit on the grounds of an alleged failure to provide information, the appeal tribunal has to satisfy itself of the reasonableness of the request for information (or a home visit) in the individual case before it as part of its deciding whether the failure to provide the information provided sufficient grounds to alter or stop the benefit award. Accordingly, in cases where the need for a particular piece of information or a home visit is challenged on an appeal the appeal tribunal must decide for itself on the facts whether the information or home visit was reasonably required, rather than limiting itself to deciding (on judicial review type grounds) whether the request under regulation 86(1) was one which a reasonable local authority could make.

pp390-391 HB Regs reg 88

Para (3)(d) amended by reg 3(9) of the Social Security (Miscellaneous Amendments)(No.2) Regulations 2008 SI No.1042 as from 19 May 2008.

p404 HB Regs reg 95

Para (2A) inserted by reg 17(1) of the Housing Benefit (Local Housing Allowance and Information Sharing) Amendment Regulations 2007 SI No.2868 as from 7 April 2008, save that for someone to whom reg 1(5) of those regulations apply, the amendments come into force on the day on or after 7 April 2008 when the first of the events specified in reg 1(6) applies to her/him, or on 6 April 2009 if none have before that date.

pp407-408 HB Regs reg 96

Paras (1) and (3) amended and paras (3A) and (3B) inserted by reg 17(2) of the Housing Benefit (Local Housing Allowance and Information Sharing) Amendment Regulations 2007 SI No.2868 as from 7 April 2008, save that for someone to whom reg 1(5) of those regulations apply, the amendments come into force on the day on or after 7 April 2008 when the first of the events specified in reg 1(6) applies to her/him, or on 6 April 2009 if none have before that date.

pp411-419   HB Regs reg 100

[p414: in the analysis to paragraphs (2) and (3), at the end of the first paragraph on p414 add:]

In *CH 3586/2007*, the Deputy Commissioner said that a tribunal must consider and determine whether the overpayment was caused by a wholly uninduced official error or was rather the result of the claimant's own failings – ie, her/his failure to inform the 'designated office' of a change in circumstances under reg 88 HB Regs (or reg 69 HB(SPC) Regs).

[p415: in the analysis to paragraphs (2) and (3), Who must make the mistake? replace the paragraphs starting (1) and (2) with:]

(1) The relevant authority. 'Relevant authority' is defined in reg 2 as an authority administering HB.

(2) An officer or person acting for the 'relevant authority'. This includes employees of bodies carrying out HB functions which have been privatised or put out to tender under an enforcement determination issued by the Secretary of State (see SSAA s139G). The officer need not be an officer working in the HB section: *CH 2321/2002* para 37. For example, if a claimant is visited by an officer from the social services department, who then promises to notify the HB department of a change in the claimant's circumstances and fails to do so, that will be a relevant mistake. In *CH 3586/2007*, the Deputy Commissioner agreed. He could see no justification for construing the term 'relevant authority' in a way which confines it to one department within the authority. It would have been easy to limit the term expressly. He noted the contrast between the absence of a restrictive definition of the term 'relevant authority' with the deliberately restrictive way in which the separate duty imposed on claimants to report change of circumstances was drafted. There, the claimant is required to report changes to the 'designated office' as defined in reg 2, not to the authority generally. However, it would be insufficient to base a conclusion that a mistake had been made on the mere fact that information was given to a department, or an officer in a department, other than the HB department. A tribunal would need to be satisfied that either the claimant had a reasonably based expectation that the information would be passed on, for example, because s/he was told, or could reasonably infer, that this would happen, or because there were internal arrangements or practices within the authority for dealing with information potentially relevant to entitlement to HB and CTB and that those arrangements or practices had not been followed.

[p417: after the 4th complete paragraph ending ' ... relevant to her/his HB entitlement.' add a new paragraph:]

In *CH 2943/2007*, the claimant had correctly stated her earnings in her HB and CTB claims and in later enquiries, but the local authority had calculated her benefit on incorrect (lower) earnings and these were shown on its decision notices. The commissioner pointed out that a claimant cannot reasonably be expected to seek advice about a local authority's decision notice because s/he does not understand all the figures unless s/he has some reason to believe that the figures are wrong. A claimant who has given clear and correct information is entitled to start from the basis that the local authority has such information when stating her/his weekly earnings.

pp419-420   HB Regs reg 101

Para (2A) inserted and para (3) amended by reg 2 of the Housing Benefit (Local Housing Allowance, Information Sharing and Miscellaneous) Amendment Regulations 2008 SI No. 586 as from 7 April 2008.

pp424-429   HB Regs reg 102

[p426: at the end of the second paragraph of the analysis delete '(but note that ... Court of Appeal)' and then add:]

The Court of Appeal dismissed the Secretary of State's appeal against the decision in *Secretary of State for Work and Pensions v Balding* [2007] 13 December, EWCA Civ 1327.

p437   HB Regs new reg 114A

New reg 114A inserted by reg 3(2) of the Housing Benefit (Local Housing Allowance and Information Sharing) Amendment Regulations 2007 SI No.2868, as amended by reg 4(2)(b) of the Housing Benefit (Local Housing Allowance, Information Sharing and Miscellaneous) Amendment Regulations 2008 SI No.586, as from 7 April 2008.

pp437-438   HB Regs reg 114

Reg 114 omitted by reg 3(3) of the Housing Benefit (Local Housing Allowance and Information Sharing) Amendment Regulations 2007 SI No.2868 as from 7 April 2008.

p444   HB Regs reg 122

Part 15 and reg 122 substituted by reg 20(1) of the Housing Benefit (Local Housing Allowance and Information Sharing) Amendment Regulations 2007 SI No.2868 as from 7 April 2008.

pp448-451   HB Regs Sch 2

Sch 2 substituted by reg 18 of the Housing Benefit (Local Housing Allowance and Information Sharing) Amendment Regulations 2007 SI No.2868 as from 7 April 2008, save that for someone to whom reg 1(5) of those regulations apply, the amendments come into force on the day on or after 7 April 2008 when the first of the events specified in reg 1(6) applies to her/him, or on 6 April 2009 if none have before that date.

pp451-465   HB Regs Sch 3

Paras 3, 13 and 20 amended, para 6 substituted and paras 9, 10 and 11 omitted by reg 3(10) of the Social Security (Miscellaneous Amendments)(No.2) Regulations 2008 SI No.1042 as from 19 May 2008.

pp465-472   HB Regs Sch 4

Paras 3, 9 and 17 amended by reg 3(11) of the Social Security (Miscellaneous Amendments)(No.2) Regulations 2008 SI No.1042 as from 19 May 2008.

pp472-486   HB Regs Sch 5

Sub-paras (a) and (b) of para 22 substituted by reg 11(12) of the Social Security (Miscellaneous Amendments)(No.5) Regulations 2007 SI No.2618 as from 1 April 2008 (7 April 2008 where rent payable weekly or at intervals of a week).

Para 28A inserted by reg 6(5)(a) of the Social Security (Miscellaneous Amendments) Regulations 2008 SI No.698 as from, as they relate to a particular beneficiary, the first day of the benefit week on or after 7 April 2008.

Paras 37 and 48 omitted and para 41 amended by reg 6(5)(b) and (c) of the Social Security (Miscellaneous Amendments) Regulations 2008 SI No.698 as from 14 April 2008.

Para 15 substituted, para 18 omitted and paras 25, 44 and 45 amended by reg 3(12) of the Social Security (Miscellaneous Amendments)(No.2) Regulations 2008 SI No.1042 as from 19 May 2008.

[p485: at the end of the analysis to paragraph 57, delete 'Note that leave to appeal ... Pensions' and replace with:]

The Court of Appeal upheld the decision in *Casewell v Secretary of State for Work and Pensions* [2008] 11 March, WLR (D) 86.

pp486-499   HB Regs Sch 6

Para 19A inserted by reg 6(6)(b) of the Social Security (Miscellaneous Amendments) Regulations 2008 SI No.698 as from, as they relate to a particular beneficiary, the first day of the benefit week on or after 7 April 2008.

Para 9(1)(b) substituted and para 29 omitted and para 41 amended by reg 6(6)(a) and (c) of the Social Security (Miscellaneous Amendments) Regulations 2008 SI No.698 as from 14 April 2008.

Paras 16, 40, 41, 43 and 55 amended by reg 3(13) of the Social Security (Miscellaneous Amendments)(No.2) Regulations 2008 SI No.1042 as from 19 May 2008.

[p489: at the end of the second paragraph of the analysis to paragraph 9 add:]

The decision was approved by *CIS 3760/2006*.

[p490: in the analysis to paragraph 12, after 'cars, etc' add:]

, or even a caravan based at a non-residential site. In *R(H) 7/08*, Commissioner Jacobs concluded that 'personal possessions' mean any physical assets other than land and assets used for business purposes.

[p494: in the analysis of paragraph 26, after 'in the circumstances.' add:]

In *CIS 1915/2007*, the claimant had fled domestic violence and an arranged marriage and began divorce proceedings. However, under family pressure these were temporarily suspended. The DWP decided that value of her interest in the former matrimonial home could no longer be disregarded as she was no longer taking reasonable steps to dispose of it. Deputy Commissioner Mark allowed the claimant's appeal. He said that in considering the reasonableness of the period taken by the claimant to secure a divorce (and the resulting disposal of the premises), including any temporary suspension of such action, it was necessary to look at all the facts, including the pressures that were brought on her. The steps she took to temporarily suspend her divorce proceedings until she had moved to a new address and changed her name to secure her safety did not mean that she was no longer taking reasonable steps to dispose of the premises through divorce proceedings.

pp499-503   HB Regs Sch 7
Para 3(3) amended by reg 19 of the Housing Benefit (Local Housing Allowance and Information Sharing) Amendment Regulations 2007 SI No.2868, as amended by reg 4(6) of the Housing Benefit (Local Housing Allowance, Information Sharing and Miscellaneous) Amendment Regulations 2008 SI No.586, as from 7 April 2008, save that for someone to whom reg 1(5) of those regulations apply, the amendments come into force on the day on or after 7 April 2008 when the first of the events specified in reg 1(6) applies to her/him, or on 6 April 2009 if none have before that date.

pp503-504   HB Regs Sch 8
Para 2(3) amended by reg 19 of the Housing Benefit (Local Housing Allowance and Information Sharing) Amendment Regulations 2007 SI No.2868 as from 7 April 2008, save that for someone to whom reg 1(5) of those regulations apply, the amendments come into force on the day on or after 7 April 2008 when the first of the events specified in reg 1(6) applies to her/him, or on 6 April 2009 if none have before that date.

pp510-518   HB Regs Sch 10
Sch 10 substituted by reg 20(2) of the Housing Benefit (Local Housing Allowance and Information Sharing) Amendment Regulations 2007 SI No.2868 as from 7 April 2008.

pp520-521   RO(HBF) Order Art 2
Definitions of 'broad rental market area', 'broad rental market area determination' and 'local housing allowance determination' amended and definition of 'working day' inserted by Art 4(1) of the Rent Officers (Housing Benefit Functions) Amendment Order 2007 SI No.2871 as from 20 March 2008.

Definitions of 'broad rental market area', 'broad rental market area determination', 'local housing allowance determination' and 'relevant date' substituted and definition of 'pathfinder authority' omitted by Art 6(3) of the Rent Officers (Housing Benefit Functions) Amendment Order 2007 SI No.2871 as from 7 April 2008, save where Art 6(1)(a), (b) or (c) of that order applies.

Definitions of 'hostel' and 'rent' substituted, definitions of 'the Housing Benefit Regulations' and 'the Housing Benefit (State Pension Credit) Regulations' inserted and definition of '1987 Regulations' omitted by Art 10(1) of the Rent Officers (Housing Benefit Functions) Amendment Order 2007 SI No.2871 as from 7 April 2008.

pp522-523   RO(HBF) Order Art 3
Para (2)(a) amended by Art 5(1) of the Rent Officers (Housing Benefit Functions) Amendment Order 2007 SI No.2871 as from 7 April 2008.

p523   RO(HBF) Order Art 3A
Art 3A amended by Art 10(2) of the Rent Officers (Housing Benefit Functions) Amendment Order 2007 SI No.2871 as from 7 April 2008.

p524   RO(HBF) Order Art 4A
Art 4A amended by Art 10(3) of the Rent Officers (Housing Benefit Functions) Amendment Order 2007 SI No.2871 as from 7 April 2008.

pp524-525   RO(HBF) Order Art 4B
Para (1) amended and paras (1A), (2A), (3A) and (6) inserted by Art 4(2) of the Rent Officers (Housing Benefit Functions) Amendment Order 2007 SI No.2871 as from 20 March 2008.

Para (6) amended by Art 5(2) of the Rent Officers (Housing Benefit Functions) Amendment Order 2007 SI No.2871 as from 7 April 2008.

Paras (1), (2) and (3) omitted, para (4) substituted, para (4A) inserted and para (5) amended by Art 6(4) of the Rent Officers (Housing Benefit Functions) Amendment Order 2007 SI No.2871, as amended by Art 2(3) of the Rent Officers (Housing Benefit Functions) Amendment Order 2008 SI No.587, as from 7 April 2008, save where Art 6(1)(a), (b) or (c) of that order applies.

Para (4A) amended by Art 2(2) of the Rent Officers (Housing Benefit Functions) Amendment Order 2008 SI No.587 as from 7 April 2008.

pp525-526   RO(HBF) Order Art 4C
Paras (1) and (2) substituted by Art 6(5) of the Rent Officers (Housing Benefit Functions) Amendment Order 2007 SI No.2871 as from 7 April 2008, save where Art 6(1)(a), (b) or (c) of that order applies.

Para (4) substituted by Art 7(2) of the Rent Officers (Housing Benefit Functions) Amendment Order 2007 SI No.2871 as from 7 April 2008, save where Art 7(1) of that order applies.

p526   RO(HBF) Order Art 4D
Art 4D amended by Art 6(6) of the Rent Officers (Housing Benefit Functions) Amendment Order 2007 SI No.2871 as from 7 April 2008, save where Art 6(1)(a), (b) or (c) of that order applies.

p526   RO(HBF) Order Art 4E
Art 4E amended by Art 6(6) of the Rent Officers (Housing Benefit Functions) Amendment Order 2007 SI No.2871 as from 7 April 2008, save where Art 6(1)(a), (b) or (c) of that order applies.

Art 4E amended by Art 10(4) of the Rent Officers (Housing Benefit Functions) Amendment Order 2007 SI No.2871 as from 7 April 2008.

p527 RO(HBF) Order Art 5
Art 5 amended by Art 7(3) of the Rent Officers (Housing Benefit Functions) Amendment Order 2007 SI No.2871 as from 7 April 2008, save where Art 7(1) of that order applies.

p527 RO(HBF) Order Art 6
Paras (2) and (3) amended by Art 10(5) of the Rent Officers (Housing Benefit Functions) Amendment Order 2007 SI No.2871 as from 7 April 2008.

p527 RO(HBF) Order Art 7
Art 7 amended by Art 10(6) of the Rent Officers (Housing Benefit Functions) Amendment Order 2007 SI No.2871 as from 7 April 2008.

pp527-528 RO(HBF) Order Art 7A
Para (3) amended and para (4) inserted by Art 4(3) of the Rent Officers (Housing Benefit Functions) Amendment Order 2007 SI No.2871 as from 20 March 2008.

Para (2) amended and para (3) omitted by Art 6(7) of the Rent Officers (Housing Benefit Functions) Amendment Order 2007 SI No.2871 as from 7 April 2008, save where Art 6(1)(a), (b) or (c) of that order applies.

pp529-536 RO(HBF) Order Sch 1
Para 7(3) substituted by Art 7(4) of the Rent Officers (Housing Benefit Functions) Amendment Order 2007 SI No.2871 as from 7 April 2008, save where Art 7(1) of that order applies.

Para 7(1) substituted by Art 8(2) of the Rent Officers (Housing Benefit Functions) Amendment Order 2007 SI No.2871 as from 7 April 2008, save where Art 8(1)(a) or (b) of that order applies.

Para 6(1) substituted, para 6(2A) inserted, para 6(2) omitted and para 6(3) amended by Art 9(2) of the Rent Officers (Housing Benefit Functions) Amendment Order 2007 SI No.2871 as from 7 April 2008, save where Art 9(1)(a) or (b) of that order applies.

Para 9(1)(c) substituted and para 9(1)(da) inserted by Art 9(3) of the Rent Officers (Housing Benefit Functions) Amendment Order 2007 SI No.2871 as from 7 April 2008, save where Art 9(1)(a) or (b) of that order applies.

Paras 4(4) and 11(5)(b) amended by Art 10(7) of the Rent Officers (Housing Benefit Functions) Amendment Order 2007 SI No.2871 as from 7 April 2008.

pp536-538 RO(HBF) Order Sch 3A
Sch 3A omitted by Art 6(8) of the Rent Officers (Housing Benefit Functions) Amendment Order 2007 SI No.2871 as from 7 April 2008, save where Art 6(1)(a), (b) or (c) of that order applies.

Para 1(2)(b) amended by Art 10(8) of the Rent Officers (Housing Benefit Functions) Amendment Order 2007 SI No.2871 as from 7 April 2008.

p538 RO(HBF) Order new Sch 3B
New Sch 3B inserted by Art 4(4) of the Rent Officers (Housing Benefit Functions) Amendment Order 2007 SI No.2871 as from 20 March 2008.

pp540-541 RO(HBF)(Scotland) Order Art 2
Definitions of 'broad rental market area', 'broad rental market area determination' and 'local housing allowance determination' amended and definition of 'working day' inserted by Art 13(1) of the Rent Officers (Housing Benefit Functions) Amendment Order 2007 SI No.2871 as from 20 March 2008.

Definitions of 'broad rental market area', 'broad rental market area determination', 'local housing allowance determination' and 'relevant date' substituted and definition of 'pathfinder authority' omitted by Art 15(3) of the Rent Officers (Housing Benefit Functions) Amendment Order 2007 SI No.2871 as from 7 April 2008, save where Art 15(1)(a), (b) or (c) of that order applies.

Definitions of 'hostel' and 'rent' substituted, definitions of 'the Housing Benefit Regulations' and 'the Housing Benefit (State Pension Credit) Regulations' inserted and definition of '1987 Regulations' omitted by Art 19(1) of the Rent Officers (Housing Benefit Functions) Amendment Order 2007 SI No.2871 as from 7 April 2008.

pp541-542 RO(HBF)(Scotland) Order Art 3
Para (2)(a) amended by Art 14(1) of the Rent Officers (Housing Benefit Functions) Amendment Order 2007 SI No.2871 as from 7 April 2008.

p542 RO(HBF)(Scotland) Order Art 3A
Art 3A amended by Art 19(2) of the Rent Officers (Housing Benefit Functions) Amendment Order 2007 SI No.2871 as from 7 April 2008.

p543 RO(HBF)(Scotland) Order Art 4A
Art 4A amended by Art 19(3) of the Rent Officers (Housing Benefit Functions) Amendment Order 2007 SI No.2871 as from 7 April 2008.

pp543-544 RO(HBF)(Scotland) Order Art 4B
Para (1) amended and paras (1A), (2A), (3A) and (6) inserted by Art 13(2) of the Rent Officers (Housing Benefit Functions) Amendment Order 2007 SI No.2871 as from 20 March 2008.

Para (6) amended by Art 14(2) of the Rent Officers (Housing Benefit Functions) Amendment Order 2007 SI No.2871 as from 7 April 2008.

Paras (1), (2) and (3) omitted, para (4) substituted, para (4A) inserted and para (5) amended by Art 15(4) of the Rent Officers (Housing Benefit Functions) Amendment Order 2007 SI No.2871, as amended by Art 2(5) of the Rent Officers (Housing Benefit Functions) Amendment Order 2008 SI No.587, as from 7 April 2008, save where Art 15(1)(a), (b) or (c) of that order applies.

Para (4A) amended by Art 2(4) of the Rent Officers (Housing Benefit Functions) Amendment Order 2008 SI No.587 as from 7 April 2008.

p544 RO(HBF)(Scotland) Order Art 4C
Paras (1) and (2) substituted by Art 15(5) of the Rent Officers (Housing Benefit Functions) Amendment Order 2007 SI No.2871 as from 7 April 2008, save where Art 15(1)(a), (b) or (c) of that order applies.

Para (4) substituted by Art 16(2) of the Rent Officers (Housing Benefit Functions) Amendment Order 2007 SI No.2871 as from 7 April 2008, save where Art 16(1) of that order applies.

p545 RO(HBF)(Scotland) Order Art 4D
Art 4D amended by Art 15(6) of the Rent Officers (Housing Benefit Functions) Amendment Order 2007 SI No.2871 as from 7 April 2008, save where Art 15(1)(a), (b) or (c) of that order applies.

p545 RO(HBF)(Scotland) Order Art 4E
Art 4E amended by Art 19(4) of the Rent Officers (Housing Benefit Functions) Amendment Order 2007 SI No.2871 as from 7 April 2008.

p545   RO(HBF)(Scotland) Order Art 5
Art 5 amended by Art 16(3) of the Rent Officers (Housing Benefit Functions) Amendment Order 2007 SI No.2871 as from 7 April 2008, save where Art 16(1) of that order applies.

p546   RO(HBF)(Scotland) Order Art 6
Paras (2) and (3) amended by Art 19(5) of the Rent Officers (Housing Benefit Functions) Amendment Order 2007 SI No.2871 as from 7 April 2008.

p546   RO(HBF)(Scotland) Order Art 7
Art 7 amended by Art 19(6) of the Rent Officers (Housing Benefit Functions) Amendment Order 2007 SI No.2871 as from 7 April 2008.

pp546-547   RO(HBF)(Scotland) Order Art 7A
Para (3) amended and para (4) inserted by Art 13(3) of the Rent Officers (Housing Benefit Functions) Amendment Order 2007 SI No.2871 as from 20 March 2008.

Para (2) amended and para (3) omitted by Art 15(7) of the Rent Officers (Housing Benefit Functions) Amendment Order 2007 SI No.2871 as from 7 April 2008, save where Art 15(1)(a), (b) or (c) of that order applies.

pp547-553   RO(HBF)(Scotland) Order Sch 1
Para 7(3) substituted by Art 16(4) of the Rent Officers (Housing Benefit Functions) Amendment Order 2007 SI No.2871 as from 7 April 2008, save where Art 16(1) of that order applies.

Para 7(1) substituted by Art 17(2) of the Rent Officers (Housing Benefit Functions) Amendment Order 2007 SI No.2871 as from 7 April 2008, save where Art 17(1)(a) or (b) of that order applies.

Para 6(1) substituted, para 6(2A) inserted, para 6(2) omitted and para 6(3) amended by Art 18(2) of the Rent Officers (Housing Benefit Functions) Amendment Order 2007 SI No.2871 as from 7 April 2008, save where Art 18(1)(a) or (b) of that order applies.

Para 9(1)(c) substituted and para 9(1)(da) inserted by Art 18(3) of the Rent Officers (Housing Benefit Functions) Amendment Order 2007 SI No.2871 as from 7 April 2008, save where Art 18(1)(a) or (b) of that order applies.

Paras 4(4) and 11(5)(b) amended by Art 19(7) of the Rent Officers (Housing Benefit Functions) Amendment Order 2007 SI No.2871 as from 7 April 2008.

pp553-555   RO(HBF)(Scotland) Order Sch 3A
Sch 3A omitted by Art 15(8) of the Rent Officers (Housing Benefit Functions) Amendment Order 2007 SI No.2871 as from 7 April 2008, save where Art 15(1)(a), (b) or (c) of that order applies.

Para (1)(2)(b) amended by Art 19(8) of the Rent Officers (Housing Benefit Functions) Amendment Order 2007 SI No.2871 as from 7 April 2008.

p555   RO(HBF)(Scotland) Order new Sch 3B
New Sch 3B inserted by Art 13(4) of the Rent Officers (Housing Benefit Functions) Amendment Order 2007 SI No.2871 as from 20 March 2008.

pp564-571   CTB Regs reg 2
Definitions of 'Intensive Activity Period for 50 plus' and 'supplementary benefit' omitted by reg 7(2) of the Social Security (Miscellaneous Amendments) Regulations 2008 SI No.698 as from 14 April 2008.

Definition of 'person on state pension credit' omitted by reg 5(2) of the Social Security (Miscellaneous Amendments)(No.2) Regulations 2008 SI No.1042 as from 19 May 2008.

pp583-586   CTB Regs reg 18
Paras (11)(a), (b) and (g) amended by reg 5(3) of the Social Security (Miscellaneous Amendments)(No.2) Regulations 2008 SI No.1042 as from 19 May 2008.

pp590-591   CTB Regs reg 27
Paras (3) and (4) inserted by reg 7(3) of the Social Security (Miscellaneous Amendments) Regulations 2008 SI No.698 as from, as they relate to a particular beneficiary, the first day of the benefit week on or after 7 April 2008.

pp595-598   CTB Regs reg 32
Paras 7(c)(iii) and (10)(b)(i) amended by reg 7(4) of the Social Security (Miscellaneous Amendments) Regulations 2008 SI No.698 as from 14 April 2008.

Paras (3) to (5) omitted by reg 5(4) of the Social Security (Miscellaneous Amendments)(No.2) Regulations 2008 SI No.1042 as from 19 May 2008.

pp599-601   CTB Regs reg 39
Para 4(b)(iii) amended by reg 7(4) of the Social Security (Miscellaneous Amendments) Regulations 2008 SI No.698 as from 14 April 2008.

pp604-607   CTB Regs reg 43
Definition of 'sandwich course' substituted and definition of 'student loan' amended by reg 5(5) of the Social Security (Miscellaneous Amendments)(No.2) Regulations 2008 SI No.1042 as from 19 May 2008.

p612   CTB Regs reg 50
Para (2) amended by reg 5(6) of the Social Security (Miscellaneous Amendments)(No.2) Regulations 2008 SI No.1042 as from 19 May 2008.

pp627-628   CTB Regs reg 70
Para (1) amended by reg 5(7) of the Social Security (Miscellaneous Amendments)(No.2) Regulations 2008 SI No.1042 as from 19 May 2008.

pp628-629   CTB Regs reg 71
Para (1) amended by reg 5(8) of the Social Security (Miscellaneous Amendments)(No.2) Regulations 2008 SI No.1042 as from 19 May 2008.

pp629-630   CTB Regs reg 72
Para (1) amended by reg 5(9) of the Social Security (Miscellaneous Amendments)(No.2) Regulations 2008 SI No.1042 as from 19 May 2008.

p635   CTB Regs reg 82

[at the end of the General Note to reg 82 add:]

It is common practice for local authorities to make awards of CTB until the end of the council tax year on the 31 March each year, and thus 'credit' the claimant's council tax account with CTB up to the 31 March. However, in the context of excess CTB, Commissioner Rowland has ruled in *CH 3076/2006* that such a credit may be treated as a credit of CTB only as each week of entitlement under the award passes. Accordingly where an award of CTB is superseded on, say, 1 November and entitlement to CTB removed from that date, then the amount credited to the council tax account for the period from 1 November to 31 March will not constitute excess CTB under regulation 82. This is also the case, in the commissioner's view, where benefit is suspended and not then reinstated; so the credit is not a payment of excess CTB for the period of the suspension. Accordingly, there will only have been a payment of excess benefit in a 'credit' case where entitlement to CTB has been removed retrospectively and payment of benefit was not suspended for that period.

pp642-650   CTB Regs Sch 1
Paras 3, 13 and 20 amended, para 6 substituted and paras 9, 10 and 11 omitted by reg 5(10) of the Social Security (Miscellaneous Amendments)(No.2) Regulations 2008 SI No.1042 as from 19 May 2008.

pp651-654   CTB Regs Sch 3
Paras 3, 9 and 16 amended by reg 5(11) of the Social Security (Miscellaneous Amendments)(No.2) Regulations 2008 SI No.1042 as from 19 May 2008.

pp654-661   CTB Regs Sch 4
Para 29A inserted by reg 7(5)(a) of the Social Security (Miscellaneous Amendments) Regulations 2008 SI No.698 as from, as they relate to a particular beneficiary, the first day of the benefit week on or after 7 April 2008.

Paras 39 and 49 omitted and para 43 amended by reg 7(5)(b) and (c) of the Social Security (Miscellaneous Amendments) Regulations 2008 SI No.698 as from 14 April 2008.

Paras 16, 45 and 46 amended and para 64 omitted by reg 5(12) of the Social Security (Miscellaneous Amendments)(No.2) Regulations 2008 SI No.1042 as from 19 May 2008.

pp662-669   CTB Regs Sch 5
Para 19A inserted by reg 7(6)(b) of the Social Security (Miscellaneous Amendments) Regulations 2008 SI No.698 as from, as they relate to a particular beneficiary, the first day of the benefit week on or after 7 April 2008.

Para 9(1)(b) substituted and paras 30 and 44 omitted by reg 7(6)(a) and (c) of the Social Security (Miscellaneous Amendments) Regulations 2008 SI No.698 as from 14 April 2008.

Paras 40, 41, 43 and 57 amended by reg 5(13) of the Social Security (Miscellaneous Amendments)(No.2) Regulations 2008 SI No.1042 as from 19 May 2008.

pp654-662   CTB Regs Sch 4
Sub-paras (a) and (b) of para 22 substituted by reg 13(10) of the Social Security (Miscellaneous Amendments)(No.5) Regulations 2007 SI No.2618 as from 1 April 2008.

pp683-691   HB (SPC) Regs reg 2
Definitions of 'eligible rent', 'housing association', 'maximum rent', 'non-dependant deduction' and 'Rent Officers Order' substituted and definitions of 'amended determination', 'broad rental market area', 'broad rental market area determination', 'change of dwelling', 'linked person', 'local housing allowance', 'maximum rent (LHA)', 'reckonable rent', 'registered housing association' and 'relevant information' inserted by reg 4(1) of the Housing Benefit (State Pension Credit)(Local Housing Allowance and Information Sharing) Amendment Regulations 2007 SI No.2869, as amended by reg 5(3) of the Housing Benefit (Local Housing Allowance, Information Sharing and Miscellaneous) Amendment Regulations 2008 SI No.586, as from 7 April 2008, save that for someone to whom reg 1(5) of those regulations apply, the amendments come into force on the day on or after 7 April 2008 when the first of the events specified in reg 1(6) applies to her/him, or on 6 April 2009 if none have before that date.

Definition of 'concessionary payment' amended, definition of 'the former regulations' omitted and definition of 'sandwich course' substituted by reg 4(2) of the Social Security (Miscellaneous Amendments)(No.2) Regulations 2008 SI No.1042 as from 19 May 2008.

p692   HB (SPC) Regs reg 3
Para (4) amended by reg 4(2) of the Housing Benefit (State Pension Credit)(Local Housing Allowance and Information Sharing) Amendment Regulations 2007 SI No.2869 as from 7 April

2008, save that for someone to whom reg 1(5) of those regulations apply, the amendments come into force on the day on or after 7 April 2008 when the first of the events specified in reg 1(6) applies to her/him, or on 6 April 2009 if none have before that date.

pp694-698   HB (SPC) Regs reg 7
Para (8)(c)(ii) amended by reg 4(3) of the Social Security (Miscellaneous Amendments)(No.2) Regulations 2008 SI No.1042 as from 19 May 2008.

p702   HB (SPC) Regs reg 11
Para (1) substituted and para (3) amended by reg 4(3) of the Housing Benefit (State Pension Credit)(Local Housing Allowance and Information Sharing) Amendment Regulations 2007 SI No.2869 as from 7 April 2008, save that for someone to whom reg 1(5) of those regulations apply, the amendments come into force on the day on or after 7 April 2008 when the first of the events specified in reg 1(6) applies to her/him, or on 6 April 2009 if none have before that date.

pp702-704   HB (SPC) Regs reg 12
Paras (3) to (7) omitted and para (8) amended by reg 4(4) of the Housing Benefit (State Pension Credit)(Local Housing Allowance and Information Sharing) Amendment Regulations 2007 SI No.2869 as from 7 April 2008, save that for someone to whom reg 1(5) of those regulations apply, the amendments come into force on the day on or after 7 April 2008 when the first of the events specified in reg 1(6) applies to her/him, or on 6 April 2009 if none have before that date.

p704   HB (SPC) Regs new regs 12B, 12C and 12D
New regs 12B, 12C and 12D inserted by reg 5 of the Housing Benefit (State Pension Credit)(Local Housing Allowance and Information Sharing) Amendment Regulations 2007 SI No.2869 as from 7 April 2008, save that for someone to whom reg 1(5) of those regulations apply, the amendments come into force on the day on or after 7 April 2008 when the first of the events specified in reg 1(6) applies to her/him, or on 6 April 2009 if none have before that date.

pp704-707   HB (SPC) Regs regs 13, 13ZA and 13ZB
Regs 13, 13ZA and 13ZB substituted by reg 6 of the Housing Benefit (State Pension Credit)(Local Housing Allowance and Information Sharing) Amendment Regulations 2007 SI No.2869 as from 7 April 2008, save that for someone to whom reg 1(5) of those regulations apply, the amendments come into force on the day on or after 7 April 2008 when the first of the events specified in reg 1(6) applies to her/him, or on 6 April 2009 if none have before that date.

p707   HB (SPC) Regs new regs 13C, 13D and 13E
New regs 13C, 13D and 13E inserted by reg 7 of the Housing Benefit (State Pension Credit)(Local Housing Allowance and Information Sharing) Amendment Regulations 2007 SI No.2869, as amended by reg 5(4) of the Housing Benefit (Local Housing Allowance, Information Sharing and Miscellaneous) Amendment Regulations 2008 SI No.586, as from 7 April 2008, save that for someone to whom reg 1(5) of those regulations apply, the amendments come into force on the day on or after 7 April 2008 when the first of the events specified in reg 1(6) applies to her/him, or on 6 April 2009 if none have before that date.

pp707-709   HB (SPC) Regs reg 14
Paras (2), (3) and (9) omitted and para (4A) inserted by reg 3(1) of the Housing Benefit (State Pension Credit)(Local Housing Allowance and Information Sharing) Amendment Regulations 2007 SI No.2869, as amended by reg 5(2)(a) of the Housing Benefit (Local Housing Allowance, Information Sharing and Miscellaneous) Amendment Regulations 2008 SI No.586, as from 7 April 2008.

Reg 14 substituted by reg 8 of the Housing Benefit (State Pension Credit)(Local Housing Allowance and Information Sharing) Amendment Regulations 2007 SI No. 2869, as amended by reg 5(5) of the Housing Benefit (Local Housing Allowance, Information Sharing and Miscellaneous) Amendment Regulations 2008 SI No.586, as from 7 April 2008, save that for someone to whom reg 1(5) of those regulations apply, the amendments come into force on the day on or after 7 April 2008 when the first of the events specified in reg 1(6) applies to her/ him, or on 6 April 2009 if none have before that date.

pp709-711   HB (SPC) Regs regs 15 to 18
Regs 15 to 18 substituted by reg 9 of the Housing Benefit (State Pension Credit) (Local Housing Allowance and Information Sharing) Amendment Regulations 2007 SI No.2869 as from 7 April 2008, save that for someone to whom reg 1(5) of those regulations apply, the amendments come into force on the day on or after 7 April 2008 when the first of the events specified in reg 1(6) applies to her/him, or on 6 April 2009 if none have before that date.

p711   HB (SPC) Regs new reg 18A
New reg 18A inserted by reg 10 of the Housing Benefit (State Pension Credit) (Local Housing Allowance and Information Sharing) Amendment Regulations 2007 SI No.2869 as from 7 April 2008, save that for someone to whom reg 1(5) of those regulations apply, the amendments come into force on the day on or after 7 April 2008 when the first of the events specified in reg 1(6) applies to her/him, or on 6 April 2009 if none have before that date.

pp713-714   HB (SPC) Regs reg 22
Para (5) amended by reg 4(4) of the Social Security (Miscellaneous Amendments)(No.2) Regulations 2008 SI No.1042 as from 19 May 2008.

pp721-724   HB (SPC) Regs reg 31
Para (11)(f) amended by reg 4(5) of the Social Security (Miscellaneous Amendments)(No.2) Regulations 2008 SI No.1042 as from 19 May 2008.

pp737-739   HB (SPC) Regs reg 48
Para (4)(a) amended by reg 11 of the Housing Benefit (State Pension Credit)(Local Housing Allowance and Information Sharing) Amendment Regulations 2007 SI No.2869 as from 7 April 2008, save that for someone to whom reg 1(5) of those regulations apply, the amendments come into force on the day on or after 7 April 2008 when the first of the events specified in reg 1(6) applies to her/him, or on 6 April 2009 if none have before that date.

pp739-740   HB (SPC) Regs reg 50
Reg 50 substituted by reg 12 of the Housing Benefit (State Pension Credit) (Local Housing Allowance and Information Sharing) Amendment Regulations 2007 SI No.2869 as from 7 April 2008, save that for someone to whom reg 1(5) of those regulations apply, the amendments come into force on the day on or after 7 April 2008 when the first of the events specified in reg 1(6) applies to her/him, or on 6 April 2009 if none have before that date.

pp740-741   HB (SPC) Regs reg 53
Para (4) amended by reg 13 of the Housing Benefit (State Pension Credit) (Local Housing Allowance and Information Sharing) Amendment Regulations 2007 SI No.2869 as from 7 April 2008, save that for someone to whom reg 1(5) of those regulations apply, the amendments come into force on the day on or after 7 April 2008 when the first of the events specified in reg 1(6) applies to her/him, or on 6 April 2009 if none have before that date.

pp742-744   HB (SPC) Regs reg 55
Reg 55 substituted by reg 14 of the Housing Benefit (State Pension Credit) (Local Housing Allowance and Information Sharing) Amendment Regulations 2007 SI No.2869 as from 7 April 2008, save that for someone to whom reg 1(5) of those regulations apply, the amendments

come into force on the day on or after 7 April 2008 when the first of the events specified in reg 1(6) applies to her/him, or on 6 April 2009 if none have before that date.

pp746-748   HB (SPC) Regs reg 59
Paras (1) and (3) amended by reg 15(1) of the Housing Benefit (State Pension Credit) (Local Housing Allowance and Information Sharing) Amendment Regulations 2007 SI No.2869, as amended by reg 5(6) of the Housing Benefit (Local Housing Allowance, Information Sharing and Miscellaneous) Amendment Regulations 2008 SI No.586, as from 7 April 2008, save that for someone to whom reg 1(5) of those regulations apply, the amendments come into force on the day on or after 7 April 2008 when the first of the events specified in reg 1(6) applies to her/him, or on 6 April 2009 if none have before that date.

pp748-750   HB (SPC) Regs reg 60
Para (9) amended by reg 15(2) of the Housing Benefit (State Pension Credit) (Local Housing Allowance and Information Sharing) Amendment Regulations 2007 SI No.2869 as from 7 April 2008, save that for someone to whom reg 1(5) of those regulations apply, the amendments come into force on the day on or after 7 April 2008 when the first of the events specified in reg 1(6) applies to her/him, or on 6 April 2009 if none have before that date.

pp750-752   HB (SPC) Regs regs 61 and 62
Regs 61 and 62 substituted by reg 16 of the Housing Benefit (State Pension Credit) (Local Housing Allowance and Information Sharing) Amendment Regulations 2007 SI No.2869 as from 7 April 2008, save that for someone to whom reg 1(5) of those regulations apply, the amendments come into force on the day on or after 7 April 2008 when the first of the events specified in reg 1(6) applies to her/him, or on 6 April 2009 if none have before that date.

pp757-759   HB (SPC) Regs reg 67
Para (4)(a)(ii) amended by reg 4(6) of the Social Security (Miscellaneous Amendments)(No.2) Regulations 2008 SI No.1042 as from 19 May 2008.

pp763-764   HB (SPC) Regs reg 76
Para (2A) inserted by reg 17(1) of the Housing Benefit (State Pension Credit) (Local Housing Allowance and Information Sharing) Amendment Regulations 2007 SI No.2869 as from 7 April 2008, save that for someone to whom reg 1(5) of those regulations apply, the amendments come into force on the day on or after 7 April 2008 when the first of the events specified in reg 1(6) applies to her/him, or on 6 April 2009 if none have before that date.

p764   HB (SPC) Regs reg 77
Paras (1) and (3) amended and paras (3A) and (3B) inserted by reg 17(2) of the Housing Benefit (State Pension Credit) (Local Housing Allowance and Information Sharing) Amendment Regulations 2007 SI No.2869 as from 7 April 2008, save that for someone to whom reg 1(5) of those regulations apply, the amendments come into force on the day on or after 7 April 2008 when the first of the events specified in reg 1(6) applies to her/him, or on 6 April 2009 if none have before that date.

pp766-767   HB(SPC) Regs reg 82
Para (2A) inserted and para (3) amended by reg 3 of the Housing Benefit (Local Housing Allowance, Information Sharing and Miscellaneous) Amendment Regulations 2008 SI No.586 as from 7 April 2008.

pp767-768   HB (SPC) Regs reg 83
Para (4) amended by reg 4(7) of the Social Security (Miscellaneous Amendments)(No.2) Regulations 2008 SI No.1042 as from 19 May 2008.

p772   HB (SPC) Regs new reg 95A

New reg 95A inserted by reg 3(2) of the Housing Benefit (State Pension Credit) (Local Housing Allowance and Information Sharing) Amendment Regulations 2007 SI No.2869, as from 7 April 2008. Note that reg 5(2)(b) of the Housing Benefit (Local Housing Allowance, Information Sharing and Miscellaneous) Amendment Regulations 2008 SI No. 586 says to amend 'the inserted regulation 114A'.

pp772-773   HB (SPC) Regs reg 95

Reg 95 omitted by reg 3(3) of the Housing Benefit (State Pension Credit) (Local Housing Allowance and Information Sharing) Amendment Regulations 2007 SI No.2869 as from 7 April 2008.

p777   HB (SPC) Regs reg 103

Reg 103 substituted by reg 20 of the Housing Benefit (State Pension Credit) (Local Housing Allowance and Information Sharing) Amendment Regulations 2007 SI No.2869 as from 7 April 2008, save that for someone to whom reg 1(5) of those regulations apply, the amendments come into force on the day on or after 7 April 2008 when the first of the events specified in reg 1(6) applies to her/him, or on 6 April 2009 if none have before that date.

pp780-781   HB (SPC) Regs Sch 2

Sch 2 substituted by reg 18 of the Housing Benefit (State Pension Credit) (Local Housing Allowance and Information Sharing) Amendment Regulations 2007 SI No.2869 as from 7 April 2008, save that for someone to whom reg 1(5) of those regulations apply, the amendments come into force on the day on or after 7 April 2008 when the first of the events specified in reg 1(6) applies to her/him, or on 6 April 2009 if none have before that date.

pp788-791   HB (SPC) RegsSch 5

Paras 1 and 12 amended by reg 4(8) of the Social Security (Miscellaneous Amendments)(No.2) Regulations 2008 SI No.1042 as from 19 May 2008.

pp792-797   HB (SPC) RegsSch 6

Para 22 amended by reg 4(9) of the Social Security (Miscellaneous Amendments)(No.2) Regulations 2008 SI No.1042 as from 19 May 2008.

pp797-799   HB (SPC) Regs Sch 7

Para 2 amended by reg 19 of the Housing Benefit (State Pension Credit) (Local Housing Allowance and Information Sharing) Amendment Regulations 2007 SI No.2869 as from 7 April 2008, save that for someone to whom reg 1(5) of those regulations apply, the amendments come into force on the day on or after 7 April 2008 when the first of the events specified in reg 1(6) applies to her/him, or on 6 April 2009 if none have before that date.

pp799-801   HB (SPC) RegsSch 8

Para 9 amended by reg 4(10) of the Social Security (Miscellaneous Amendments)(No.2) Regulations 2008 SI No.1042 as from 19 May 2008.

pp801-810   HB (SPC) Regs Sch 9

Sch 9 substituted by reg 20 of the Housing Benefit (State Pension Credit) (Local Housing Allowance and Information Sharing) Amendment Regulations 2007 SI No.2869 as from 7 April 2008, save that for someone to whom reg 1(5) of those regulations apply, the amendments come into force on the day on or after 7 April 2008 when the first of the events specified in reg 1(6) applies to her/him, or on 6 April 2009 if none have before that date.

pp815-821   CTB(SPC) Regs reg 2

Definition of 'sandwich course' substituted by reg 6(2) of the Social Security (Miscellaneous Amendments)(No.2) Regulations 2008 SI No.1042 as from 19 May 2008.

pp834-837   CTB(SPC) Regs reg 21
Para (11)(f) amended by reg 6(3) of the Social Security (Miscellaneous Amendments)(No.2) Regulations 2008 SI No.1042 as from 19 May 2008.

pp860-863   CTB(SPC) Regs reg 53
Para (12A) inserted by reg 6(4) of the Social Security (Miscellaneous Amendments)(No.2) Regulations 2008 SI No.1042 as from 19 May 2008.

pp882-885   CTB(SPC) Regs Sch 3
Paras 1 and 12 amended and para 24 inserted by reg 6(5) of the Social Security (Miscellaneous Amendments)(No.2) Regulations 2008 SI No.1042 as from 19 May 2008.

pp885-889   CTB(SPC) Regs Sch 4
Para 26A inserted by reg 6(6) of the Social Security (Miscellaneous Amendments)(No.2) Regulations 2008 SI No.1042 as from 19 May 2008.

pp939-940   SS&CS(DA) Regs reg 55

[p940: in the General Note, delete 'Given that there is . . . in point of law.' and replace the text with:]

A Tribunal of Commissioners dealt with the issue of the availability (and illegibility) of the record of proceedings in *CSDLA 500/2007* and *CSDLA 524/2007*. It did not accept that any breach of reg 55 rendered a tribunal's decision erroneous in law. It decided that there was no requirement for an appeal to be allowed where there is a lack of a record of proceedings, if immaterial. It said at paragraph 27:

' ... we are satisfied that Parliament cannot have intended that all breaches of regulation 55, whatever their materiality, should render appeal proceedings defective such that a tribunal's decision is necessarily erroneous in point of law on that ground alone. We would stress that to make, preserve and upon request produce a record of proceedings is a regulatory requirement: chairmen and administrators charged with making, keeping and producing records should appreciate both the mandatory nature of regulation 55 obligations and their practical importance. However, where there is no record of proceedings, that is not necessarily fatal to the integrity of the appeal proceedings. On an appeal to disturb a decision, an appellant must show that the failure to comply with regulation 55 was material to the decision in the sense that it has resulted in a real possibility of unfairness or injustice. Insofar as they suggest otherwise, *CDLA 4110/1997*, *CIB 3013/1997* and *CA 3479/2000* should no longer be followed.'

pp961-963   D&A Regs reg 7
Paras (2ZA), (2B) and (2C) omitted and para (3) amended by reg 4(2) of the Housing Benefit (Local Housing Allowance, Miscellaneous and Consequential) Amendment Regulations 2007 SI No.2870 as from 7 April 2008, save that for someone to whom reg 1(3) of those regulations apply, the amendments come into force on the day on or after 7 April 2008 when the first of the events specified in reg 1(6) applies to her/him, or on 6 April 2009 if none have before date.

pp961-965   D&A Regs reg 7

[p963: in the first paragraph under General Note, at the end of the sentence beginning 'The commissioners ruled that . . . ' add:]

: and see further *CIS 3655/2007* below

[p964: at the end of paragraph (4) in the Analysis add:]

Superseding a tribunal or commissioner's decision on the basis that it was made in ignorance of, or was based upon a mistake as to, some material fact involves identifying on the evidence a fact which the tribunal or commissioner was not aware of and that fact *would* justify a different outcome decision: *CIS 3655/2007* (at para 29, following *Wood v Secretary of State for Work and Pensions* [2003] EWCA Civ 53, CA (reported as *R(DLA) 1/03*) and, in effect, restoring *R(I) 56/54* to orthodoxy). The decision of the Court of Appeal in *Saker R(I) 2/88*, in which it was held that a fact was 'material' if it might make a difference to the decision being sought to be reviewed is, accordingly, no longer relevant.

p965   D&A Regs new reg 7A
New reg 7A inserted by reg 4(3) of the Housing Benefit (Local Housing Allowance, Miscellaneous and Consequential) Amendment Regulations 2007 SI No.2870, as amended by reg 6(2)(a) of the Housing Benefit (Local Housing Allowance, Information Sharing and Miscellaneous) Amendment Regulations 2008 SI No.586, as from 7 April 2008, save that for someone to whom reg 1(3) of those regulations apply, the amendments come into force on the day on or after 7 April 2008 when the first of the events specified in reg 1(6) applies to her/him, or on 6 April 2009 if none have before date.

pp965-967   D&A Regs reg 8
Para (6A)amended and para (15) substituted by reg 4(4) of the Housing Benefit (Local Housing Allowance, Miscellaneous and Consequential) Amendment Regulations 2007 SI No.2870, as amended by reg 6(2)(b) of the Housing Benefit (Local Housing Allowance, Information Sharing and Miscellaneous) Amendment Regulations 2008 SI No.586, as from 7 April 2008, save that for someone to whom reg 1(3) of those regulations apply, the amendments come into force on the day on or after 7 April 2008 when the first of the events specified in reg 1(6) applies to her/him, or on 6 April 2009 if none have before date.

pp986-988   D&A Regs reg 21

[p987: in the sixth and seventh paragraphs of the analysis substitute 'CH 3631/2006' for 'CH 3631/2007'.]

pp1035-37   Social Security Fraud Act 2001 s7
Para 1(b) amended by s49(1) of the Welfare Reform Act 2007 as from 1 April 2008.

pp1074-76   SS(I&A) Consequential Amendment Regs Sch
[p1075: in the analysis of paragraph 1, in the paragraph starting with ' ... is temporarily without funds', after 'have been disrupted may benefit.' add:]

The phrase 'is temporarily without funds' refers to the state of affairs at the date of the claim or the date of the award:*CH 4248/2006*. It is not sufficient that the claimant has been without funds at some point in the past, but that ceased before the date of claim.

pp1080-81   Discretionary Financial Assistance Regulations 2001 reg 3
Paras (d), (f) and (g) amended and para (n) inserted by reg 2 of the Discretionary Financial Assistance (Amendment) Regulations 2008 SI No.637.

p1082   Discretionary Financial Assistance Regulations 2001 reg 4
Reg 4(a) substituted by reg 5 of the Housing Benefit (Local Housing Allowance, Miscellaneous and Consequential) Amendment Regulations 2007 SI No.2870 as from 7 April 2008, save that for someone to whom reg 1(3) of those regulations apply, the amendments come into force on the day on or after 7 April 2008 when the first of the events specified in reg 1(6) applies to her/him, or on 6 April 2009 if none have before date.

p1082   Discretionary Financial Assistance Regulations 2001 reg 5
Reg 5 substituted by reg 3 of the Discretionary Financial Assistance (Amendment) Regulations 2008 SI No.637 as from 7 April 2008.

pp1087-88   Social Security (Loss of Benefit) Regulations 2001 reg 2
Para (2) amended by Art 3 of the Welfare Reform Act 2007 (Commencement No.6 and Consequential Provisions) Order 2008 SI No.787 as from 1 April 2008.

pp1099-   Housing Benefit and Council Tax Benefit (Consequential Provisions) Regulations
1125   2006 Sch 3
Paras 4, 5 and 8 substituted by reg 6(2) and (3) of the Housing Benefit (Local Housing Allowance, Miscellaneous and Consequential) Amendment Regulations 2007 SI No.2870 as from 7 April 2008, save that for someone to whom reg 1(3) of those regulations apply, the amendments come into force on the day on or after 7 April 2008 when the first of the events specified in reg 1(6) applies to her/him, or on 6 April 2009 if none have before date.

Paras 3(1), 5(2) and 9(3)(a)(ii) amended by reg 7(2) to (4) of the Social Security (Miscellaneous Amendments) (No.2) Regulations 2008 SI No.1042 as from 19 May 2008.

[p1103: in the analysis to sub-paragraph 10: Exempt accommodation, after the paragraph ending '... token or minimal amount.' add:]

The care, support or supervision must be provided either by, or on behalf of the landlord. The words 'or acting on its behalf' in sub-paragraph (b) of the definition mean acting on its behalf in providing the care support, or supervision. It is not sufficient that a third party is acting on behalf of the landlord in some other respect. The third party must also be acting on the landlord's behalf in providing care, etc: *R(H) 6/08*, an interim decision of Commissioner Turnbull.

[p1104: in the analysis to sub-paragraph 10: Exempt accommodation, after ' ... additional support.' add:]

The final decisions in *CH 779/2007* and *R(H) 6/08* (and a third appeal, *CH 2805/2007*) will be made by Commissioner Turnbull after a joint hearing.

[p1121: in the first paragraph of the analysis to paragraphs (11)(a) and (13): Those who claimed asylum ... 'on arrival', delete 'However ... October 2007.' And replace with:]

A definitive answer to this debate has now been given in *Kola and Another v Secretary of State for Work and Pensions* [2007] 28 November, UKHL 54, reported as *R(IS) 1/08* . The House of Lords decided that an asylum seeker could have submitted her/his asylum claim 'on arrival' even if s/he did not submit the claim to an immigration officer on duty at the port of entry. It held that the provision is ambiguous as to what is meant by 'on arrival' and that the Secretary of State's very narrow interpretation of it would produce obvious unfairness in many cases. Lord Brown of Eaton-Under-Haywood said: 'If the asylum seeker could not reasonably have been expected to claim asylum any earlier than he did, having regard both to his practical opportunity for doing so and to his state of mind at the time, including the effect on him of anything said by his facilitating agent, then I see no good reason why his claim should not properly be accepted as one made 'on his arrival.''

pp1125-33   Housing Benefit and Council Tax Benefit (Consequential Provisions) Regulations
2006 Sch 4
Reg 10A and paras 3 and 7 of Sch A1 as inserted by Sch 4 substituted by reg 6(4) of the Housing Benefit (Local Housing Allowance, Miscellaneous and Consequential) Amendment Regulations 2007 SI No.2870 as from 7 April 2008, save that for someone to whom reg 1(3) of those regulations apply, the amendments come into force on the day on or after 7 April 2008 when the first of the events specified in reg 1(6) applies to her/him, or on 6 April 2009 if none have before date.

Paras 3(4) amended by reg 7(5) of the Social Security (Miscellaneous Amendments)(No.2) Regulations 2008 SI No.1042 as from 19 May 2008.

pp1163-64 Income-Related Benefits (Subsidy to Authorities) Order 1998 Art 13
Art 13 amended by Art 2(2) of the Income-related Benefits (Subsidy to Authorities) Amendment Order 2008 SI No.196 with retrospective effect from 1 April 2006.

pp1169-72 Income-Related Benefits (Subsidy to Authorities) Order 1998 Art 18
Para 1 amended and paras (10) and (11) omitted by Art 2(3) of the Income-related Benefits (Subsidy to Authorities) Amendment Order 2008 SI No.196 with retrospective effect from 1 April 2006.

p1175   Income-Related Benefits (Subsidy to Authorities) Order 1998 Art 21
Art 21 omitted by Art 2(4) of the Income-related Benefits (Subsidy to Authorities) Amendment Order 2008 SI No.196 with retrospective effect from 1 April 2006.

pp1176-83 Income-Related Benefits (Subsidy to Authorities) Order 1998 Sch 1
Sch 1 substituted by Art 3 of the Income-related Benefits (Subsidy to Authorities) Amendment Order 2008 SI No.196 with retrospective effect from 1 April 2006.

pp1191-96 Income-Related Benefits (Subsidy to Authorities) Order 1998 Sch 4A
Paras 2 and 4 amended, Parts 3 and 5 substituted, by the Income-related Benefits (Subsidy to Authorities) Amendment (No.2) Order 2008 SI No.695 as from 1 April 2008.

Welfare Reform Act 2007
Part 2
Housing Benefit and Council Tax benefit

Local housing allowance

30.–(1)   In section 130 of the Contributions and Benefits Act (housing benefit) subsection (4) ceases to have effect.

(2)   After that section insert–

"130A   Appropriate maximum housing benefit

(1)   For the purposes of section 130 above, the appropriate maximum housing benefit (in this section referred to as "the AMHB") is determined in accordance with this section.

(2)   Regulations must prescribe the manner in which the AMHB is to be determined.

(3)   The regulations may provide for the AMHB to be ascertained in the prescribed manner by reference to rent officer determinations.

(4)   The regulations may require an authority administering housing benefit in any prescribed case–

(a)   to apply for a rent officer determination, and

(b)   to do so within such time as may be specified in the regulations.

(5)   The regulations may make provision as to the circumstances in which, for the purpose of determining the AMHB, the amount of the liability mentioned in section 130(1)(a) above must be taken to be the amount of a rent officer determination instead of the actual amount of that liability.

(6)   Regulations under subsection (5) may also make provision for the liability of a person who, by virtue of regulations under section 137(2)(j) below, is treated as having a liability mentioned in section 130(1)(a) above to be the amount of a rent officer determination.

(7)   A rent officer determination is a determination made by a rent officer in the exercise of functions under section 122 of the Housing Act 1996."

(3)   In Schedule 7 to the Child Support, Pensions and Social Security Act 2000 (c. 19) (housing benefit and council tax benefit: revisions and appeals), in paragraph 4–

(a)   in sub-paragraph (1) for "sub-paragraph (4)" substitute "sub-paragraphs (4) and (4A)";

(b)   after sub-paragraph (4) insert–

"(4A)   Regulations may prescribe the cases and circumstances in which, and the procedure by which, a decision relating to housing benefit must be made by the appropriate relevant authority."

Information relating to housing benefit

35.–(1)   Section 5 of the Administration Act (regulations about claims and benefits) is amended as follows.

(2)   After subsection (2) insert–

"(2A)   The regulations may also require such persons as are prescribed to provide a rent officer with information or evidence of such description as is prescribed.

(2B)   For the purposes of subsection (2A), the Secretary of State may prescribe any description of information or evidence which he thinks is necessary or expedient to enable rent officers to carry out their functions under section 122 of the Housing Act 1996.

(2C)   Information or evidence required to be provided by virtue of subsection (2A) may relate to an individual claim or award or to any description of claims or awards.''

(3)   Subsection (3) ceases to have effect.

Directions by Secretary of State

39.–(1)   Section 139D of the Administration Act (power to give directions) is amended in accordance with subsections (2) to (8) below.

(2)   In subsection (1) (reports that trigger the section), for paragraph (c) substitute–

''(c)   a copy of a report under section 102(1)(b) or (c) of the Local Government (Scotland) Act 1973 which to any extent relates to the administration of benefit has been sent to a local authority and the Secretary of State under section 102(2) of that Act;''.

(3)   In subsection (1), after paragraph (c) insert–

''(ca)   a copy of a report which has been sent to a local authority under section 13A(3) of the Local Government Act 1999 and to the Secretary of State under section 13A(4A) of that Act;''.

(4)   In subsection (2) for ''invite'' substitute ''require''.

(5)   After subsection (2) insert–

''(2A)   A requirement under subsection (2) above may specify–
(a)   any information or description of information to be provided;
(b)   the form and manner in which the information is to be provided.
(2B)   The authority must respond to a requirement under subsection (2) above before the end of such period (not less than one month after the day on which the requirement is made) as the Secretary of State specifies in the requirement.
(2C)   The Secretary of State may extend the period specified under subsection (2B) above.''

(6)   For subsection (3) substitute–

''(3)   After considering–
(a)   the report,
(b)   any proposals made by the authority in response to it, and
(c)   any other information he thinks is relevant,
the Secretary of State may give directions to the authority under subsection (3A) or (3B) or both.
(3A)   Directions under this subsection are directions as to–
(a)   standards which the authority is to attain in the prevention and detection of fraud relating to benefit or otherwise in the administration of benefit;
(b)   the time within which the standards are to be attained.
(3B)   Directions under this subsection are directions to take such action as the Secretary of State thinks necessary or expedient for the purpose of improving the authority's exercise of its functions–
(a)   in relation to the prevention and detection of fraud relating to benefit;
(b)   otherwise in relation to the administration of benefit.
(3C)   A direction under subsection (3B) may specify the time within which anything is to be done.''

(7)   In subsection (4), for "subsection (3)" substitute "subsection (3A)".

(8)   After subsection (4) insert–

"(4A)   If the Secretary of State proposes to give a direction under this section he must give the authority to which the direction is to be addressed an opportunity to make representations about the proposed direction.

(4B)   The Secretary of State may specify a period within which representations mentioned in subsection (4A) above must be made.

(4C)   The Secretary of State may extend a period specified under subsection (4B) above.

(4D)   Subsections (4A) to (4C) do not apply if the Secretary of State thinks that it is necessary for a direction to be given as a matter of urgency.

(4E)   If the Secretary of State acts under subsection (4D) he must give in writing to the authority to which the direction is addressed his reasons for doing so."

(9)   After section 139D of that Act insert–

"139DA   Directions: variation and revocation

(1)   The Secretary of State may at any time in accordance with this section vary or revoke a direction under section 139D above.

(2)   A direction may be varied or revoked only if the Secretary of State thinks it is necessary to do so–

(a)   in consequence of representations made by the authority to which the direction is addressed,

(b)   to rectify an omission or error, or

(c)   in consequence of a material change in circumstances.

(3)   The Secretary of State must not vary a direction unless he first–

(a)   sends a copy of the proposed variation to the authority concerned,

(b)   gives the authority his reasons for making the variation, and

(c)   gives the authority an opportunity to make representations about the proposed variation.

(4)   The Secretary of State may specify a period of not less than one month within which representations mentioned in subsection (3)(c) above must be made.

(5)   The Secretary of State may extend a period specified under subsection (4) above."

Minor and consequential amendments relating to Part 2

40.   Schedule 5 (which makes miscellaneous minor amendments and amendments consequential on this Part) has effect.

Local authority powers to investigate benefit fraud

46.–(1)   Section 110A of the Administration Act (authorisation of investigations by authorities administering housing benefit or council tax benefit) is amended as follows.

(2)   In subsection (1) for "any one or more of the purposes mentioned in subsection (2) below" substitute "a relevant purpose".

(3)   After subsection (1) insert–

"(1A)   Each of the following is a relevant purpose–

(a)   a purpose mentioned in subsection (2) below;

(b)   a purpose mentioned in section 109A(2)(a), (c) or (d).

(1B)   If the Secretary of State prescribes conditions for the purposes of this section, an authority must not proceed under this section for a purpose mentioned in section 109A(2)(a), (c) or (d) unless any such condition is satisfied.

(1C)   An authorisation made for a purpose mentioned in section 109A(2)(a), (c) or (d)–

(a)   is subject to such restrictions as may be prescribed;
(b)   is not valid in such circumstances as may be prescribed.''

(4)   In subsection (2) for ''Those purposes'' substitute ''The purposes in this subsection''.
(5)   In subsection (8), after paragraph (c) insert–

''but paragraphs (a) and (b) above do not apply in any case where the relevant purpose is as mentioned in subsection (1A)(b) above.''

Local authority powers to prosecute benefit fraud

47.   After section 116 of the Administration Act (legal proceedings) insert–

''116A   Local authority powers to prosecute benefit fraud

(1)   This section applies if an authority administering housing benefit or council tax benefit has power to bring proceedings for a benefit offence relating to that benefit.
(2)   The authority may bring proceedings for a benefit offence relating to any other relevant social security benefit unless–
(a)   the proceedings relate to any benefit or circumstances or any description of benefit or circumstances which the Secretary of State prescribes for the purposes of this paragraph, or
(b)   the Secretary of State has directed that the authority must not bring the proceedings,
and a direction under paragraph (b) may relate to a particular authority or description of authority or to particular proceedings or any description of proceedings.
(3)   If the Secretary of State prescribes conditions for the purposes of this section, an authority must not bring proceedings under this section unless any such condition is satisfied.
(4)   The Secretary of State may continue proceedings which have been brought by an authority under this section as if the proceedings had been brought in his name or he may discontinue the proceedings if–
(a)   he makes provision under subsection (2)(a), such that the authority would no longer be entitled to bring the proceedings under this section,
(b)   he gives a direction under subsection (2)(b) in relation to the proceedings, or
(c)   a condition prescribed under subsection (3) ceases to be satisfied in relation to the proceedings.
(5)   In the exercise of its power under subsection (2), a local authority must have regard to the Code for Crown Prosecutors issued by the Director of Public Prosecutions under section 10 of the Prosecution of Offences Act 1985–
(a)   in determining whether the proceedings should be instituted;
(b)   in determining what charges should be preferred;
(c)   in considering what representations to make to a magistrates' court about mode of trial;
(d)   in determining whether to discontinue proceedings.
(6)   An authority must not bring proceedings for a benefit offence which does not relate to housing benefit or council tax benefit otherwise than in accordance with this section.
(7)   In subsection (2), ''relevant social security benefit'' has the same meaning as in section 121DA below.
(8)   This section does not apply to Scotland.''

Loss of benefit for commission of benefit offences

49.–(1)   In section 7 of the Social Security Fraud Act 2001 (c. 11) (loss of benefit for commission of benefit offences) in subsection (1)(b) (period within which later offence must be committed), for ''three years'' substitute ''five years''.

(2)   The amendment made by subsection (1) shall be disregarded insofar as the application of section 7(1)(b) of that Act involves considering whether an offence committed before the day on which this section comes into force was committed within the relevant period.

SCHEDULE 5

Section 40

Minor and consequential amendments relating to Part 2

5. In section 139E (information about attainment of standards), in subsection (1)–
(a)   for ''section 139D(3)'' substitute ''section 139D(3A) or (3B)'';
(b)   after paragraph (a) insert–

''(aa)   whether the authority has taken the action which it has been directed to take;'';

(c)   in paragraph (b) after ''those standards'' insert ''or take that action''.
6. (1)   Section 139F (enforcement notices) is amended as follows.
(2)   In subsection (1)–
(a)   for ''section 139D(3)'' substitute ''section 139D(3A) or (3B)'';
(b)   after paragraph (a) insert–

''(aa)   is not satisfied that the authority has taken the action which it has been directed to take;'';

(c)   in paragraph (b) after ''those standards'' insert ''or take that action''.
(3)   In subsection (2)(a), after ''paragraph (a)'' insert '', (aa)''.
(4)   In subsection (4), at the beginning insert ''If the notice identifies directions under section 139D(3A),''.
(5)   After subsection (4) insert–

''(4A)   If the notice identifies directions under section 139D(3B), the authority's response shall either–
(a)   state that the authority has taken the action, or is likely to take it within the time specified in the directions, and justify that statement; or
(b)   state that the authority has not taken the action, or is not likely to take it within that time, and (if the authority wishes) give reasons why a determination under section 139G below should not be made or should not include any particular provision.''

7. (1)   Section 139G (enforcement determinations) is amended as follows.
(2)   In subsection (1)–
(a)   in paragraph (a) after ''the standards'' insert ''or taken the action'';
(b)   in paragraph (b) after ''those standards'' insert ''or take that action''.
(3)   In subsections (3) and (5)(c), after ''the standards'' insert ''or the taking of the action''.
9.   In section 140B(5A) (calculation of amount of subsidy), for ''section 139D(3)'' substitute ''section 139D(3A) or (3B)''.

Local Government and Public Involvement in Health Act 2007
Chapter 2
Audit Commission and auditors: functions and procedure
Benefits inspections

Powers of the Audit Commission relating to benefits
147.–(1)   *Omitted*

(2)   In section 139D of the Social Security Administration Act 1992 (c. 5) (power of Secretary of State to give directions following report), in subsection (1), after paragraph (ba) insert–

''(bb)   a copy of a report has been sent to a local authority under subsection (3) of section 13 of the Local Government Act 1999 and to the Secretary of State under subsection (4A) of that section;''.

Interaction of benefits inspectors with the Audit Commission

150.   After section 139B of the Social Security Administration Act 1992 (c. 5) insert–

''139BA   Interaction with Audit Commission

(1)   A person authorised under section 139A(1) must from time to time, or at such times as the Secretary of State may specify by order, prepare–

(a)   a document setting out what inspections of English authorities he proposes to carry out (an ''inspection programme'');

(b)   a document setting out the way in which he proposes to carry out his functions of inspecting and reporting on such authorities (an ''inspection framework'').

(2)   The person authorised under section 139A(1) must–

(a)   consult the Audit Commission before preparing an inspection programme or an inspection framework; and

(b)   once an inspection programme or inspection framework is prepared, send a copy of it to–

(i)   the Secretary of State; and

(ii)   the Audit Commission.

(3)   The Secretary of State may by order specify the form that inspection programmes or inspection frameworks must take.

(4)   A person authorised under section 139A(1)–

(a)   must co-operate with the Audit Commission, and

(b)   may act jointly with the Audit Commission,

where it is appropriate to do so for the efficient and effective discharge of the person's functions in relation to English authorities.

(5)   In this section–

''the Audit Commission'' means the Audit Commission for Local Authorities and the National Health Service in England;

''English authorities'' means authorities administering housing benefit or council tax benefit in England;

''person'' does not include the Audit Commission.''

SCHEDULE 9

s146

Consequential amendments relating to change of name of the Audit Commission

Amendment of references to the current name of the Commission

1.–(1)   In the provisions listed in sub-paragraph (2), in the expression ''Audit Commission for Local Authorities and the National Health Service in England and Wales'', omit ''and Wales''.

(2)   The provisions are–

(h)   section 123(8)(ja) of the Social Security Administration Act 1992 (c. 5) (unauthorised disclosure of information relating to particular persons);

The Social Security (Miscellaneous Amendments) (No.5) Regulations 2007

(SI 2007 No.2618)

Made	*6th September 2007*
Laid before Parliament	*10th September 2007*
Coming into force in accordance with regulation 1	

The Secretary of State for Work and Pensions makes the following Regulations in the exercise of powers conferred by–
– sections 30C(3), 30E(1), 70(8), 123(1)(a), (d) and (e), 130(2), 135(1) and (2), 136(3), (5)(a) to (c), 136A(3), 137(1) and (2)(d) and (h), 171D, 171G(2), 175(1) to (4) of, and paragraph 2(3) of Schedule 7 to, the Social Security Contributions and Benefits Act 1992,
– sections 5(1)(a), (g), (hh), (i) and (q), 6(1)(a), (g), (hh), (i) and (q) and 189(1), (3) and (5) of the Social Security Administration Act 1992,
– sections 4(5) and (12), 12(1), (2), (4)(a) to (c), 19(8), 20A(9), 35(1) and 36(1), (2) and (4) of, and paragraph 1(2)(a) of Schedule 1 to, the Jobseekers Act 1995,
– paragraphs 4(6), 20(1)(b) and 23(1) of Schedule 7 to the Child Support, Pensions and Social Security Act 2000, and
– sections 2(6), 15(3) and (6)(a), 17(1) and 19(1) of the State Pension Credit Act 2002.
The Social Security Advisory Committee and the Industrial Injuries Advisory Council have agreed that the proposals in respect of these Regulations should not be referred to them.
In respect of the provisions in these Regulations relating to housing benefit and council tax benefit, the Secretary of State has consulted the organisations appearing to him to be representative of the authorities concerned.

Citation, commencement and interpretation

1.–(1) *Omitted*
(2) *Omitted*
(3) Regulation 11(12) shall come into force–
(a) in relation to any case where rent is payable at intervals of a whole number of weeks, on 7th April 2008;
(b) in any other case, on 1st April 2008.
(4) Regulation 13(10) shall come into force on 1st April 2008.
(5) *Omitted*

Amendment of the Housing Benefit Regulations 2006

11.–(1) The Housing Benefit Regulations 2006 are amended as follows.
(12) In paragraph 22 of Schedule 5 (sums to be disregarded in the calculation of income other than earnings) for sub-paragraphs (a) and (b) substitute–

"(a) where the aggregate of any payments made in respect of any one week in respect of the occupation of the dwelling by that person or a member of his family, or by that person and a member of his family, is less than £20, the whole of that amount; or
(b) where the aggregate of any such payments is £20 or more per week, £20.".

Amendment of the Council Tax Benefit Regulations 2006

13.–(1) The Council Tax Benefit Regulations 2006 are amended as follows.
(10) In paragraph 22 of Schedule 4 (sums to be disregarded in the calculation of income other than earnings) for sub-paragraphs (a) and (b) substitute–

"(a) where the aggregate of any payments made in respect of any one week in respect of the occupation of the dwelling by that person or a member of his family, or by that person and a member of his family, is less than £20, the whole of that amount; or

(b) where the aggregate of any such payments is £20 or more per week, £20.".

The Housing Benefit (Local Housing Allowance and Information Sharing) Amendment Regulations 2007

(SI 2007 No. 2868)

Made	*2nd October 2007*
Laid before Parliament	*8th October 2007*
Coming into force in accordance with regulation 1	

The Secretary of State for Work and Pensions makes the following Regulations in exercise of the powers conferred by sections 123(1)(d), 130(2), 130A(2) to (6), 137(1) and 175(1) and (3) to (6) of the Social Security Contributions and Benefits Act 1992 and sections 5(1)(p), (2A) to (2C) and (6), 189(4) to (6) and 191 of the Social Security Administration Act 1992.

This instrument contains only regulations made by virtue of, or consequential upon, sections 30 and 35 of the Welfare Reform Act 2007 and is made before the end of the period of six months beginning with the coming into force of those sections.

In accordance with section 176(1) of the Social Security Administration Act 1992, the Secretary of State has consulted with organisations appearing to him to be representative of the authorities concerned.

Citation and commencement

1.—(1) These Regulations may be cited as the Housing Benefit (Local Housing Allowance and Information Sharing) Amendment Regulations 2007.

(2) This regulation and regulations 2 (amendment of the Housing Benefit Regulations 2006) and 3 (amendments relating to information sharing) shall come into force on 7th April 2008.

(3) Subject to paragraph (6) (which relates to non-local housing allowance cases), regulations 4 to 19 (amendment of the Housing Benefit Regulations 2006 relating to determination of appropriate maximum housing benefit) shall come into force on 7th April 2008 immediately following the coming into force of regulation 3.

(4) Regulation 20 (substitution of Part 15 of and Schedule 10 to the Housing Benefit Regulations 2006 in relation to former pathfinder authorities) shall come into force immediately following the coming into force of regulations 4 to 19 and in this paragraph "former pathfinder authorities" means those relevant authorities specified in Part 1 of Schedule 10 of the Housing Benefit Regulations.

(5) This paragraph applies to a case where no reference was made to a maximum rent (standard local rate) in determining the amount of the eligible rent which applied immediately before 7th April 2008 and in this paragraph–

"eligible rent" shall be construed in accordance with–
　(i) regulations 12 or 12A of the Housing Benefit Regulations 2006 as in force immediately before 7th April 2008; or
　(ii) in a case to which paragraph 4 of Schedule 3 to the Housing Benefit and Council Tax Benefit (Consequential Provisions) Regulations 2006 applies, regulations 12 and 13 of those Regulations as set out in paragraph 5 of that Schedule as in force immediately before 7th April 2008; and

"maximum rent (standard local rate)" means a maximum rent (standard local rate) determined in accordance with regulation 13A of the Housing Benefit Regulations 2006 as in force immediately before 7th April 2008.

(6)   In a case to which paragraph (5) applies regulations 4 to 19 shall come into force on the day when, on or after 7th April 2008, the first of the following sub-paragraphs applies–

(a)   a relevant authority is required to apply to a rent officer by virtue of regulation 14 of the Housing Benefit Regulations;

(b)   sub-paragraph (a) would apply but for the case falling within regulation 14(4)(a) of, or 14(4)(b) of and paragraph 2 of Schedule 2 to, the Housing Benefit Regulations (no application to rent officer required as an existing rent officer determination may be used);

(c)   a relevant authority is required to determine an eligible rent in accordance with regulation 12(3)(b) of the Housing Benefit Regulations; or

(d)   a relevant authority is required to determine an eligible rent in accordance with regulation 12(3) of the Housing Benefit Regulations 2006 as set out in paragraph 5 of Schedule 3 to the Consequential Provisions Regulations,

and in this paragraph "relevant authority" means an authority administering housing benefit.

(7)   Where paragraph (6) does not apply before 6th April 2009, regulations 4 to 19 shall come into force on that date.

(8)   In this regulation–

(a)   "the Housing Benefit Regulations" means the Housing Benefit Regulations 2006 as in force immediately before the coming into force of regulations 4 to 19 in that case; and

(b)   "the Consequential Provisions Regulations" means the Housing Benefit and Council Tax Benefit (Consequential Provisions) Regulations 2006 as in force immediately before the coming into force of regulations 4 to 19 in that case.

Amendment of the Housing Benefit Regulations 2006

2.   The Housing Benefit Regulations 2006 shall be amended in accordance with the following provisions of these Regulations.

Amendment of the Housing Benefit Regulations 2006 relating to information sharing

3.–(1)   In regulation 14 (requirement to refer to rent officers)–

(a)   omit paragraphs (2), (3) and (9);

(b)   after paragraph (4) insert–

"(4A)   The provision of information to the rent officer in accordance with [¹ regulation 114A(5)] shall be treated as an application to the rent officer under paragraph (1).".

(2)   After regulation 113 (interpretation) insert–

"Information to be provided to rent officers

114A.–(1)   This paragraph applies to every claim for or award of housing benefit in the form of a rent allowance where the eligible rent has been, or is to be determined, in accordance with–

(a)   regulation 12(3)(a) (rent) or 12C (eligible rent and maximum rent), as the case may require;

(b)   [¹ regulation 12D] (eligible rent and the maximum rent (LHA)) or any of regulations 12E to 12K (transitional protection for pathfinder cases), as the case may require; or

(c)   regulations 12 (rent) and 13 (maximum rent) as set out in paragraph 5 of Schedule 3 to the Consequential Provisions Regulations.

(2)   No earlier than the first, and no later than the fifth, working day of every month a relevant authority shall provide the following information to the rent officer

in relation to every claim for or award of housing benefit to which paragraph (1) applied in the preceding month–

(a) the address, including any room or unit number, house or flat number or name, and the postcode of the dwelling to which the claim or award relates;

(b) where the claim or award relates to mooring charges for a houseboat, or payments in respect of the site on which a caravan or mobile home stands, the mooring or plot number and the address of the mooring or site, including the postcode;

(c) the date on which the tenancy began;

(d) the amount of rent and the rental period, whether calendar monthly, four weekly, weekly or some other period;

(e) where the claimant has the use of two or more bedrooms, the number of bedrooms and rooms suitable for living in that there are in the dwelling, and in this sub-paragraph "bedroom" does not include a bedroom which the claimant shares with any person other than a member of his household, a non-dependant of his, or a person who pays rent to him or his partner;

(f) whether the tenant (together with his partner where he has one) has exclusive use of only one bedroom, and if so, whether they have exclusive use of a kitchen, bathroom, toilet and a room suitable for living in;

(g) whether the tenant has exclusive use of only one bedroom, and if so, which, if any, of the following the tenancy provides for him to share–

(i) a kitchen;

(ii) a bathroom;

(iii) a toilet; or

(iv) a room suitable for living in;

(h) the date on which entitlement to housing benefit began; and

(i) where applicable, the date on which entitlement to housing benefit ended.

(3) Where the relevant authority is required to apply to the rent officer for a board and attendance determination by virtue of regulation 13D(10) (determination of a maximum rent (LHA)), it shall provide the following information in the application to the Rent Officer–

(a) the address, including any room or unit number, house or flat number or name and the postcode of the dwelling to which the claim or award relates;

(b) the date on which the tenancy began;

(c) the length of the tenancy;

(d) the total amount of those payments referred to in regulation 12(1) (rent) which the claimant is liable to make in respect of the dwelling which he occupies as his home;

(e) whether those payments include any charges for water, sewerage or allied environmental services or charges in respect of meals or fuel which are ineligible for housing benefit; and

(f) where those payments include any charges that are ineligible for housing benefit by reason of paragraph 1(a)(iv) and (c) to (f) of Schedule 1 (ineligible service charges), that such charges are included, and the value of those charges as determined by that authority pursuant to regulation 12B(2) and that Schedule.

(4) Where the relevant authority has identified charges to which paragraph (3)(f) applies, it shall–

(a) deduct those charges from the total amount of those payments which, in accordance with paragraph (3)(d), it has stated that the claimant is liable to make in respect of the dwelling which he occupies as his home; and

(b) notify that total so reduced to the rent officer in its application.

(5) Where a relevant authority has received notification from the rent officer that a substantial part of the rent is attributable to board and attendance, it shall

provide the information referred to in paragraphs (7) and (8), except for such information as it has already provided in accordance with paragraphs (3) and (4).

(6)   Where the relevant authority is required to apply to the rent officer for a determination by virtue of regulation 14(1) (requirement to refer to rent officers), it shall provide the information referred to in paragraphs (7) to (9) in the application to the rent officer.

(7)   In relation to the dwelling to which the claim or award relates, the relevant authority shall provide the following information–

(a)   the address, including any room or unit number, house or flat number or name and the postcode of the dwelling;

(b)   where the claim or award relates to mooring charges for a houseboat, or payments in respect of the site on which a caravan or mobile home stands, the mooring or plot number and the address of the mooring or site, including the postcode;

(c)   whether the dwelling is–
(i)   a detached house;
(ii)   a semi-detached house;
(iii)   a terraced house;
(iv)   a maisonette;
(v)   a detached bungalow;
(vi)   a semi-detached bungalow;
(vii)   a flat in a house;
(viii) a flat in a block;
(ix)   a flat over a shop;
(x)   a bedsit or rooms or a studio flat;
(xi)   a hostel;
(xii)   a caravan, mobile home or houseboat;
(xiii) board and lodgings;
(xiv)   a hotel;
(xv)   a care home;
(xvi)   an independent hospital; or
(xvii) some other description of dwelling, and if so what;

(d)   whether the dwelling has central heating, a garden, a garage or a parking space;

(e)   how many rooms suitable for living in there are–
(i)   in the dwelling;
(ii)   in the dwelling which the claimant shares with any person other than a member of his household, a non-dependant of his, or a person who pays rent to him or his partner;

(f)   how many bedsitting rooms there are in the categories (e)(i) and (ii);

(g)   how many bedrooms there are in the categories (e)(i) and (ii);

(h)   how many bathrooms or toilets there are in the categories (e)(i) and (ii); and

(i)   such other information as the rent officer may reasonably require to make a determination.

(8)   In relation to the tenancy to which the claim or award relates, the relevant authority shall provide the following information–

(a)   the information referred to in paragraphs (3)(d) to (f) and (4);

(b)   if the tenancy is furnished, and if so, to what extent;

(c)   the rental period, whether calendar monthly, four weekly, weekly or some other period;

(d)   the length of the tenancy;

(e)   when the tenancy began and, if appropriate, when it ended;

(h)   the landlord's or letting agent's name;

(i)   the landlord's or letting agent's business address;

(j)   whether the landlord is a housing association or registered social landlord; and

(k)   such other information as the rent officer may reasonably require to make a determination.

(9)   In relation to the claimant and the other occupiers of the dwelling to which the claim or award relates, the relevant authority shall provide the following information–

(a)   such information regarding the relationship of the claimant to the occupiers and the occupiers to each other, as is necessary for the rent officer to make the determination;

(b)   the age and sex of each occupier under 18;

(c)   whether the claimant is or may be a young individual; and

(d)   any other information that is relevant to the rent officer in making the determination, including visits to the dwelling.

(10)   Where a rent officer serves a notice under article 5 (insufficient information) of the Rent Officers Order the relevant authority shall supply the further information required under this regulation, or confirm whether information already supplied is correct and, if it is not, supply the correct information.

(11)   Where the relevant authority refers a case to the rent officer in accordance with regulation 14 as in force before the coming into force of regulation 8 of the Housing Benefit (Local Housing Allowance and Information Sharing) Amendment Regulations 2007, it shall notify the rent officer that the referral is made in accordance with regulation 14 as in force before the coming into force of regulation 8 of those Regulations.

(12)   In this regulation–

"tenancy" includes–

(a)   in Scotland, any other right of occupancy; and

(b)   in any other case, a licence to occupy premises,

and reference to a tenant, landlord or any other expression appropriate to a tenancy shall be construed accordingly;

"working day" means any day other than a Saturday, a Sunday, Christmas Day, Good Friday or a day which is a bank holiday under the Banking and Financial Dealings Act 1971 in the jurisdiction in which the area of the relevant authority is situated.".

(3)   Omit regulation 114 (evidence and information required by rent officers).

Amendment

1.   Amended by reg 4(2) of SI 2008 No 586 as from 7.4.08.

Amendments to regulations 2, 3, 11 and 12 of the Housing Benefit Regulations 2006

4.–(1)   In regulation 2(1) (interpretation)–

(a)   for the definition of "eligible rent" substitute–

" "eligible rent" means, as the case may require, an eligible rent determined in accordance with–

(a)   regulations 12B (eligible rent), 12C (eligible rent and maximum rent) or 12D (eligible rent and maximum rent (LHA)); or

(b)   regulations 12 (rent) and 13 (restrictions on unreasonable payments) as set out in paragraph 5 of Schedule 3 to the Consequential Provisions Regulations in a case to which paragraph 4 of that Schedule applies;";

(b)   for the definition of "housing association" substitute–

" "housing association" has the meaning assigned to it by section 1(1) of the Housing Associations Act 1985;";

(c)   for the definition of "maximum rent" substitute–

" "maximum rent" means the amount to which the eligible rent is restricted in a case where regulation 13 applies;";

(d)   for the definition of "non-dependant deduction" substitute–

" "non-dependant deduction" means a deduction that is to be made under regulation 74 (non-dependant deductions);";

(e)   for the definition of "Rent Officers Order" substitute–

"Rent Officers Order" means the Rent Officers (Housing Benefit Functions) Order 1997 or, as the case may be, the Rent Officers (Housing Benefit Functions) (Scotland) Order 1997;";

(f)   for the definition of "young individual" substitute–
"young individual" means a single claimant who has not attained the age of 25 years, but does not include such a claimant–
    (a)   whose landlord is a registered housing association;
    (b)   who has not attained the age of 22 years and has ceased to be the subject of a care order made pursuant to section 31(1)(a) of the Children Act 1989 which had previously been made in respect to him either–
        (i)   after he attained the age of 16 years; or
        (ii)   before he attained the age of 16 years, but had continued after he attained that age;
    (c)   who has not attained the age of 22 years and was formerly provided with accommodation under section 20 of the Children Act 1989;
    (d)   who has not attained the age of 22 years and has ceased to be subject to a supervision requirement by a children's hearing under section 70 of the Children (Scotland) Act 1995 ("the 1995 Act") made in respect of him which had continued after he attained the age of 16 years, other than a case where–
        (i)   the ground of referral was based on the sole condition as to the need for compulsory measures of care specified in section 52(1)(i) of the 1995 Act (commission of offences by child); or
        (ii)   he was required by virtue of the supervision requirement to reside with a parent or guardian of his within the meaning of the 1995 Act, or with a friend or relative of his or of his parent or guardian;
    (e)   who has not attained the age of 22 years and has ceased to be a child in relation to whom the parental rights and responsibilities were transferred to a local authority under a parental responsibilities order made in accordance with section 86 of the 1995 Act or treated as so vested in accordance with paragraph 3 of Schedule 3 to that Act, either–
        (i)   after he attained the age of 16 years; or
        (ii)   before he attained the age of 16 years, but had continued after he attained that age; or
    (f)   who has not attained the age of 22 years and has ceased to be provided with accommodation by a local authority under section 25 of the 1995 Act where he has previously been provided with accommodation by the authority under that provision either–

      (i)   after he attained the age of 16 years; or

      (ii)   before he attained the age of 16 years, but had continued to be in such accommodation after he attained that age;'';

(g)   at the appropriate places insert–

'' ''amended determination'' means a determination made in accordance with article 7A of the Rent Officers Order;

''broad rental market area'' has the meaning specified in paragraph 4 of Schedule 3B to the Rent Officers Order;

''broad rental market area determination'' means a determination made in accordance with article 4B(1A) of the Rent Officers Order;

''change of dwelling'' means, for the purposes of regulations 13C and 14, a change of dwelling occupied by a claimant as his home during the award where the dwelling to which the claimant has moved is one in respect of which the authority may make a rent allowance;

''linked person'' means–

(a)   any member of the claimant's family;

(b)   if the claimant is a member of a polygamous marriage, any partners of his and any child or young person for whom he or a partner is responsible and who is a member of the same household; or

(c)   any relative of the claimant or his partner who occupies the same dwelling as the claimant, whether or not they reside with him, except for a relative who has a separate right of occupation of the dwelling which would enable them to continue to occupy it even if the claimant ceased his occupation of it;

''local housing allowance'' means an allowance determined in accordance with paragraph 2 of Schedule 3B to the Rent Officers Order;

''maximum rent (LHA)'' means the amount determined in accordance with regulation 13D;

''reckonable rent'' means payments which a person is liable to make in respect of the dwelling which he occupies as his home, and which are eligible, or would, but for regulation 13, be eligible for housing benefit;

[1 ''registered housing association'' means a housing association which–

(a)   is registered in a register maintained by the Corporation or the National Assembly for Wales under Chapter 1 of Part 1 of the Housing Act 1996; or

(b)   in Scotland, is registered by Scottish Ministers by virtue of section 57(3)(b) of the Housing (Scotland) Act 2001,

and ''the Corporation'' has the same meaning as in section 56 of the Housing Act 1996;]

''relevant information'' means information or evidence forwarded to the relevant authority by an appropriate DWP office regarding a claim on which rent allowance may be awarded, which completes the transfer of all information or evidence held by the appropriate DWP office relating to that claim;

''single room rent'' means the rent determined by a rent officer under paragraph 5 of Schedule 1 to the Rent Officers Order;''.

(2)   In regulation 3(4) (definition of non-dependant) for ''and regulation 9'' substitute '', regulations 9 and 13(6)(c) and the definition of ''linked person'' in regulation 2''.

(3)   In regulation 11 (eligible housing costs)–

(a)   for paragraph (1) substitute–

''(1)   Subject to the following provisions of this regulation, housing benefit shall be payable in respect of the payments specified in regulation 12(1) (rent) and a claimant's maximum housing benefit shall be calculated under Part 8 (amount of benefit) by reference to the amount of his eligible rent determined in accordance with–

  (a)   regulation 12B (eligible rent);

  (b)   regulations 12C (eligible rent and maximum rent), 13 (maximum rent), 13ZA (protection on death and 13 week protection) and 13ZB (change in reckonable rent);

  (c)   regulations 12D (eligible rent and maximum rent (LHA)), 13C (when a maximum rent (LHA) is to be determined) and 13D (determination of a maximum rent (LHA)); or

  (d)   regulations 12 (rent) and 13 (restrictions on unreasonable payments) as set out in paragraph 5 of Schedule 3 to the Consequential Provisions Regulations,

whichever is applicable in his case.'';

  (b)   in paragraph (3) for ''paragraphs (1) to (3) of that regulation'' substitute ''paragraphs (1) or (2) of that regulation or paragraph (2) of regulation 12B''.

  (4)   In regulation 12 (rent)–

  (a)   omit paragraphs (3) to (7);

  (b)   in paragraph (8) after ''regulation'' insert '', regulation 12B (eligible rent)''.

Amendment

1.   Substituted by reg 4(3) of SI 2008 No 586 as from 7.4.08.

Insertion of regulations 12B, 12C and 12D into the Housing Benefit Regulations 2006

  5.   After regulation 12 (rent) insert–

''Eligible rent

12B.–(1) The amount of a person's eligible rent shall be determined in accordance with the provisions of this regulation except where regulations 12C (eligible rent and maximum rent) or 12D (eligible rent and maximum rent (LHA)) apply, or paragraph 4 of Schedule 3 to the Consequential Provisions Regulations applies.

  (2)   Subject to paragraphs (3), (4) and (6), the amount of a person's eligible rent shall be the aggregate of such payments specified in regulation 12(1) as that person is liable to pay less–

  (a)   except where he is separately liable for charges for water, sewerage or allied environmental services, an amount determined in accordance with paragraph (5);

  (b)   where payments include service charges which are wholly or partly ineligible, an amount in respect of the ineligible charges determined in accordance with Schedule 1; and

  (c)   where he is liable to make payments in respect of any service charges to which regulation 12(1)(e) does not apply, but to which paragraph 3(2) of Part 1 of Schedule 1 (unreasonably low service charges) applies in the particular circumstances, an amount in respect of such charges determined in accordance with paragraph 3(2) of Part 1 of Schedule 1.

  (3)   Where the payments specified in regulation 12(1) are payable in respect of accommodation which consists partly of residential accommodation and partly of other accommodation, only such proportion of those payments as is referable to the residential accommodation shall count as eligible rent for the purposes of these Regulations.

  (4)   Where more than one person is liable to make payments in respect of a dwelling, the payments specified in regulation 12(1) shall be apportioned for the

purpose of calculating the eligible rent for each such person having regard to all the circumstances, in particular, the number of such persons and the proportion of rent paid by each such person.

(5)   The amount of the deduction referred to in paragraph (2) shall be–

(a)   if the dwelling occupied by the claimant is a self-contained unit, except in a case to which sub-paragraph (c) applies, the amount of the charges;

(b)   in any other case, except one to which sub-paragraph (c) applies, the proportion of those charges in respect of the self-contained unit which is obtained by dividing the area of the dwelling occupied by the claimant by the area of the self-contained unit of which it forms part;

(c)   where the charges vary in accordance with the amount of water actually used, the amount which the appropriate authority considers to be fairly attributable to water, and sewerage services, having regard to the actual or estimated consumption of the claimant.

(6)   In any case where it appears to the relevant authority that in the particular circumstances of that case the eligible rent as determined in accordance with the preceding paragraphs of this regulation is greater than it is reasonable to meet by way of housing benefit, the eligible rent shall be such lesser sum as seems to that authority to be an appropriate rent in that particular case.

Eligible rent and maximum rent

12C.–(1)   This regulation applies where a maximum rent has been, or is to be, determined in accordance with regulation 13 (maximum rent).

(2)   Where this regulation applies, except where paragraph (3) applies, the amount of a person's eligible rent shall be the maximum rent, subject to paragraphs (3), (4) and (6) of regulation 12B.

(3)   In a case where the maximum rent is derived from a single room rent determined by a rent officer under paragraph 5 of Schedule 1 to the Rent Officers Order the eligible rent shall be the maximum rent subject to paragraphs (3) and (6) of regulation 12B.

Eligible rent and maximum rent (LHA)

12D.–(1)   This regulation applies where, by virtue of paragraphs (2) or (3) of regulation 13C (when a maximum rent (LHA) is to be determined), a maximum rent (LHA) has been, or is to be, determined in accordance with regulation 13D (determination of a maximum rent (LHA)).

(2)   Where this regulation applies, except where paragraphs (3)(a) (protection on death) or (5)(a) (13 week protection) apply,–

(a)   the amount of a person's eligible rent shall be the maximum rent (LHA); and

(b)   it shall apply until the earlier of–

(i)   the determination of a maximum rent (LHA) by virtue of regulation 13C(2)(d) (change of category of dwelling, death or change of dwelling for an LHA case);

(ii)   the determination of a maximum rent (LHA) by virtue of regulation 13C(3) (anniversary of LHA date); or

(iii)   the determination of a maximum rent by virtue of regulation 13 or an eligible rent under regulation 12B.

(3)   Subject to paragraph (7), where the relevant authority is required to determine a maximum rent (LHA) by virtue of regulation 13C(2)(a), (b) (new claim on or after 7th April 2008) or (d)(i) or (ii) (change of category of dwelling or death relating to an LHA case) and the claimant occupies a dwelling which is the same as that occupied by him at the date of death of any linked person, the eligible rent shall be–

(a)   either–

> (i) the eligible rent which applied on the day before the death occurred; or
>
> (ii) in a case where there was no eligible rent, subject to regulation 12B(3) (mixed use accommodation), (4) (more than one person liable to make payments) and (6) (discretion in relation to eligible rent), the reckonable rent due on that day; or

(b) the eligible rent determined in accordance with paragraph (2), where it is equal to or more than the eligible rent determined in accordance with sub-paragraph (a).

(4) For the purpose of paragraph (3), a claimant shall be treated as occupying the dwelling if paragraph (13) of regulation 7 (circumstances in which a person is or is not to be treated as occupying a dwelling as his home) is satisfied and for that purpose paragraph (13) shall have effect as if sub-paragraph (b) of that paragraph were omitted.

(5) Subject to paragraphs (6) and (7), where a relevant authority is required to determine a maximum rent (LHA) by virtue of regulation 13C(2)(a) or (b) (new claim on or after 7th April 2008) and the relevant authority is satisfied that the claimant or a linked person was able to meet the financial commitments for his dwelling when they were entered into, the eligible rent shall be–

(a) an eligible rent determined in accordance with regulation 12B(2); or

(b) the eligible rent determined in accordance with paragraph (2), where it is equal to or more than the eligible rent referred to in sub-paragraph (a).

(6) Paragraph (5) shall not apply where a claimant or the claimant's partner, was previously entitled to benefit in respect of an award of housing benefit which fell wholly or partly less than 52 weeks before the commencement of the claimant's current award of housing benefit.

(7) Where a person's eligible rent has been determined in accordance with–

(a) paragraph (3)(a) (protection on death), it shall apply until the first of the following events occurs–

> (i) the period of 12 months from the date of death has expired;
>
> (ii) the relevant authority determines an eligible rent in accordance with paragraph (2) which is equal to or exceeds it or is based on a maximum rent (LHA) determined by virtue of regulation 13C(2)(d)(iii) (change of dwelling);
>
> (iii) the determination of an eligible rent in accordance with paragraph (3)(a) (protection on death) in relation to a subsequent death; or
>
> (iv) the determination of a maximum rent by virtue of regulation 13 or an eligible rent under regulation 12B.

(b) paragraph (5)(a) (13 week protection), it shall apply until the first of the following events occurs–

> (i) the first 13 weeks of the claimant's award of housing benefit have expired;
>
> (ii) the relevant authority determines an eligible rent in accordance with paragraph (2) which is equal to or exceeds it or is based on a maximum rent (LHA) determined by virtue of regulation 13C(2)(d)(iii) (change of dwelling);
>
> (iii) the determination of an eligible rent in accordance with paragraph (3)(a) (protection on death); or
>
> (iv) the determination of a maximum rent by virtue of regulation 13 or an eligible rent under regulation 12B.

(8) Where an eligible rent ceases to apply by virtue of paragraph (7)(a)(i) (expiry of protection on death) or (7)(b)(i) (expiry of 13 week protection), the eligible rent that shall apply instead shall be the one which would have applied but for paragraphs (3)(a) and (5)(a).''.

Substitution of regulations 13, 13ZA and 13ZB for regulation 13 of the Housing Benefit Regulations 2006

6. For regulation 13 (maximum rent) substitute–

"Maximum rent

13.–(1) The maximum rent shall be determined in accordance with paragraphs (2) to (8) where–

(a) a local authority has applied for a determination in accordance with regulation 14 (requirement to refer to rent officers), a redetermination in accordance with regulation 15 or 16, or a substitute determination or substitute redetermination in accordance with regulation 17 and a rent officer has made a determination, redetermination, substitute determination or substitute redetermination in exercise of the Housing Act functions; or

(b) an authority is not required to apply to the rent officer for a determination because–

    (i) regulation 14(2)(a) applies; or

    (ii) regulation 14(2)(b) applies because paragraph 2(2) of Schedule 2 applies.

(2) In a case where the rent officer has determined a claim-related rent, but is not required to notify the relevant authority of a local reference rent or a single room rent, the maximum rent shall be that claim-related rent.

(3) Subject to the limit specified in paragraph (4), in a case where the rent officer has determined both a local reference rent of which he is required to notify the relevant authority and a claim-related rent, the maximum rent shall be the local reference rent.

(4) In a case to which paragraph 8 of Schedule 3 to the Consequential Provisions Regulations applies, where the rent officer has determined and is required to notify the relevant authority of a local reference rent the maximum rent shall not exceed twice that local reference rent.

(5) Subject to paragraph (6), in the case of a young individual–

(a) except where sub-paragraph (b) applies, where the rent officer has determined a single room rent and is required to notify the relevant authority of it, the maximum rent shall not exceed that single room rent;

(b) where–

    (i) the rent officer has determined a single room rent and a claim-related rent and is required to notify the authority of them;

    (ii) the claim-related rent includes payment in respect of meals; and

    (iii) the single room rent is greater than the claim-related rent less an amount in respect of meals determined in accordance with paragraph 2 of Part 1 of Schedule 1 (ineligible service charges),

the maximum rent shall not exceed the claim-related rent less that amount in respect of meals.

(6) Paragraph (5) shall not apply in the case of a claimant–

(a) to whom paragraph 4 of Schedule 3 to the Consequential Provisions Regulations (saving provision) applies;

(b) to whom paragraph 14 of Schedule 3 (severe disability premium) applies; or

(c) where a non-dependant resides with him.

(7) Where the maximum rent is derived from–

(a) a claim-related rent and the notification under paragraph 9(1)(c) of Schedule 1 to the Rent Officers Order states that an ineligible amount in respect of meals has been included in that claim-related rent; or

(b) a local reference rent and the notification under paragraph 9(1)(da) of Schedule 1 to the Rent Officers Order states that an ineligible amount in respect of meals has been included in that local reference rent, in determining the maximum rent the relevant authority shall deduct an amount determined in accordance with paragraph 2 of Schedule 1 to these Regulations in respect of meals.

(8)　This regulation is subject to regulations 13ZA (protection on death and 13 week protection) and 13ZB (change in reckonable rent).

(9)　In this regulation–

"claim-related rent" means the rent notified by the rent officer under paragraph 9(1) of Schedule 1 to the Rent Officers Order;

"local reference rent" means the rent determined by a rent officer under paragraph 4 of Schedule 1 to the Rent Officers Order.

Protection on death and 13 week protection

13ZA.–(1)　In a case where the claimant occupies a dwelling which is the same as that occupied by him at the date of death of a linked person, the maximum rent shall be either–

(a)　the maximum rent which applied before the death occurred; or

(b)　in a case where there was no maximum rent, the reckonable rent due before the death occurred,

for a period of 12 months from the date of such a death.

(2)　For the purposes of paragraph (1), a claimant shall be treated as occupying the dwelling if paragraph (13) of regulation 7 (circumstances in which a person is or is not to be treated as occupying a dwelling as his home) is satisfied and for that purpose sub-paragraph (b) of that paragraph of that regulation shall be treated as if it were omitted.

(3)　Subject to paragraph (4), where the relevant authority is satisfied that the claimant or a linked person was able to meet the financial commitments for his dwelling when they were entered into, there shall be no maximum rent during the first 13 weeks of the claimant's award of housing benefit.

(4)　Paragraph (3) shall not apply where a claimant or the claimant's partner was previously entitled to benefit in respect of an award of housing benefit which fell wholly or partly less than 52 weeks before the commencement of the claimant's current award of housing benefit.

Change in reckonable rent

13ZB.–(1)　In a case where–

(a)　the authority has determined a maximum rent under regulation 13 or 13ZA; and

(b)　during the period for which that maximum rent applies the reckonable rent in respect of the dwelling by reference to which that maximum rent was determined is reduced to a sum which is less than that maximum rent,

the maximum rent shall be reduced to an amount equal to the reduced reckonable rent.

(2)　This paragraph applies in a case where–

(a)　a rent officer has made a determination in exercise of the Housing Act functions pursuant to an application by an authority under regulation 14(1)(e) (pre-tenancy determination);

(b)　subsequent to that determination the reckonable rent for that dwelling is changed; and

(c)　a maximum rent is to be determined in relation to a claim for housing benefit by a claimant.

(3)　In a case to which paragraph (2) applies, where the reckonable rent is reduced to a figure below the figure that would have been the maximum rent if the reckonable rent had not changed, the maximum rent shall be the reckonable rent as so reduced.

(4)   In any other case to which paragraph (2) applies, the authority shall treat the reckonable rent to be that applicable to the determination by the rent officer referred to in paragraph (2)(a).''.

Insertion of regulations 13C, 13D and 13E into the Housing Benefit Regulations 2006
7.   After regulation 13ZB (change in reckonable rent), as substituted by regulation 6, insert–

''When a maximum rent (LHA) is to be determined
13C.–(1)   A relevant authority shall determine a maximum rent (LHA) in accordance with regulation 13D (determination of a maximum rent (LHA)) in any case where paragraphs (2) or (3) apply.
(2)   This paragraph applies where a relevant authority has received–
(a)   a claim on which a rent allowance may be awarded, where the date of claim falls on or after 7th April 2008;
(b)   relevant information regarding a claim on which a rent allowance may be awarded, where the date of claim falls on or after 7th April 2008;
(c)   in relation to an award of housing benefit where the eligible rent was determined without reference to regulation 13A or 13D, a notification of a change of dwelling (as defined in regulation 2) where the change occurs on or after 7th April 2008; or
(d)   in relation to an award of housing benefit where a maximum rent (LHA) was determined in accordance with regulation 13D–
(i)   notification of a change of a kind which affects the category of dwelling applicable to the claim;
(ii)   notification of the death of a linked person, where the notification does not fall within head (i); or
(iii)   notification of a change of dwelling.
(3)   This paragraph applies on the anniversary of the LHA date.
(4)   Where the LHA date is 29th February, the anniversary of the LHA date shall be 28th February.
(5)   This regulation does not apply in a case where–
(a)   the landlord is a registered social landlord;
(b)   paragraph 4(1)(b) of Schedule 3 to the Consequential Provisions Regulations (savings provision) applies;
(c)   the tenancy is an excluded tenancy of a type [¹ mentioned in any of paragraphs 4 to 11] of Schedule 2;
(d)   the claim or award relates to–
(i)   periodical payments of kind falling within regulation 12(1) (rent) which a person is liable to make in relation to a houseboat, caravan or mobile home which he occupies as his home; or
(ii)   rent payable in relation to a hostel; or
(e)   rent under the tenancy is attributable to board and attendance, and–
(i)   the relevant authority has made an application to the rent officer in accordance with regulation 13D(10) (board and attendance determination), regulation 15 (applications to the rent officer for determinations) or regulation 17 (substitute determinations or substitute redeterminations); and
(ii)   the rent officer has determined that a substantial part of the rent under the tenancy is fairly attributable to board and attendance and has notified the relevant authority of this in accordance with article 4C, 4D or 4E of the Rent Officers Order.

(6)   In this regulation–

"the LHA date" means the date by reference to which the local housing allowance used to determine the maximum rent (LHA) was identified;

"registered social landlord" has the same meaning as in Part 1 of the Housing Act 1996 or, in Scotland, sections 57 and 59 of the Housing (Scotland) Act 2001.

Amendment

1.   Amended by reg 4(4)(a) of SI 2008 No 586 as from 7.4.08.

Determination of a maximum rent (LHA)

13D.–(1)   Subject to paragraph (3) to (11), the maximum rent (LHA) shall be the local housing allowance determined by the rent officer by virtue of article 4B(2A) or (4) of the Rent Officers Order which is applicable to–

(a)   the broad rental market area in which the dwelling to which the claim or award of housing benefit relates is situated at the relevant date; and

(b)   the category of dwelling which applies at the relevant date in accordance with paragraph (2).

(2)   The category of dwelling which applies is–

(a)   the category specified in paragraph 1(1)(a) of Schedule 3B to the Rent Officers Order (one bedroom shared accommodation) where–

    (i)   the claimant is a young individual who has no non-dependant residing with him and to whom paragraph 14 of Schedule 3 (severe disability premium) does not apply; or

    (ii)   paragraph (b) does not apply because neither sub-paragraph (b)(i) nor (ii) are satisfied in the claimant's case and neither the claimant nor his partner (where he has one) is a person to whom paragraph 14 of Schedule 3 (severe disability premium) applies, or to whom the circumstances in any of paragraphs (b) to (f) of the definition of young individual applies (certain care leavers);

(b)   except where paragraph (a)(i) applies, the category specified in paragraph 1(1)(b) of Schedule 3B to the Rent Officers Order (one bedroom self-contained accommodation) where that applies in the claimant's case at the relevant date in accordance with the size criteria [1 as set out in paragraph (3)] and–

    (i)   the claimant (together with his partner where he has one) has the exclusive use of two or more rooms; or

    (ii)   the claimant (together with his partner where he has one) has the exclusive use of one room, a bathroom and toilet and a kitchen or facilities for cooking,

and in this sub-paragraph "room" means a bedroom or room suitable for living in except for a room which the claimant shares with any person other than a member of his household, a non-dependant of his, or a person who pays rent to him or his partner;

(c)   in any other case, the category which corresponds with the number of bedrooms to which the claimant is entitled in accordance with paragraph (3).

(3)   The claimant shall be entitled to one bedroom for each of the following categories of occupier (and each occupier shall come within the first category only which applies to him)–

(a)   a couple (within the meaning of Part 7 of the Act);

(b)   a person who is not a child;

(c)   two children of the same sex;

(d)   two children who are less than 10 years old;

(e)   a child.

(4)   The relevant authority shall determine–

    (a)   the cap rent (in accordance with the definition in paragraph (12)); and

    (b)   whether the cap rent exceeds the applicable local housing allowance.

    (5)   Where the applicable local housing allowance exceeds the cap rent, for the purpose of determining the appropriate maximum housing benefit, the amount of the claimant's liability shall be the amount of the applicable local housing allowance.

    (6)   Where paragraph (5) applies, the maximum rent (LHA) shall be the lower of–

    (a)   the applicable local housing allowance; or

    (b)   the amount equal to the cap rent determined in accordance with paragraph (4)(a) plus £15.

    (7)   Where no local housing allowance applicable to a claim or award of housing benefit falling within paragraph (2)(c) has been determined, the relevant authority shall–

    (a)   apply to the rent officer for local housing allowance determinations for the category of dwelling applicable to the claim or award of housing benefit for each broad rental market area falling within its area, in whole or in part, at the relevant date, which shall be specified in the application; and

    (b)   apply the local housing allowance so determined for the broad rental market area in which the dwelling to which the claim or award of housing benefit relates is situated at the relevant date.

    (8)   Subject to paragraph (9), where–

    (a)   the relevant authority receives a request from a person stating that–

        (i)   he is contemplating occupying as his home a dwelling within the area of the relevant authority which contains a specified number of bedrooms, exceeding five, and

        (ii)   that if he does so, he is likely to claim housing benefit; and

    (b)   no local housing allowance determination is in effect for a broad rental market area falling within, in whole or in part, the area of the relevant authority for the category of dwelling containing the number of bedrooms specified in the request,

the relevant authority shall apply to the rent officer for local housing allowance determinations for each broad rental market area falling within its area, in whole or in part, for the category of dwelling containing the number of bedrooms specified in the request, and in this sub-paragraph "bedroom" means has the meaning specified in paragraph 1(2) of Schedule 3B to the Rent Officers Order.

    (9)   The request must–

    (a)   be made on a form approved by the relevant authority for the purpose of making a request under paragraph (8);

    (b)   be properly completed; and

    (c)   contain the following matters–

        (i)   the signature of the prospective occupier;

        (ii)   the signature of the person to whom the prospective occupier would incur liability to make such payments;

        (iii)   a statement that the person in paragraph (ii) agrees to the application being made for that determination; and

        (iv)   an indication that the prospective occupier is contemplating occupying the dwelling as his home and that if he does so, he is likely to claim housing benefit.

    (10)   The relevant authority shall apply to the rent officer for a board and attendance determination to be made in accordance with article 4C of the Rent Officers Order where–

    (a)   the relevant authority is required to determine a maximum rent (LHA) by virtue of regulation 13C; and

    (b)   part of the rent under the tenancy appears to the relevant authority to be likely to be attributable to board and attendance.

(11)   Where an application to a rent officer is required in accordance with paragraph (10) it shall be made within the same period following the day on which the relevant authority becomes obliged to determine a maximum rent (LHA) by virtue of regulation 13C as would be required if the application were to be made under regulation 14(1).

(12)   In this regulation–

"cap rent" means the aggregate of such payments specified in regulation 12(1) (rent) which the claimant is liable to pay, or is treated as liable to pay by virtue of regulation 8 (circumstances in which a person is treated as liable to make payments in respect of a dwelling), subject to regulation 12B(3) (mixed use accommodation), (4) (more than one person liable to make payments) and (6) (discretion in relation to eligible rent);

"occupiers" means the persons whom the relevant authority is satisfied occupy as their home the dwelling to which the claim or award relates except for any joint tenant who is not a member of the claimant's household;

"relevant date" means, as the case may require–

(a)   the date of the claim to which the claim or relevant information referred to in regulation 13C(2)(a) or (b) relates;

(b)   the date of the change of dwelling, change which affects the category of dwelling, or date of death, to which a notification referred to in regulation 13C(2)(c) or (d) relates; or

(c)   the date on which the anniversary of the LHA date referred to in regulation 13C(3) falls.

"tenancy" includes

(a)   in Scotland, any other right of occupancy; and

(b)   in any other case, a licence to occupy premises,

and reference to a tenant, landlord or any other expression appropriate to a tenancy shall be construed accordingly.

Amendment

1.   Amended by reg 4(4)(b) of SI 2008 No 586 as from 7.4.08.

Publication of local housing allowances

13E.–(1)   A relevant authority shall take such steps as appear to it to be appropriate for the purpose of securing that information in relation to broad rental market areas falling in whole or in part within its area, and local housing allowances applicable to such broad rental market areas, is brought to the attention of persons who may be entitled to housing benefit from the authority.".

Substitution of regulation 14 of the Housing Benefit Regulations 2006

8.   For regulation 14 (requirement to refer to rent officers), substitute–

"Requirement to refer to rent officers

14.–(1)   Subject to the following provisions of this regulation, a relevant authority shall apply to a rent officer for a determination to be made in pursuance of the Housing Act functions where–

(a)   it has received a claim on which rent allowance may be awarded and any of the circumstances specified in regulation 13C(5)(a) to (e) (rent allowance cases for which a maximum rent (standard local rent) is not to be determined) apply;

(b)   it has received relevant information regarding a claim on which rent allowance may be awarded and any of the circumstances specified in regulation 13C(5)(a) to (e) apply;

(c)   it has received a notification of a change relating to a rent allowance and a maximum rent (LHA) does not fall to be determined under regulation 13C (determination of a maximum rent (LHA));

(d)   it has received a notification of a change of dwelling and any of the circumstances specified in regulation 13C(5)(a) to (e) apply;

(e)   it has received, except in the case where any liability to make payments in respect of a dwelling would be to a housing authority, a request from a person (''the prospective occupier''), on a properly completed form approved for the purpose by the relevant authority, which includes the specified matters and any of the circumstances specified in regulation 13C(5)(a) to (d) apply;

(f)   52 weeks have expired since it last made an application under sub-paragraph (a), (b), (c), (d) [¹ , (e) or (h)] in relation to the claim or award in question and–

    (i)   a maximum rent (LHA) determined under regulation 13D does not apply; and

    (ii)   a maximum rent (LHA) is not to be determined under regulation 13D; [¹]

(g)   52 weeks have expired since an application was made under sub-paragraph (f) or a previous application was made under this sub-paragraph, whichever last occurred, and–

    (i)   a maximum rent (LHA) determined under regulation 13D does not apply; and

    (ii)   a maximum rent (LHA) is not to be determined under regulation 13D. [¹ or

(h)   has received notification that any of the circumstances in regulation 13C(5) apply.]

(2)   An application shall not be required under paragraph (1) where a claim, relevant information regarding a claim, notification or request relates to either–

(a)   a dwelling in a hostel if, during the period of 12 months ending on the day on which that claim, relevant information regarding a claim, notification or request is received by the relevant authority–

    (i)   a rent officer has already made a determination in the exercise of the Housing Act functions in respect of a dwelling in that hostel which is a similar dwelling to the dwelling to which the claim, relevant information regarding a claim, notification or request relates; and

    (ii)   there has been no change relating to a rent allowance that has affected the dwelling in respect of which that determination was made; or

(b)   an ''excluded tenancy'' within the meaning of Schedule 2 (excluded tenancies).

(3)   The provision of information to the rent officer in accordance with regulation 114A(5) shall be treated as an application to the rent officer under paragraph (1).

(4)   Where a relevant authority receives a request pursuant to paragraph (1)(e) (request from prospective occupier) and it is a case where, by reason of paragraph (2) (hostels or excluded tenancies), an application to a rent officer is not required, the authority shall–

(a)   return it to the prospective occupier, indicating why no such application is required; and

(b)   where it is not required by reason of either paragraph (2)(a) (hostels) of this regulation or paragraph 2 of Schedule 2 (cases where the rent officer has already made a determination), shall also send him a copy of that determination within 4 days of the receipt of that request by the authority.

(5)   Where an application to a rent officer is required by paragraph (1) it shall be made within 3 days, or as soon as practicable after that date, of–

(a)   the relevant authority receiving a claim on which rent allowance may be awarded;
(b)   the relevant authority receiving relevant information regarding a claim on which rent allowance may be awarded;
(c)   the relevant authority receiving a notification of a change relating to a rent allowance;
(d)   the relevant authority receiving a notification of a change of dwelling; or
(e)   the day on which the period mentioned in paragraph (1)(f) or (g) expired,
except that, in the case of a request to which paragraph (1)(e) (request from prospective occupier) applies, the application shall be made within 2 days of the receipt of that request by the authority.

(6)   In calculating any period of days mentioned in paragraphs (4) or (5), no regard shall be had to a day on which the offices of the relevant authority are closed for the purposes of receiving or determining claims.

(7)   For the purpose of this regulation a dwelling in a hostel shall be regarded as similar to another dwelling in that hostel if each dwelling provides sleeping accommodation for the same number of persons.

(8)   In this regulation–
"change relating to a rent allowance" means a change or increase to which paragraph 2(3)(a), (b), (c) or (d) of Schedule 2 applies;
"prospective occupier" shall include a person currently in receipt of housing benefit in respect of a dwelling which he occupies as his home and who is contemplating entering into a new agreement to occupy that dwelling, but only where his current agreement commenced 11 months or more before the request under paragraph (1)(e);
"specified matters" means–
(a)   the signature of the prospective occupier;
(b)   the signature of the person to whom the prospective occupier would incur liability to make such payments;
(c)   a statement that the person in paragraph (b) agrees to the application being made for that determination; and
(d)   an indication that the prospective occupier is contemplating occupying the dwelling as his home and that if he does so, he is likely to claim housing benefit;
"tenancy" includes–
(a)   in Scotland, any other right of occupancy; and
(b)   in any other case, a licence to occupy premises,
and reference to a tenant, landlord or any other expression appropriate to a tenancy shall be construed accordingly;
[¹]

Amendment
1.   Amended by reg 4(5) of SI 2008 No 586 as from 7.4.08.

Substitution of regulations 15 to 18 of the Housing Benefit Regulations 2006

9.   For regulations 15 (applications to the rent officer for redetermination) to 18 (application of provisions to substitute determinations or substitute redeterminations) substitute–

"Application to the rent officer for redeterminations

15.–(1)   Subject to paragraph (2) and regulation 16 (application for redetermination by rent officer), where a relevant authority has obtained from a rent officer either or both of the following–
(a)   a determination on a reference made under regulation 13D(10) (board and attendance determination) or regulation 14 (requirement to refer to rent officers);

(b)   a redetermination on a reference made under regulation 16(2) (application for redetermination by rent officer),

the authority may apply to the rent officer for a redetermination of any determination or redetermination he has made which has effect at the date of the application.

(2)   No application shall be made for a further redetermination of a redetermination made in response to an application under paragraph (1).

Application for a redetermination by a rent officer

16.–(1)   This paragraph applies where–

(a)   a person affected makes written representations which are signed by him, to a relevant authority concerning a decision which it makes in relation to him;

(b)   those representations relate, in whole or in part, to a rent officer's determination or redetermination in exercise of the Housing Act functions except for functions relating to broad rental market area determinations and local housing allowance determinations or amended determinations; and

(c)   those representations are made no later than one month after the day on which the person affected was notified of the decision by the relevant authority.

(2)   Subject to paragraphs (3) and (4), where paragraph (1) applies, the relevant authority shall, within 7 days of receiving the representations, apply to the rent officer for a redetermination or, as the case may be, a further redetermination in exercise of the Housing Act functions and a copy of those representations shall accompany the local authority's application.

(3)   Except where paragraph (4) applies, a relevant authority, in relation to any determination by a rent officer of an application under regulation 13D(10) (board and attendance determination) or 14(1) (requirement to refer to rent officers), shall not apply for a redetermination under paragraph (2) more than once in respect of an individual claimant's dwelling to which that determination relates.

(4)   Paragraph (2) shall operate so as to require a relevant authority to make a second application where the following conditions are met in addition to those imposed by that paragraph–

(a)   the written representations made under paragraph (1) relate to a redetermination by a rent officer made in response to an application by the relevant authority under regulation 15 (application to the rent officer for redetermination);

(b)   by the time of that application, the rent officer has already provided a redetermination under this regulation of a determination made in response to an application under regulation 13D(10) or 14(1); and

(c)   both the application under this regulation referred to in sub-paragraph (b) and the second application for which this paragraph provides relate to the same claimant.

(5)   Where a decision has been revised in consequence of a redetermination, substitute determination or substitute redetermination by a rent officer in exercise of the Housing Act functions (except for those relating to broad rental market area determinations and local housing allowance determinations or amended determinations) and that redetermination, substitute determination or substitute redetermination has led to–

(a)   a reduction in the maximum rent, the redetermination, substitute determination or substitute redetermination shall be a change of circumstances;

(b)   an increase in the maximum rent, the redetermination, substitute determination or substitute redetermination shall have effect in place of the original determination.

Substitute determinations or substitute redeterminations

17.–(1)   In a case where either–

(a)   the appropriate authority discovers that an application it has made to the rent officer contained an error in respect of any of the following–

(i)   the size of the dwelling;

(ii)   the number of occupiers;

(iii)   the composition of the household;

(iv)   the terms of the tenancy; or

(b)   the rent officer has, in accordance with article 7A(1) or (2) of the Rent Officers Order, notified an appropriate authority of an error he has made (other than in the application of his professional judgement),

the authority shall apply to the rent officer for a substitute determination, substitute redetermination, board and attendance redetermination, substitute board and attendance determination or substitute board and attendance redetermination, as the case may be.

(2)   In its application to the rent officer the relevant authority shall state the nature of the error and withdraw any previous application relating to the same case for a redetermination or substitute determination or substitute redetermination, which it has made but to which the rent officer has not yet responded.

Application of provisions to substitute determinations or substitute redeterminations

18.   Regulations 15, 16 and 17 apply to a substitute determination or substitute redetermination as they apply to the determination or redetermination it replaces.''.

Insertion of regulation 18A into the Housing Benefit Regulations 2006

10.   After regulation 18 (application of provisions to substitute determinations or substitute redeterminations) insert–

''Amended determinations

18A.–(1)   This regulation applies where a decision has been revised in consequence of an amended broad rental market area determination or amended local housing allowance determination by a rent officer.

(2)   Where that amended determination has led to a reduction in the maximum rent (LHA) applicable to a claimant, the amended determination shall be a change of circumstances in relation to that claimant.

(3)   Where that amended determination has led to an increase in the maximum rent (LHA) applicable to a claimant, the amended determination shall have effect in place of the original determination.''.

Amendment of regulation 50 of the Housing Benefit Regulations 2006

11.   In regulation 50(4)(a) (diminishing notional capital rule) for ''regulation 80(4)(a)'' substitute ''regulation 80(3)(a)''.

Substitution of regulation 70 of the Housing Benefit Regulations 2006

12.   For regulation 70 (maximum housing benefit) substitute–

''**70.**   The amount of a person's appropriate maximum housing benefit in any week shall be 100 per cent. of his eligible rent calculated on a weekly basis in accordance with regulations 80 and 81 (calculation of weekly amounts and rent free periods) less any deductions in respect of non-dependants which fall to be made under regulation 74 (non-dependant deductions).''

Amendment of regulations 72 and 73 of the Housing Benefit Regulations 2006

13. In regulations 72(4) (extended payments) and 73(4) (extended payments (severe disablement allowance and incapacity benefit)) for ''regulation 80(7)'' substitute ''regulation 80(6)''.

Substitution of regulation 74 of the Housing Benefit Regulations 2006

14. For regulation 74 (non-dependant deductions) substitute–

''**74.**–(1) Subject to the following provisions of this regulation, the deductions referred to in regulation 70 (maximum housing benefit) shall be–

   (a) in respect of a non-dependant aged 18 or over in remunerative work, £47.75 per week;

   (b) in respect of a non-dependant aged 18 or over to whom sub-paragraph (a) does not apply, £7.40 per week.

(2) In the case of a non-dependant aged 18 or over to whom paragraph (1)(a) applies because he is in remunerative work, where it is shown to the appropriate authority that his normal weekly gross income is–

   (a) less than £111.00, the deduction to be made under this regulation shall be that specified in paragraph (1)(b);

   (b) not less than £111.00 but less than £164.00, the deduction to be made under this regulation shall be £17.00;

   (c) not less than £164.00 but less than £213.00, the deduction to be made under this regulation shall be £23.35;

   (d) not less than £213.00 but less than £283.00, the deduction to be made under this regulation shall be £38.20;

   (e) not less than £283.00 but less than £353.00, the deduction to be made under this regulation shall be £43.50.

(3) Only one deduction shall be made under this regulation in respect of a couple or, as the case may be, members of a polygamous marriage and, where, but for this paragraph, the amount that would fall to be deducted in respect of one member of a couple or polygamous marriage is higher than the amount (if any) that would fall to be deducted in respect of the other, or any other, member, the higher amount shall be deducted.

(4) In applying the provisions of paragraph (2) in the case of a couple or, as the case may be, a polygamous marriage, regard shall be had, for the purpose of paragraph (2) to the couple's or, as the case may be, all members of the polygamous marriage's joint weekly gross income.

(5) Where a person is a non-dependant in respect of more than one joint occupier of a dwelling (except where the joint occupiers are a couple or members of a polygamous marriage), the deduction in respect of that non-dependant shall be apportioned between the joint occupiers (the amount so apportioned being rounded to the nearest penny) having regard to the number of joint occupiers and the proportion of the payments in respect of the dwelling payable by each of them.

(6) No deduction shall be made in respect of any non-dependants occupying a claimant's dwelling if the claimant or his partner is–

   (a) blind or treated as blind by virtue of paragraph 13 of Schedule 3 (additional condition of the higher pensioner and disability premiums); or

   (b) receiving in respect of himself either–

      (i) attendance allowance; or

      (ii) the care component of the disability living allowance.

(7) No deduction shall be made in respect of a non-dependant if–

   (a) although he resides with the claimant, it appears to the appropriate authority that his normal home is elsewhere; or

(b) he is in receipt of a training allowance paid in connection with a Youth Training Scheme established under section 2 of the 1973 Act or section 2 of the Enterprise and New Towns (Scotland) Act 1990; or

(c) he is a full-time student during a period of study within the meaning of Part 7 (Students); or

(d) he is a full-time student and during a recognised summer vacation appropriate to his course he is not in remunerative work; or

(e) he is a full-time student and the claimant or his partner has attained the age of 65; or

(f) he is not residing with the claimant because he has been a patient for a period in excess of 52 weeks, or a prisoner, and for these purposes–

    (i) "patient" has the meaning given in paragraph (18) of regulation 7 (circumstances in which a person is or is not to be treated as occupying a dwelling as his home);

    (ii) where a person has been a patient for two or more distinct periods separated by one or more intervals each not exceeding 28 days, he shall be treated as having been a patient continuously for a period equal in duration to the total of those distinct periods; and

    (iii) "prisoner" means a person who is detained in custody pending trial or sentence upon conviction or under a sentence imposed by a court other than a person who is detained in hospital under the provisions of the Mental Health Act 1983, or, in Scotland, under the provisions of the Mental Health (Care and Treatment) (Scotland) Act 2003 or the Criminal Procedure (Scotland) Act 1995.

(8) No deduction shall be made in calculating the amount of a rent rebate or allowance in respect of a non-dependant aged less than 25 who is on income support or an income-based jobseeker's allowance.

(9) In the case of a non-dependant to whom paragraph (2) applies because he is in remunerative work, there shall be disregarded from his weekly gross income–

(a) any attendance allowance or disability living allowance received by him;

(b) any payment made under the Macfarlane Trust, the Macfarlane (Special Payments) Trust, the Macfarlane (Special Payments) (No. 2) Trust, the Fund, the Eileen Trust or the Independent Living Funds which had his income fallen to be calculated under regulation 40 (calculation of income other than earnings) would have been disregarded under paragraph 23 of Schedule 5 (income in kind); and

(c) any payment which had his income fallen to be calculated under regulation 40 would have been disregarded under paragraph 35 of Schedule 5 (payments made under certain trusts and certain other payments).

(10) No deduction shall be made in respect of a non-dependant who is on state pension credit.".

Amendment of regulation 79 of the Housing Benefit Regulations 2006

15. In regulation 79(1) and (3) (date on which change of circumstances is to take effect) for "regulation 80(6)" substitute "regulation 80(5)".

Substitution of regulations 80 and 81 of the Housing Benefit Regulations 2006

16. For regulations 80 (calculation of weekly amounts) and 81 (rent free periods) substitute–

"Calculation of weekly amounts

80.–(1) A person's entitlement to housing benefit in any benefit week shall be calculated in accordance with the following provisions of this regulation.

(2) The weekly amount of a claimant's eligible rent shall be–

(a) subject to paragraph (3), where rent is payable at intervals of one week or a multiple thereof, the amount of eligible rent payable weekly or, where it is payable at intervals of a multiple of a week, the amount determined by dividing the amount of eligible rent payable by the number equal to the number of weeks in respect of which it is payable; or

(b) subject to paragraph (3), where the rent is payable at intervals of a calendar month or multiples thereof, the amount determined by dividing the amount payable by the number equal to the number of calendar months in respect of which it is payable, multiplying by 12 and dividing by 52;

(c) subject to paragraph (3), where the rent is payable at intervals of a day or multiples thereof, the amount determined by dividing the amount payable by the number equal to the number of days in respect of which it is payable and multiplying by 7.

(3) In a case–

(a) to which regulation 76(2) or (3) (date on which entitlement is to commence) applies, his eligible rent for the benefit week in which he becomes liable to make payments in respect of a dwelling which he occupies as his home shall be calculated by multiplying his daily rent by the number equal to the number of days in that benefit week for which he is liable to make such payments;

(b) where a change of circumstances takes effect in a benefit week under regulation 79(2A), (but is not a change described in sub-paragraph (c)(ii) of this regulation), (2B), (8) or (9) other than on the Monday of a benefit week then the claimant's eligible rent for that benefit week shall be calculated by multiplying his daily rent by the appropriate number of days in that benefit week;

(c) where–

(i) the amount of eligible rent which the claimant is liable to pay in respect of a dwelling is altered and that change of circumstances takes effect under regulation 79(2); or

(ii) the claimant–

(aa) moves to a new dwelling occupied as the home,

(bb) he is not entitled to be treated, immediately after that move, as occupying two dwellings as his home or as occupying his former dwelling as his home, and

(cc) that change of circumstances takes effect under regulation 79(2A),

other than on the Monday of a benefit week, then the claimant's eligible rent for that benefit week shall be calculated by multiplying his old and new daily rent by the number equal to the number of days in that week which relate respectively to the old and new amounts which he is liable to pay.

(4) In the case of a claimant whose weekly eligible rent falls to be calculated in accordance with paragraph (3)(a) or (b) by reference to the daily rent in his case, his weekly applicable amount, weekly income, the weekly amount of any non-dependant deductions and the minimum amount payable in his case shall be calculated in the same manner as his weekly eligible rent by reference to the amounts determined in his case in accordance with Parts 5 to 8 (applicable amounts, income and capital, students and amount of benefit).

(5) Where a change in the amount of a claimant's applicable amount, income or non-dependant deductions falls to be taken into account in the same benefit week as a change in his eligible rent to which paragraph (3)(c) applies, it shall be taken into account in that week on a daily basis in the same manner and as if it had occurred on the same day as that change in his eligible rent.

(6) In any case where a claimant has received an extended payment or an extended payment (severe disablement allowance and incapacity benefit), his

entitlement shall be adjusted in such circumstances and by such amount as are prescribed in Part 3 of Schedule 7 or paragraph 9 of Schedule 8, as the case may be.

(7) Any amount determined under these Regulations may, if it is appropriate, be rounded to the nearest whole penny by disregarding any amount less than half a penny and treating any amount of half a penny or more as a whole penny.

(8) In this regulation "daily rent" shall mean the amount determined by dividing by 7 the amount determined under whichever sub-paragraph of paragraph (2) is appropriate in each case.

(9) Where a claimant is entitled to benefit in respect of two (but not more than two) dwellings in accordance with regulation 7(6) his eligible rent shall be calculated in respect of each dwelling in accordance with this regulation.

Rent free periods

81.–(1) This regulation applies to a claimant for any period (referred to in this regulation as a rent free period) in, or in respect of, which he is not liable to pay rent except for any period to which regulation 8(1)(d) (waiver of rent by landlord in return for work done) applies.

(2) In the case of the beginning or ending of a claimant's rent-free period, his eligible rent for the benefit week in which the rent free period begins and ends shall be calculated on a daily basis as if those benefit weeks were weeks to which regulation 80(3) applies.

(3) For the purpose of determining the weekly applicable amount and income of a claimant to whom this regulation applies, the weekly amount of any non-dependant deductions and the minimum amount payable in his case–

(a) in a case to which regulation 80(2)(a) applies, the amounts determined in his case in accordance with Parts 5 to 8 (applicable amounts, income and capital, students and amount of benefit) shall be multiplied by 52 or 53, whichever is appropriate, and divided by the number equal to the number of weeks in that 52 or 53 week period in respect of which he is liable to pay rent;

(b) subject to paragraph (4), in a case to which regulation 80(2)(b) or (c) applies, the amounts determined in his case in accordance with Parts 5 to 8 shall be multiplied by 365 or 366, whichever is appropriate and divided by the number of days in that 365 or 366 day period in respect of which he is liable to pay rent.

(4) In a case to which paragraph (3)(b) applies, where either regulation 80(4) or (5) also applies or it is the beginning or end of a rent-free period, the weekly amounts referred to in paragraph (3) shall first be calculated in accordance with sub-paragraph (b) of that paragraph and then determined on a daily basis in the same manner as the claimant's eligible rent.''.

Amendment of regulations 95 and 96 of the Housing Benefit Regulations 2006

17.–(1) In regulation 95 (circumstances in which payment is to be made to a landlord) after paragraph (2) insert–

''(2A) In a case where–

(a) a relevant authority has determined a maximum rent (LHA) in accordance with regulation 13D; and

(b) the rent allowance exceeds the amount which the claimant is liable to pay his landlord by way of rent,

any payment of rent allowance made to a landlord pursuant to this regulation or to regulation 96 may include all or part of any amount by which the rent allowance exceeds the amount which the claimant is liable to pay his landlord as rent but shall not include any amount by which the rent allowance exceeds the amount which the claimant is liable to pay his landlord as rent and arrears of rent.''.

(2)   In regulation 96 (circumstances in which payment may be made to a landlord)–
(a)   in paragraph (1) for "paragraph (3)" substitute "paragraphs (3) and (3A)";
(b)   in paragraph (3) after "paragraph (1)" insert ", (3A) or (3B)";
(c)   after paragraph (3) insert–

"(3A)In a case where a relevant authority has determined a maximum rent in accordance with regulation 13D–
(a)   sub-paragraphs (a) and (b) of paragraph (1) shall not apply; and
(b)   payment of a rent allowance to a person's landlord may be made where–
(i)   the relevant authority considers that the claimant is likely to have difficulty in relation to the management of his financial affairs;
(ii)   the relevant authority considers that it is improbable that the claimant will pay his rent; or
(iii) a direct payment has previously been made by the relevant authority to the landlord in accordance with regulation 95 in respect of the current award of housing benefit.

(3B)   Where the relevant authority suspects that the grounds in paragraph (3A)(b)(i) or (ii) apply and is considering whether to make payments on one of those grounds, it may make a payment of a rent allowance to the person's landlord for a period not exceeding 8 weeks.".

Substitution of Schedule 2 to the Housing Benefit Regulations 2006
18.   For Schedule 2 (excluded tenancies) substitute–

"SCHEDULE 2

Excluded tenancies

1.   An excluded tenancy is any tenancy to which any of the following paragraphs applies.
2.–(1)   Subject to the following sub-paragraphs, where a rent officer has made a determination, which relates to the tenancy in question or any other tenancy of the same dwelling this paragraph applies to–
(a)   the tenancy in respect of which that determination was made; and
(b)   any other tenancy of the same dwelling on terms which are substantially the same, other than the term relating to the amount of rent, as those terms were at the time of that determination or, if earlier, at the end of the tenancy.
(2)   For the purposes of any claim, notification, request or application under regulation 14(1) ("the later application"), a tenancy shall not be an excluded tenancy by virtue of sub-paragraph (1) by reference to a rent officer's determination made in consequence of an earlier claim, notification, request or application ("the earlier application") where–
(a)   the earlier and later applications were made in respect of the same claimant or different claimants; and
(b)   the earlier application was made more than 52 weeks before the later application was made.
(3)   Sub-paragraph (1) shall not apply where subsequent to the making of the determination mentioned in that sub-paragraph–
(a)   the number of occupiers of the dwelling has changed and that dwelling is not in a hostel;
(b)   there has been a substantial change in the condition of the dwelling (including the making of improvements) or the terms of the tenancy other than a term relating to rent;
(c)   there has been a rent increase under a term of the tenancy and the term under which that increase was made was either included in the tenancy at the time when the application for that determination was made (or was a term substantially the same as such a term) and that determination was not made under paragraph 1(2), 2(2) or 3(3) of Schedule 1 to the Rent Officers Order;
(d)   in a case where the rent officer has made a determination under paragraph 2(2) of Schedule 1 to the Rent Officers Order (size and rent determinations), but since the date of the application for that determination–
(i)   a child, who is a member of the household occupying the dwelling, has attained the age of 10 years; or
(ii)   a young person, who is a member of the household occupying that dwelling, has attained the age of 16 years; or

      (iii)   there is a change in the composition of the household occupying the dwelling;

  (e)   the claimant is a young individual, except in a case where the determination mentioned in sub-paragraph (1) was, or was made in conjunction with, a determination of a single room rent pursuant to paragraph 5 of Schedule 1 to the Rent Officers Order on or after 2nd July 2001.

3.–(1)   This paragraph applies where the landlord is a registered housing association, except in a case where the local authority considers that–

  (a)   the claimant occupies a dwelling larger than is reasonably required by him and any others who occupy that dwelling (including any non-dependants of his and any person paying rent to him); or

  (b)   the rent payable for that dwelling is unreasonably high.

  (2)   Where the circumstances set out in head (a) or (b) of sub-paragraph (1) above exist, the authority shall so state in their application for a determination.

4.   This paragraph applies to a tenancy entered into before–

  (a)   in Scotland, 2nd January 1989; and

  (b)   in any other case, 15th January 1989.

5.   This paragraph applies to a regulated tenancy within the meaning of–

  (a)   in Scotland, the Rent (Scotland) Act 1984; and

  (b)   in any other case, the Rent Act 1977.

6.   This paragraph applies to a housing association tenancy which–

  (a)   in Scotland, is a tenancy to which Part 6 of the Rent (Scotland) Act 1984 applies; and

  (b)   in any other case, is a housing association tenancy to which Part 6 of the Rent Act 1977 applies.

7.   This paragraph applies to a protected occupancy or statutory tenancy within the meaning of the Rent (Agriculture) Act 1976.

8.   This paragraph applies to a tenancy at a low rent within the meaning of Part 1 of the Landlord and Tenant Act 1954 or Schedule 10 to the Local Government and Housing Act 1989.

9.   This paragraph applies to a tenancy of any dwelling which is a bail hostel or probation hostel approved by the Secretary of State under section 9(1) of the Criminal Justice and Court Services Act 2000.

10.   This paragraph applies to a tenancy of a housing action trust established under Part 3 of the Housing Act 1988.

11.–(1)   Subject to sub-paragraphs (2) and (3) this paragraph applies to a tenancy–

  (a)   in respect of a dwelling comprised in land which has been disposed of under section 32 of the Housing Act 1985 or section 12 of the Housing (Scotland) Act 1987;

  (b)   in respect of a dwelling comprised in land which has been disposed of with the consent required by section 43 of the Housing Act 1985 or section 12 of the Housing (Scotland) Act 1987;

  (c)   in respect of which the fee simple estate has been acquired, under the right conferred by Chapter 2 of Part 1 of the Housing Act 1996, otherwise than from a housing action trust within the meaning of Part 3 of the Housing Act 1988, or in respect of which the house has been acquired under the right conferred by Part 3 of the Housing (Scotland) Act 1988; or

  (d)   in respect of a dwelling disposed of under the New Towns (Transfer of Housing Stock) Regulations 1990 to a person who is an approved person for the purposes of disposal under those Regulations or in respect of a dwelling disposed of pursuant to powers contained in the New Towns (Scotland) Act 1968 to a housing association.

  (2)   This paragraph shall not apply to a tenancy to which sub-paragraph (1) refers if–

  (a)   there has been an increase in rent since the disposal or acquisition, as the case may be, occurred; and

  (b)   the local authority stated in the application for determination that–

      (i)   the claimant occupies a dwelling larger than is reasonably required by him and any others who occupy that dwelling (including any non-dependant of his and any person paying rent to him); or

      (ii)   the rent payable for that dwelling is unreasonably high.

  (3)   Where the disposal or acquisition, as the case may be, took place on or after 7th October 2002, sub-paragraph (2)(b) shall apply to a tenancy to which sub-paragraph (1) refers as if head (i) were omitted.

12.   This paragraph applies to a shared ownership tenancy.

13.   In this Schedule, "rent" shall be construed in accordance with paragraph (8) of regulation 14 (interpretation of "tenancy" and other expressions appropriate to a tenancy) and, subject to that paragraph, has the same meaning–

  (a)   in Scotland, as in section 25 of the Housing (Scotland) Act 1988, except that the reference to the house in subsection (3) shall be construed as a reference to the dwelling;

  (b)   in any other case, as in section 14 of the Housing Act 1988, except that the reference to the dwelling-house in subsection (4) shall be construed as a reference to the dwelling,

  and–

(i)   other expressions have the same meanings as in regulation 14(8);

(ii)   in the case of a determination by a rent officer pursuant to a request for such a determination under regulation 14(1)(e), any reference to a "tenancy" shall be taken as a reference to a prospective tenancy and any reference to an "occupier" or any person "occupying" a dwelling shall, in the case of such a determination, be taken to be a reference to a potential occupier or potential occupation of that dwelling.".

Amendment of Schedules 7 and 8 to the Housing Benefit Regulations 2006

19. In [¹ paragraph 3(3)] of Schedule 7 (extended payments of housing benefit) and paragraph 2(3) of Schedule 8 (extended payments (severe disablement allowance and incapacity benefit) of housing benefit) for "regulation 80(4)(c)" substitute "regulation 80(3)(c)".

Amendment

1.   Amended by reg 4(6) of SI 2008 No 586 as from 7.4.08.

Substitution of Part 15 of and Schedule 10 to the HousingBenefit Regulations 2006

20.–(1)   For Part 15 substitute–

"PART 15
Former pathfinder authorities
Modifications in respect of former pathfinder authorities
122.–(1)   In this regulation and in Schedule 10, "former pathfinder authority" means a relevant authority specified in Part 1 of that Schedule.

(2)   The provisions of Part 2 of Schedule 10 apply in relation to the area of a former pathfinder authority.".

(2)   For Schedule 10 (pathfinder authorities) substitute–

"SCHEDULE 10

Former pathfinder authorities

PART 1

Former pathfinder authorities
Argyll and Bute
Blackpool
Brighton and Hove
Conwy
Coventry
East Riding of Yorkshire
Edinburgh
Guildford
Leeds
Lewisham
North East Lincolnshire
Norwich
Pembrokeshire
St Helens
Salford
South Norfolk
Teignbridge
Wandsworth

PART 2

Application of the Regulations
1.   These Regulations shall apply to former pathfinder authorities subject to the provisions of this Part of this Schedule.

Amendment of regulation 2

2.　　In regulation 2(1) (interpretation)–

(a)　　in the definition of "eligible rent", in sub-paragraph (a) for "or 12D (eligible rent and maximum rent (LHA))" substitute ", 12D (eligible rent and maximum rent (LHA)) or any of regulations 12E to 12K (transitional protection for pathfinder cases)";

(b)　　after the definition of "maximum rent (LHA)" insert–

""maximum rent (standard local rent)" means a maximum rent (standard local rate) determined in accordance with regulation 13A;".

Amendment of regulation 11

3.　　In regulation 11(1) (eligible housing costs)–

(a)　　in paragraph (c) omit "or"; and

(b)　　after sub-paragraph (d) insert–

"; or

(e)　　any of regulations 12E to 12K (transitional protection for pathfinder cases) and regulations 13C (when a maximum rent (LHA) is to be determined) and 13D (determination of a maximum rent (LHA)),".

Amendment of regulation 12B

4.　　In regulation 12B(1) (eligible rent) for "or 12D (eligible rent and maximum rent (LHA))" substitute ", 12D (eligible rent and maximum rent (LHA)) or any of regulations 12E to 12K (transitional protection for pathfinder cases)".

Amendment of regulation 12D

5.　　In regulation 12D (eligible rent and maximum rent (LHA)) before paragraph (1) insert–

"(A1)　　This regulation shall not apply where any of regulations 12E to 12K (transitional protection for pathfinder cases) apply."

Insertion of regulations 12E to 12K

6.　　After regulation 12D (eligible rent and maximum rent (LHA)) insert–

"Basic transitional protection for pathfinder cases

12E.–(1)　　This regulation applies where–

(a)　　reference was made to a maximum rent (standard local rate) in determining the amount of the eligible rent which applied immediately before 7th April 2008;

(b)　　on 7th April 2008 the local authority determines a maximum rent (LHA) by virtue of regulation 13C(4A)(a); and

(c)　　regulations 12F (cases where the claimant enjoyed protection on death before 7th April 2008) and 12G (cases where the claimant enjoyed 13 week protection before 7th April 2008) do not apply.

(2)　　Where this regulation applies, the claimant's eligible rent is–

(a)　　the maximum rent (LHA) where that is higher than the eligible rent which applied immediately before 7th April 2008; or

(b)　　the amount of the eligible rent which applied immediately before 7th April 2008.

(3)　　Where the eligible rent is the amount of the eligible rent which applied immediately before 7th April 2008, it will continue to apply until, on or after 7th April 2008, the first of the following events occurs–

(a)　　the relevant authority is required to determine a maximum rent (LHA) by virtue of regulation 13C(2)(d)(i) (change of category of dwelling) because the claimant has become entitled to a larger category of dwelling and the maximum rent (LHA) is higher than that eligible rent;

(b)　　the relevant authority is required to determine a maximum rent (LHA) by virtue of regulation 13C(2)(d)(i) (change of category of dwelling) because the claimant has become entitled to a smaller category of dwelling;

(c)　　the relevant authority is required to determine an eligible rent following a change of dwelling;

(d)　　the relevant authority is required to determine an eligible rent in accordance with regulation 12H (cases where a death occurs in the first year on or after 7th April 2008) following the death of a linked person;

(e)　　the relevant authority determines a maximum rent (LHA) on 7th April 2009 by virtue of regulation 13C(4A)(b).

(4)　　Where the eligible rent is the maximum rent (LHA), it shall be treated as if it had been determined in accordance with regulation 12D(2)(a) (eligible rent is maximum rent (LHA)) and shall apply according to the provisions of regulation 12D (eligible rent and maximum rent (LHA)).

Cases where the claimant enjoyed protection on death before 7th April 2008

12F.–(1)   This regulation applies where–
(a)   immediately before 7th April 2008 the claimant enjoyed protection on death in accordance with regulation 12A(4)(a)(ii) (pathfinder protection on death based on reckonable rent); and
(b)   on 7th April 2008 the local authority determines a maximum rent (LHA) by virtue of regulation 13C(4A)(a).
(2)   Where this regulation applies, the claimant's eligible rent is–
(a)   the maximum rent (LHA) where that is higher than the eligible rent which applied immediately before 7th April 2008; or
(b)   the amount of the eligible rent which applied immediately before 7th April 2008.
(3)   Where the eligible rent is the amount of the eligible rent which applied immediately before 7th April 2008, it will continue to apply until, on or after 7th April 2008, the first of the following events occurs–
(a)   the end of 12 months after the death to which the protection relates;
(b)   the relevant authority is required to determine a maximum rent (LHA) by virtue of regulation 13C(2)(d)(i) (change of category of dwelling) and it is higher than that eligible rent;
(c)   the relevant authority is required to determine an eligible rent following a change of dwelling;
(d)   the relevant authority is required to determine an eligible rent in accordance with regulation 12H (cases where a death occurs in the first year on or after 7th April 2008) following the death of a linked person;
(4)   Where the eligible rent ceases to apply because of paragraph (3)(a), the eligible rent will be the maximum rent (LHA) which would have applied but for the transitional protection.
(5)   Where the eligible rent is the maximum rent (LHA), it shall be treated as if it had been determined in accordance with regulation 12D(2)(a) (eligible rent is maximum rent (LHA)) and shall apply according to the provisions of regulation 12D (eligible rent and maximum rent (LHA)).

Cases where the claimant enjoyed 13 week protection before 7th April 2008

12G.–(1)   This regulation applies where–
(a)   immediately before 7th April 2008 the claimant enjoyed 13 week protection in accordance with regulation 12A(6)(a) (local housing allowance pathfinder 13 week protection); and
(b)   on 7th April 2008 the local authority determines a maximum rent (LHA) by virtue of regulation 13C(4A)(a).
(2)   Where this regulation applies, the claimant's eligible rent is–
(a)   the maximum rent (LHA) where that is higher than the eligible rent which applied immediately before 7th April 2008; or
(b)   the amount of the eligible rent which applied immediately before 7th April 2008.
(3)   Where the eligible rent is the amount of the eligible rent which applied immediately before 7th April 2008, it will continue to apply until, on or after 7th April 2008, the first of the following events occurs–
(a)   the end of the day when the protection expires, namely 13 weeks after the date of the claim;
(b)   the relevant authority is required to determine a maximum rent (LHA) by virtue of regulation 13C(2)(d)(i) (change of category of dwelling) and it is higher than that eligible rent;
(c)   the relevant authority is required to determine an eligible rent following a change of dwelling;
(d)   the relevant authority is required to determine an eligible rent in accordance with regulation 12H (cases where a death occurs in the first year on or after 7th April 2008) following the death of a linked person.
(4)   Where the eligible rent ceases to apply because of paragraph (3)(a), the eligible rent will be the maximum rent (LHA) which would have applied but for the transitional protection.
(5)   Where the eligible rent is the maximum rent (LHA), it shall be treated as if it had been determined in accordance with regulation 12D(2)(a) (eligible rent is maximum rent (LHA)) and shall apply according to the provisions of regulation 12D (eligible rent and maximum rent (LHA)).

Cases where a death occurs in the first year on or after 7th April 2008

12H.–(1)   This regulation applies where–
(a)   the eligible rent is that specified in regulation 12E(2)(b) (basic transitional protection for pathfinder cases), 12F(2)(b) (transitional protection where the claimant enjoyed protection on death before 7th April 2008), 12G(2)(b) (transitional protection where the claimant enjoyed 13 week protection before 7th April 2008) or paragraph (2)(b) of this regulation;
(b)   a linked person dies on or after 7th April 2008 and before 7th April 2009;
(c)   the claimant occupies the same dwelling as the linked person at the date of death; and
(d)   the relevant authority determines a maximum rent (LHA) by virtue of regulation 13C(2)(d)(i) or (ii) (change of category of dwelling or death of a linked person).
(2)   Where this regulation applies, the claimant's eligible rent is–
(a)   the maximum rent (LHA) where that is higher than the eligible rent which applied immediately before the date of the death; or

(b)   the amount of the eligible rent which applied immediately before the date of the death.

(3)   Where the eligible rent is the amount of the eligible rent which applied immediately before the date of death, it will continue to apply until, on or after the date of the death, the first of the following events occurs–

(a)   the end of 12 months from the date of the death;

(b)   the relevant authority is required to determine a maximum rent (LHA) by virtue of regulation 13C(2)(d)(i) (change of category of dwelling) and it is higher than that eligible rent;

(c)   the relevant authority is required to determine an eligible rent following a change of dwelling;

(d)   the relevant authority is required to determine an eligible rent in accordance with this regulation following the death of another linked person.

(4)   Where the eligible rent is the maximum rent (LHA), it shall be treated as if it had been determined in accordance with regulation 12D(2)(a) (eligible rent is maximum rent (LHA)) and shall apply according to the provisions of regulation 12D (eligible rent and maximum rent (LHA)).

(5)   For the purposes of paragraph (1)(c), a claimant shall be treated as occupying the dwelling if regulation 7(13) is satisfied and for that purpose paragraph (13) of regulation 7 shall have effect as if sub-paragraph (b) were omitted.

Basic transitional protection in the second year and subsequent years after 7th April 2008

12I.–(1)   This regulation applies where–

(a)   immediately before 7th April 2009 the claimant was enjoying basic transitional protection under regulation 12E; and

(b)   the local authority determines a maximum rent (LHA) by virtue of 13C(4A)(b) on 7th April 2009.

(2)   Where this regulation applies, the claimant's eligible rent is–

(a)   the maximum rent (LHA) where it is higher than the eligible rent applying immediately before 7th April 2008; or

(b)   in any other case, the lower of–

(i)   the amount of the eligible rent applying immediately before 7th April 2008; or

(ii)   the amount of the cap rent by reference to which the maximum rent (LHA) was determined, plus £15.

(3)   Where the claimant's eligible rent is determined in accordance with paragraph (2)(b), it continues to apply until, on or after 7th April 2009, the first of the following events occurs–

(a)   the relevant authority is required to determine a maximum rent (LHA) by virtue of regulation 13C(2)(d)(i) (change of category of dwelling) because the claimant has become entitled to a larger category of dwelling or 13C(3) (anniversary of the LHA date) and the maximum rent (LHA) is higher than that eligible rent;

(b)   the relevant authority is required to determine a maximum rent (LHA) by virtue of regulation 13C(2)(d)(i) (change of category of dwelling) because the claimant has become entitled to a smaller category of dwelling;

(c)   the relevant authority is required to determine an eligible rent following a change of dwelling;

(d)   the relevant authority is required to determine an eligible rent in accordance with regulation 12K (protection on death in the second and subsequent years after 7th April 2008) following the death of a linked person.

(4)   Where the eligible rent is the maximum rent (LHA), it shall be treated as if it had been determined in accordance with regulation 12D(2)(a) (eligible rent is maximum rent (LHA)) and shall apply according to the provisions of regulation 12D (eligible rent and maximum rent (LHA)).

Transitional protection in the second year after 7th April 2008 where the claimant is already enjoying protection on death

12J.–(1)   This regulation applies where–

(a)   immediately before 7th April 2009 the claimant was enjoying transitional protection on death under regulation 12H (cases where a death occurs in the first year on or after 7th April 2008); and

(b)   the local authority determines a maximum rent (LHA) by virtue of regulation 13C(4A)(b) on 7th April 2009 .

(2)   Where this regulation applies, the claimant's eligible rent is–

(a)   the maximum rent (LHA) where that is higher than the eligible rent which applied immediately before the date of the death to which the protection relates; or

(b)   the amount of the eligible rent which applied immediately before the date of the death.

(3)   Where the eligible rent which applies is the one that applied immediately before the date of the death, it continues to apply until, on or after the date of the death, the first of the following events occurs–

(a)   the end of 12 months after the date of the death to which the protection relates;

(b)   the relevant authority is required to determine a maximum rent (LHA) by virtue of regulation 13C(2)(d)(i) (change of category of dwelling) and it is higher than that eligible rent;

(c)   the relevant authority is required to determine an eligible rent following a change of dwelling;

(d)   the relevant authority is required to determine an eligible rent in accordance with regulation 12K (protection on death in the second and subsequent years after 7th April 2008) following the death of a linked person.

(4)   Where the eligible rent ceases to apply because of paragraph (3)(a) the eligible rent is the one that would have applied if the relevant authority not determined an eligible rent in accordance with regulation 12H(2)(b) (transitional protection where a death occurs in the first year on or after 7th April 2008).

(5)   Where the eligible rent is the maximum rent (LHA), it shall be treated as if it had been determined in accordance with regulation 12D(2)(a) (eligible rent is maximum rent (LHA)) and shall apply according to the provisions of regulation 12D (eligible rent and maximum rent (LHA)).

Protection on death in the second and subsequent years after 7th April 2008

12K.–(1)   This regulation applies where–

(a)   the claimant's eligible rent is that specified in regulation 12I(2)(b) (basic transitional protection in the second and subsequent years after 7th April 2008), 12J(2)(b) (transitional protection in the second year after 7th April 2008 where the claimant is already enjoying protection on death) or paragraph (2)(b) of this regulation;

(b)   a linked person dies on or after 7th April 2009;

(c)   the claimant occupies the same dwelling as the linked person at the date of death; and

(d)   the relevant authority determines a maximum rent (LHA) by virtue of regulation 13C(2)(d)(i) or (ii) (change of category of dwelling or death of a linked person).

(2)   Where this regulation applies, the claimant's eligible rent is–

(a)   the maximum rent (LHA) where that is higher than the eligible rent which applied immediately before the date of the death; or

(b)   the amount of eligible rent which applied immediately before the death.

(3)   Where the eligible rent which applies is the one that applied immediately before the date of the death, it will continue to apply until, on or after the date of the death, the first of the following events occurs–

(a)   the end of 12 months from the date of the death;

(b)   the relevant authority is required to determine a maximum rent (LHA) by virtue of regulation 13C(2)(d)(i) or (3) (change of category of dwelling or anniversary of the LHA date) and it is higher than that eligible rent;

(c)   the relevant authority is required to determine an eligible rent following a change of dwelling;

(d)   the relevant authority is required to determine an eligible rent in accordance with this regulation following the death of another linked person.

(4)   Where the eligible rent ceases to apply because of paragraph (3)(a) the eligible rent is the one that would have applied but had the relevant authority not determined an eligible rent in accordance with this regulation.

(5)   Where the eligible rent is the maximum rent (LHA), it shall be treated as if it had been determined in accordance with regulation 12D(2)(a) (eligible rent is maximum rent (LHA)) and shall apply according to the provisions of regulation 12D (eligible rent and maximum rent (LHA)).

(6)   For the purposes of paragraph (1)(c), a claimant shall be treated as occupying the dwelling if regulation 7(13) is satisfied and for that purpose paragraph (13) of regulation 7 shall have effect as if sub-paragraph (b) were omitted.''.

Amendment of regulation 13C

7.   In regulation 13C (when a maximum rent (LHA) is to be determined)–

(a)   in paragraph (1) for ''paragraphs (2) or (3)'' substitute ''paragraphs (2), (3) or (4A)'';

(b)   in paragraph (3) after ''LHA date'' insert ''except where paragraph (4A)(b) applies'';

(c)   after paragraph (4) insert–

''(4A)   This paragraph applies where it is–

(a)   7th April 2008 and reference was made to a maximum rent (standard local rate) in determining the amount of the eligible rent which applied immediately before 7th April 2008; or

(b)   7th April 2009 and the eligible rent which applies on that date was determined in accordance with regulation 12E(2)(b) (basic transitional protection for pathfinder cases) or 12H(2)(b) (transitional protection where a death occurs in the first year on or after 7th April 2008).''.

Amendment of regulation 13D

8.   In regulation 13D(12) (determination of a maximum rent (LHA)) in the definition of ''relevant date'' after sub-paragraph (c) insert–

''(d)   7th April 2008;

(e)   7th April 2009.''.''.

The Housing Benefit (State Pension Credit) (Local Housing Allowance and Information Sharing) Amendment Regulations 2007

(SI 2007 No.2869)

Made	*2nd October 2007*
Laid before Parliament	*8th October 2007*
Coming into force in accordance with regulation 1	

The Secretary of State for Work and Pensions makes the following Regulations in exercise of the powers conferred by sections 123(1)(d), 130(2), 130A(2) to (6), 137(1) and 175(1) and (3) to (6) of the Social Security Contributions and Benefits Act 1992 and sections 5(1)(p), (2A) to (2C) and (6), 189(4) to (6) and 191 of the Social Security Administration Act 1992.

This instrument contains only regulations made by virtue of, or consequential upon, sections 30 and 35 of the Welfare Reform Act 2007 and is made before the end of the period of six months beginning with the coming into force of those sections.

In accordance with section 176(1) of the Social Security Administration Act 1992, the Secretary of State has consulted with organisations appearing to him to be representative of the authorities concerned.

Citation and commencement

1.–(1)   These Regulations may be cited as the Housing Benefit (State Pension Credit) (Local Housing Allowance and Information Sharing) Amendment Regulations 2007.

(2)   This regulation and regulations 2 (amendment of the Housing Benefit (Persons who have attained the qualifying age for state pension credit) Regulations 2006) and 3 (amendments relating to information sharing) shall come into force on 7th April 2008.

(3)   Subject to paragraph (6) (which relates to non-local housing allowance cases), regulations 4 to 19 (amendment of the Housing Benefit (Persons who have attained the qualifying age for state pension credit) Regulations 2006 relating to determination of appropriate maximum housing benefit) shall come into force on 7th April 2008 immediately following the coming into force of regulation 3.

(4)   Regulation 20 (substitution of Part 14 of and Schedule 9 to the Housing Benefit (Persons who have attained the qualifying age for state pension credit) Regulations 2006 in relation to former pathfinder authorities) shall come into force immediately following the coming into force of regulations 4 to 19 and in this paragraph "former pathfinder authorities" means those relevant authorities specified in Part 1 of Schedule 9 of the Housing Benefit (State Pension Credit) Regulations.

(5)   This paragraph applies to a case where no reference was made to a maximum rent (standard local rate) in determining the amount of the eligible rent which applied immediately before 7th April 2008 and in this paragraph–

"eligible rent" shall be construed in accordance with–

    (i)   regulations 12 or 12A of the Housing Benefit (Persons who have attained the qualifying age for state pension credit) Regulations 2006 as in force immediately before 7th April 2008; or

    (ii)   in a case to which paragraph 4 of Schedule 3 to the Housing Benefit and Council Tax Benefit (Consequential Provisions) Regulations 2006 applies, regulations 12 and 13 of those Regulations as set out in paragraph 5 of that Schedule as in force immediately before 7th April 2008; and

"maximum rent (standard local rate)" means a maximum rent (standard local rate) determined in accordance with regulation 13A of the Housing Benefit (Persons who have attained the qualifying age for state pension credit) Regulations 2006 as in force immediately before 7th April 2008.

(6)　In a case to which paragraph (5) applies regulations 4 to 19 shall come into force on the day when, on or after 7th April 2008, the first of the following sub-paragraphs applies–

(a)　a relevant authority is required to apply to a rent officer by virtue of regulation 14 of the Housing Benefit (State Pension Credit) Regulations;

(b)　sub-paragraph (a) would apply but for the case falling within regulation 14(4)(a) of, or 14(4)(b) of and paragraph 2 of Schedule 2 to, the Housing Benefit (State Pension Credit) Regulations (no application to rent officer required as an existing rent officer determination may be used);

(c)　a relevant authority is required to determine a new eligible rent in accordance with regulation 12(3)(b) of the Housing Benefit (State Pension Credit) Regulations; or

(d)　a relevant authority is required to determine a new eligible rent in accordance with regulation 12(3) of the Housing Benefit (Persons who have attained the qualifying age for state pension credit) Regulations 2006 as set out in paragraph 5 of Schedule 3 to the Consequential Provisions Regulations,

and in this paragraph "relevant authority" means an authority administering housing benefit.

(7)　Where paragraph (6) does not apply before 6th April 2009, regulations 4 to 19 shall come into force on that date.

(8)　In this regulation–

"the Housing Benefit (State Pension Credit) Regulations" means the Housing Benefit (Persons who have attained the qualifying age for state pension credit) Regulations 2006 as in force immediately before the coming into force of regulations 4 to 19 in that case; and

"the Consequential Provisions Regulations" means the Housing Benefit and Council Tax Benefit (Consequential Provisions) Regulations 2006 as in force immediately before the coming into force of regulations 4 to 19 in that case.

Amendment of the Housing Benefit (Persons who have attained the qualifying age for state pension credit) Regulations 2006

2.　The Housing Benefit (Persons who have attained the qualifying age for state pension credit) Regulations 2006 shall be amended in accordance with the following provisions of these Regulations.

Amendment of the Housing Benefit (Persons who have attained the qualifying age for state pension credit) Regulations 2006 relating to information sharing

3.–(1)　In regulation 14 (requirement to refer to rent officers)–

(a)　omit paragraphs (2), (3) and (9);

(b)　after paragraph (4) insert–

"(4A)　The provision of information to the rent officer in accordance with [¹ regulation 95A(5)] shall be treated as an application to the rent officer under paragraph (1).".

(2)　After regulation 94 (interpretation) insert–

" Information to be provided to rent officers

95A. –(1)　This paragraph applies to every claim for or award of housing benefit in the form of a rent allowance where the eligible rent has been, or is to be determined, in accordance with–

(a)　regulation 12(3)(a) (rent) or 12C (eligible rent and maximum rent), as the case may require;

(b)   regulation 12A (eligible rent and the maximum rent (LHA)) or any of regulations 12E to 12K (transitional protection for pathfinder cases), as the case may require; or

(c)   regulations 12 (rent) and 13 (maximum rent) as set out in paragraph 5 of Schedule 3 to the Consequential Provisions Regulations.

(2)   No earlier than the first, and no later than the fifth, working day of every month a relevant authority shall provide the following information to the rent officer in relation to every claim for or award of housing benefit to which paragraph (1) applied in the preceding month–

(a)   the address, including any room or unit number, house or flat number or name, and the postcode of the dwelling to which the claim or award relates;

(b)   where the claim or award relates to mooring charges for a houseboat, or payments in respect of the site on which a caravan or mobile home stands, the mooring or plot number and the address of the mooring or site, including the postcode;

(c)   the date on which the tenancy began;

(d)   the amount of rent and the rental period, whether calendar monthly, four weekly, weekly or some other period;

(e)   where the claimant has the use of two or more bedrooms, the number of bedrooms and rooms suitable for living in that there are in the dwelling, and in this sub-paragraph ''bedroom'' does not include a bedroom which the claimant shares with any person other than a member of his household, a non-dependant of his, or a person who pays rent to him or his partner;

(f)   whether the tenant (together with his partner where he has one) has exclusive use of only one bedroom, and if so, whether they have exclusive use of a kitchen, bathroom, toilet and a room suitable for living in;

(g)   whether the tenant has exclusive use of only one bedroom, and if so, which, if any, of the following the tenancy provides for him to share–

(i)   a kitchen;

(ii)   a bathroom;

(iii)   a toilet; or

(iv)   a room suitable for living in;

(h)   the date on which entitlement to housing benefit began; and

(i)   where applicable, the date on which entitlement to housing benefit ended.

(3)   Where the relevant authority is required to apply to the rent officer for a board and attendance determination by virtue of regulation 13D(10) (determination of a maximum rent (LHA)), it shall provide the following information in the application to the Rent Officer–

(a)   the address, including any room or unit number, house or flat number or name and the postcode of the dwelling to which the claim or award relates;

(b)   the date on which the tenancy began;

(c)   the length of the tenancy;

(d)   the total amount of those payments referred to in regulation 12(1) (rent) which the claimant is liable to make in respect of the dwelling which he occupies as his home;

(e)   whether those payments include any charges for water, sewerage or allied environmental services or charges in respect of meals or fuel which are ineligible for housing benefit; and

(f)   where those payments include any charges that are ineligible for housing benefit by reason of paragraph 1(a)(iv) and (c) to (f) of Schedule 1 (ineligible service charges), that such charges are included, and the value of those charges as determined by that authority pursuant to regulation 12B(2) and that Schedule.

(4)   where the relevant authority has identified charges to which paragraph (3)(f) applies, it shall–

(a) deduct those charges from the total amount of those payments which, in accordance with paragraph (3)(d), it has stated that the claimant is liable to make in respect of the dwelling which he occupies as his home; and

(b) notify that total so reduced to the rent officer in its application.

(5) Where a relevant authority has received notification from the rent officer that a substantial part of the rent is attributable to board and attendance, it shall provide the information referred to in paragraphs (7) and (8), except for such information as it has already provided in accordance with paragraphs (3) and (4).

(6) Where the relevant authority is required to apply to the rent officer for a determination by virtue of regulation 14(1) (requirement to refer to rent officers), it shall provide the information referred to in paragraphs (7) to (9) in the application to the rent officer.

(7) In relation to the dwelling to which the claim or award relates, the relevant authority shall provide the following information–

(a) the address, including any room or unit number, house or flat number or name and the postcode of the dwelling;

(b) where the claim or award relates to mooring charges for a houseboat, or payments in respect of the site on which a caravan or mobile home stands, the mooring or plot number and the address of the mooring or site, including the postcode;

(c) whether the dwelling is–
(i) a detached house;
(ii) a semi-detached house;
(iii) a terraced house;
(iv) a maisonette;
(v) a detached bungalow;
(vi) a semi-detached bungalow;
(vii) a flat in a house;
(viii) a flat in a block;
(ix) a flat over a shop;
(x) a bedsit or rooms or a studio flat;
(xi) a hostel;
(xii) a caravan, mobile home or houseboat;
(xiii) board and lodgings;
(xiv) a hotel;
(xv) a care home;
(xvi) an independent hospital; or
(xvii) some other description of dwelling, and if so what;

(d) whether the dwelling has central heating, a garden, a garage or a parking space;

(e) how many rooms suitable for living in there are–
(i) in the dwelling;
(ii) in the dwelling which the claimant shares with any person other than a member of his household, a non-dependant of his, or a person who pays rent to him or his partner;

(f) how many bedsitting rooms there are in the categories (e)(i) and (ii);

(g) how many bedrooms there are in the categories (e)(i) and (ii);

(h) how many bathrooms or toilets there are in the categories (e)(i) and (ii); and

(i) such other information as the rent officer may reasonably require to make a determination.

(8) In relation to the tenancy to which the claim or award relates, the relevant authority shall provide the following information–

(a) the information referred to in paragraphs (3)(d) to (f) and (4);

(b) if the tenancy is furnished, and if so, to what extent;

(c)   the rental period, whether calendar monthly, four weekly, weekly or some other period;
(d)   the length of the tenancy;
(e)   when the tenancy began and, if appropriate, when it ended;
(h)   the landlord's or letting agent's name;
(i)   the landlord's or letting agent's business address;
(j)   whether the landlord is a housing association or registered social landlord; and
(k)   such other information as the rent officer may reasonably require to make a determination.
(9)   In relation to the claimant and the other occupiers of the dwelling to which the claim or award relates, the relevant authority shall provide the following information–
(a)   such information regarding the relationship of the claimant to the occupiers and the occupiers to each other, as is necessary for the rent officer to make the determination;
(b)   the age and sex of each occupier under 18; and
(c)   any other information that is relevant to the rent officer in making the determination, including visits to the dwelling.
(10)   Where a rent officer serves a notice under article 5 (insufficient information) of the Rent Officers Order the relevant authority shall supply the further information required under this regulation, or confirm whether information already supplied is correct and, if it is not, supply the correct information.
(11)   Where the relevant authority refers a case to the rent officer in accordance with regulation 14 as in force before the coming into force of regulation 8 of the Housing Benefit (State Pension Credit) (Local Housing Allowance and Information Sharing) Amendment Regulations 2007, it shall notify the rent officer that the referral is made in accordance with regulation 14 as in force before the coming into force of regulation 8 of those Regulations.
(12)   In this regulation–
''tenancy'' includes–
(a)   in Scotland, any other right of occupancy; and
(b)   in any other case, a licence to occupy premises,
and reference to a tenant, landlord or any other expression appropriate to a tenancy shall be construed accordingly;
''working day'' means any day other than a Saturday, a Sunday, Christmas Day, Good Friday or a day which is a bank holiday under the Banking and Financial Dealings Act 1971 in the jurisdiction in which the area of the relevant authority is situated.''.

(3)   Omit regulation 95 (evidence and information required by rent officers).

Amendment
1.   Amended by reg 5(2) of SI 2008 No 586 as from 7.4.08.

Amendments to regulations 2, 3, 11 and 12 of the Housing Benefit (Persons who have attained the qualifying age for state pension credit) Regulations 2006
4.–(1)   In regulation 2(1) (interpretation)–
(a)   for the definition of ''eligible rent'' substitute–

'' ''eligible rent'' means as the case may require, an eligible rent determined in accordance with–
(a)   regulations 12B (eligible rent), 12C (eligible rent and maximum rent) or 12D (eligible rent and maximum rent (LHA)); or

(b) regulations 12 (rent) and 13 (restrictions on unreasonable payments) as set out in paragraph 5 of Schedule 3 to the Consequential Provisions Regulations in a case to which paragraph 4 of that Schedule applies;'';

(b) for the definition of ''housing association'' substitute–

'' ''housing association'' has the meaning assigned to it by section 1(1) of the Housing Associations Act 1985;'';

(c) for the definition of ''maximum rent'' substitute–

'' ''maximum rent'' means the amount to which the eligible rent is restricted in a case where regulation 13 applies;'';

(d) for the definition of ''non-dependant deduction'' substitute–

'' ''non-dependant deduction'' means a deduction that is to be made under regulation 55 (non-dependant deductions);'';

(e) for the definition of ''Rent Officers Order'' substitute–

'' ''Rent Officers Order'' means the Rent Officers (Housing Benefit Functions) Order 1997 or, as the case may be, the Rent Officers (Housing Benefit Functions) (Scotland) Order 1997;''.

(f) at the appropriate places insert–

'' ''amended determination'' means a determination made in accordance with article 7A of the Rent Officers Order;
''broad rental market area'' has the meaning specified in paragraph 4 of Schedule 3B to the Rent Officers Order;
''broad rental market area determination'' means a determination made in accordance with article 4B(1A) of the Rent Officers Order;
''change of dwelling'' means, for the purposes of regulations 13C and 14, a change of dwelling occupied by a claimant as his home during the award where the dwelling to which the claimant has moved is one in respect of which the authority may make a rent allowance;
''linked person'' means–
  (a) any member of the claimant's family;
  (b) if the claimant is a member of a polygamous marriage, any partners of his and any child or young person for whom he or a partner is responsible and who is a member of the same household; or
  (c) any relative of the claimant or his partner who occupies the same dwelling as the claimant, whether or not they reside with him, except for a relative who has a separate right of occupation of the dwelling which would enable them to continue to occupy it even if the claimant ceased his occupation of it;
''local housing allowance'' means an allowance determined in accordance with paragraph 2 of Schedule 3B to the Rent Officers Order;
''maximum rent (LHA)'' means the amount determined in accordance with regulation 13D;
''reckonable rent'' means payments which a person is liable to make in respect of the dwelling which he occupies as his home, and which are eligible, or would, but for regulation 13, be eligible for housing benefit;
[¹ ''registered housing association'' means a housing association which–
  (a) is registered in a register maintained by the Corporation or the National Assembly for Wales under Chapter 1 of Part 1 of the Housing Act 1996; or

(b)   in Scotland, is registered by Scottish Ministers by virtue of section 57(3)(b) of the Housing (Scotland) Act 2001,

and "the Corporation" has the same meaning as in section 56 of the Housing Act 1996;]

"relevant information" means information or evidence forwarded to the relevant authority by an appropriate DWP office regarding a claim on which rent allowance may be awarded, which completes the transfer of all information or evidence held by the appropriate DWP office relating to that claim;".

(2)   In regulation 3(4) (definition of non-dependant) after "and regulation 9" insert "and the definition of "linked person" in regulation 2"".

(3)   In regulation 11 (eligible housing costs)–

(a)   for paragraph (1) substitute–

" (1)   Subject to the following provisions of this regulation, housing benefit shall be payable in respect of the payments specified in regulation 12(1) (rent) and a claimant's maximum housing benefit shall be calculated under Part 7 (amount of benefit) by reference to the amount of his eligible rent determined in accordance with–

(a)   regulation 12B (eligible rent);

(b)   regulations 12C (eligible rent and maximum rent), 13 (maximum rent), 13ZA (protection on death and 13 week protection) and 13ZB (change in reckonable rent);

(c)   regulations 12D (eligible rent and maximum rent (LHA)), 13C (when a maximum rent (LHA) is to be determined) and 13D (determination of a maximum rent (LHA)); or

(d)   regulations 12 (rent) and 13 (restrictions on unreasonable payments) as set out in paragraph 5 of Schedule 3 to the Consequential Provisions Regulations,

whichever is applicable in his case.";

(b)   in paragraph (3) for " paragraphs (1) to (3) of that regulation" substitute "paragraphs (1) or (2) of that regulation or paragraph (2) of regulation 12B".

(4)   In regulation 12 (rent)–

(a)   omit paragraphs (3) to (7);

(b)   in paragraph (8) after "regulation" insert ", regulation 12B (eligible rent)".

Amendment
1.   Substituted by reg 5(3) of SI 2008 No 586 as from 7.4.08.

Insertion of regulations 12B, 12C and 12D into the Housing Benefit (Persons who have attained the qualifying age for state pension credit) Regulations 2006

5.   After regulation 12 (rent)insert–

" **Eligible rent**

12B.–(1)   The amount of a person's eligible rent shall be determined in accordance with the provisions of this regulation except where regulations 12C (eligible rent and maximum rent) or 12D (eligible rent and maximum rent (LHA)) apply, or paragraph 4 of Schedule 3 to the Consequential Provisions Regulations applies.

(2)   Subject to paragraphs (3), (4) and (6), the amount of a person's eligible rent shall be the aggregate of such payments specified in regulation 12(1) as that person is liable to pay less–

(a) except where he is separately liable for charges for water, sewerage or allied environmental services, an amount determined in accordance with paragraph (5);

(b) where payments include service charges which are wholly or partly ineligible, an amount in respect of the ineligible charges determined in accordance with Schedule 1; and

(c) where he is liable to make payments in respect of any service charges to which regulation 12(1)(e) does not apply, but to which paragraph 3(2) of Part 1 of Schedule 1 (unreasonably low service charges) applies in the particular circumstances, an amount in respect of such charges determined in accordance with paragraph 3(2) of Part 1 of Schedule 1.

(3) Where the payments specified in regulation 12(1) are payable in respect of accommodation which consists partly of residential accommodation and partly of other accommodation, only such proportion of those payments as is referable to the residential accommodation shall count as eligible rent for the purposes of these Regulations.

(4) Where more than one person is liable to make payments in respect of a dwelling, the payments specified in regulation 12(1) shall be apportioned for the purpose of calculating the eligible rent for each such person having regard to all the circumstances, in particular, the number of such persons and the proportion of rent paid by each such person.

(5) The amount of the deduction referred to in paragraph (2) shall be–

(a) if the dwelling occupied by the claimant is a self-contained unit, except in a case to which sub-paragraph (c) applies, the amount of the charges;

(b) in any other case, except one to which sub-paragraph (c) applies, the proportion of those charges in respect of the self-contained unit which is obtained by dividing the area of the dwelling occupied by the claimant by the area of the self-contained unit of which it forms part;

(c) where the charges vary in accordance with the amount of water actually used, the amount which the appropriate authority considers to be fairly attributable to water, and sewerage services, having regard to the actual or estimated consumption of the claimant.

(6) In any case where it appears to the relevant authority that in the particular circumstances of that case the eligible rent as determined in accordance with the preceding paragraphs of this regulation is greater than it is reasonable to meet by way of housing benefit, the eligible rent shall be such lesser sum as seems to that authority to be an appropriate rent in that particular case.

Eligible rent and maximum rent
12C.–(1) This regulation applies where a maximum rent has been, or is to be, determined in accordance with regulation 13 (maximum rent).

(2) Where this regulation applies the amount of a person's eligible rent shall be the maximum rent, subject to paragraphs (3), (4) and (6) of regulation 12B.

Eligible rent and maximum rent (LHA)
12D.–(1) This regulation applies where, by virtue of paragraphs (2) or (3) of regulation 13C (when a maximum rent (LHA) is to be determined), a maximum rent (LHA) has been, or is to be, determined in accordance with regulation 13D (determination of a maximum rent (LHA)).

(2) Where this regulation applies, except where paragraphs (3)(a) (protection on death) or (5)(a) (13 week protection) apply,–

(a) the amount of a person's eligible rent shall be the maximum rent (LHA); and

(b) it shall apply until the earlier of–

(i)   the determination of a maximum rent (LHA) by virtue of regulation 13C(2)(d) (change of category of dwelling, death or change of dwelling for an LHA case);

(ii)   the determination of a maximum rent (LHA) by virtue of regulation 13C(3) (anniversary of LHA date); or

(iii)   the determination of a maximum rent by virtue of regulation 13 or an eligible rent under regulation 12B.

(3)   Subject to paragraph (7), where the relevant authority is required to determine a maximum rent (LHA) by virtue of regulation 13C(2)(a), (b) (new claim on or after 7th April 2008) or (d)(i) or (ii) (change of category of dwelling or death relating to an LHA case) and the claimant occupies a dwelling which is the same as that occupied by him at the date of death of any linked person, the eligible rent shall be–

(a)   either–

    (i)   the eligible rent which applied on the day before the death occurred; or

    (ii)   in a case where there was no eligible rent, subject to regulation 12B(3) (mixed use accommodation), (4) (more than one person liable to make payments) and (6) (discretion in relation to eligible rent), the reckonable rent due on that day; or

(b)   the eligible rent determined in accordance with paragraph (2), where it is equal to or more than the eligible rent determined in accordance with sub-paragraph (a).

(4)   For the purpose of paragraph (3), a claimant shall be treated as occupying the dwelling if paragraph (13) of regulation 7 (circumstances in which a person is or is not to be treated as occupying a dwelling as his home) is satisfied and for that purpose paragraph (13) shall have effect as if sub-paragraph (b) of that paragraph were omitted.

(5)   Subject to paragraphs (6) and (7), where a relevant authority is required to determine a maximum rent (LHA) by virtue of regulation 13C(2)(a) or (b) (new claim on or after 7th April 2008) and the relevant authority is satisfied that the claimant or a linked person was able to meet the financial commitments for his dwelling when they were entered into, the eligible rent shall be–

(a)   an eligible rent determined in accordance with regulation 12B(2); or

(b)   the eligible rent determined in accordance with paragraph (2), where it is equal to or more than the eligible rent referred to in sub-paragraph (a).

(6)   Paragraph (5) shall not apply where a claimant or the claimant's partner, was previously entitled to benefit in respect of an award of housing benefit which fell wholly or partly less than 52 weeks before the commencement of the claimant's current award of housing benefit.

(7)   Where a person's eligible rent has been determined in accordance with–

(a)   paragraph (3)(a) (protection on death), it shall apply until the first of the following events occurs–

    (i)   the period of 12 months from the date of death has expired;

    (ii)   the relevant authority determines an eligible rent in accordance with paragraph (2) which is equal to or exceeds it or is based on a maximum rent (LHA) determined by virtue of regulation 13C(2)(d)(iii) (change of dwelling);

    (iii)   the determination of an eligible rent in accordance with paragraph (3)(a) (protection on death) in relation to a subsequent death; or

    (iv)   the determination of a maximum rent by virtue of regulation 13 or an eligible rent under regulation 12B.

(b)   paragraph (5)(a) (13 week protection), it shall apply until the first of the following events occurs–

    (i)   the first 13 weeks of the claimant's award of housing benefit have expired;

    (ii)   the relevant authority determines an eligible rent in accordance with paragraph (2) which is equal to or exceeds it or is based on a maximum rent (LHA) determined by virtue of regulation 13C(2)(d)(iii) (change of dwelling);

    (iii) the determination of an eligible rent in accordance with paragraph (3)(a) (protection on death); or

    (iv) the determination of a maximum rent by virtue of regulation 13 or an eligible rent under regulation 12B.

    (8)   Where an eligible rent ceases to apply by virtue of paragraph (7)(a)(i) (expiry of protection on death) or (7)(b)(i) (expiry of 13 week protection), the eligible rent that shall apply instead shall be the one which would have applied but for paragraphs (3)(a) and (5)(a).''.

Substitution of regulations 13, 13ZA and 13ZB for regulation 13 of the Housing Benefit (Persons who have attained the qualifying age for state pension credit) Regulations 2006

    6. For regulation 13 (maximum rent) substitute–

" Maximum rent

    13.–(1)   The maximum rent shall be determined in accordance with paragraphs (2) to (6) where–

    (a)   a local authority has applied for a determination in accordance with regulation 14 (requirement to refer to rent officers), a redetermination in accordance with regulation 15 or 16, or a substitute determination or substitute redetermination in accordance with regulation 17 and a rent officer has made a determination, redetermination, substitute determination or substitute redetermination in exercise of the Housing Act functions; or

    (b)   an authority is not required to apply to the rent officer for a determination because–

        (i)   regulation 14(2)(a) applies; or

        (ii)   regulation 14(2)(b) applies because paragraph 2(2) of Schedule 2 applies.

    (2)   In a case where the rent officer has determined a claim-related rent, but is not required to notify the relevant authority of a local reference rent, the maximum rent shall be that claim-related rent.

    (3)   Subject to the limit specified in paragraph (4), in a case where the rent officer has determined both a local reference rent of which he is required to notify the relevant authority and a claim-related rent, the maximum rent shall be the local reference rent.

    (4)   In a case to which paragraph 8 of Schedule 3 to the Consequential Provisions Regulations applies, where the rent officer has determined and is required to notify the relevant authority of a local reference rent the maximum rent shall not exceed twice that local reference rent.

    (5)   Where the maximum rent is derived from–

    (a)   a claim-related rent and the notification under paragraph 9(1)(c) of Schedule 1 to the Rent Officers Order states that an ineligible amount in respect of meals has been included in that claim-related rent; or

    (b)   a local reference rent and the notification under paragraph 9(1)(da) of Schedule 1 to the Rent Officers Order states that an ineligible amount in respect of meals has been included in that local reference rent,

in determining the maximum rent the relevant authority shall deduct an amount determined in accordance with paragraph 2 of Schedule 1 to these Regulations in respect of meals.

(6)   This regulation is subject to regulations 13ZA (protection on death and 13 week protection) and 13ZB (change in reckonable rent).

(7)   In this regulation–

"claim-related rent" means the rent notified by the rent officer under paragraph 9(1) of Schedule 1 to the Rent Officers Order;

"local reference rent" means the rent determined by a rent officer under paragraph 4 of Schedule 1 to the Rent Officers Order.

Protection on death and 13 week protection

13ZA.–(1)   In a case where the claimant occupies a dwelling which is the same as that occupied by him at the date of death of a linked person, the maximum rent shall be either–

(a)   the maximum rent which applied before the death occurred; or

(b)   in a case where there was no maximum rent, the reckonable rent due before the death occurred,

for a period of 12 months from the date of such a death.

(2)   For the purposes of paragraph (1), a claimant shall be treated as occupying the dwelling if paragraph (13) of regulation 7 (circumstances in which a person is or is not to be treated as occupying a dwelling as his home) is satisfied and for that purpose sub-paragraph (b) of that paragraph of that regulation shall be treated as if it were omitted.

(3)   Subject to paragraph (4), where the relevant authority is satisfied that the claimant or a linked person was able to meet the financial commitments for his dwelling when they were entered into, there shall be no maximum rent during the first 13 weeks of the claimant's award of housing benefit.

(4)   Paragraph (3) shall not apply where a claimant or the claimant's partner was previously entitled to benefit in respect of an award of housing benefit which fell wholly or partly less than 52 weeks before the commencement of the claimant's current award of housing benefit.

Change in reckonable rent

13ZB.–(1)   In a case where–

(a)   the authority has determined a maximum rent under regulation 13 or 13ZA; and

(b)   during the period for which that maximum rent applies the reckonable rent in respect of the dwelling by reference to which that maximum rent was determined is reduced to a sum which is less than that maximum rent,

the maximum rent shall be reduced to an amount equal to the reduced reckonable rent.

(2)   This paragraph applies in a case where–

(a)   a rent officer has made a determination in exercise of the Housing Act functions pursuant to an application by an authority under regulation 14(1)(e) (pre-tenancy determination);

(b)   subsequent to that determination the reckonable rent for that dwelling is changed; and

(c)   a maximum rent is to be determined in relation to a claim for housing benefit by a claimant.

(3)   In a case to which paragraph (2) applies, where the reckonable rent is reduced to a figure below the figure that would have been the maximum rent if the reckonable rent had not changed, the maximum rent shall be the reckonable rent as so reduced.

(4)   In any other case to which paragraph (2) applies, the authority shall treat the reckonable rent to be that applicable to the determination by the rent officer referred to in paragraph (2)(a).".

Insertion of regulations 13C, 13D and 13E into the Housing Benefit (Persons who have attained the qualifying age for state pension credit) Regulations 2006
    7.   After regulation 13ZB (change in reckonable rent), as substituted by regulation 6, insert–

'' When a maximum rent (LHA) is to be determined
    13C.–(1)   A relevant authority shall determine a maximum rent (LHA) in accordance with regulation 13D (determination of a maximum rent (LHA)) in any case where paragraphs (2) or (3) apply.
    (2)   This paragraph applies where a relevant authority has received–
    (a)   a claim on which a rent allowance may be awarded, where the date of claim falls on or after 7th April 2008;
    (b)   relevant information regarding a claim on which a rent allowance may be awarded, where the date of claim falls on or after 7th April 2008;
    (c)   in relation to an award of housing benefit where the eligible rent was determined without reference to regulation 13A or 13D, a notification of a change of dwelling (as defined in regulation 2) where the change occurs on or after 7th April 2008; or
    (d)   in relation to an award of housing benefit where a maximum rent (LHA) was determined in accordance with regulation 13D–
        (i)   notification of a change of a kind which affects the category of dwelling applicable to the claim;
        (ii)   notification of the death of a linked person, where the notification does not fall within head (i); or
        (iii)   notification of a change of dwelling.
    (3)   This paragraph applies on the anniversary of the LHA date.
    (4)   Where the LHA date is 29th February, the anniversary of the LHA date shall be 28th February.
    (5)   This regulation does not apply in a case where–
    (a)   the landlord is a registered social landlord;
    (b)   paragraph 4(1)(b) of Schedule 3 to the Consequential Provisions Regulations (savings provision) applies;
    (c)   the tenancy is an excluded tenancy of a type [¹ mentioned in any of paragraphs 4 to 11] of Schedule 2;
    (d)   the claim or award relates to–
        (i)   periodical payments of kind falling within regulation 12(1) (rent) which a person is liable to make in relation to a houseboat, caravan or mobile home which he occupies as his home; or
        (ii)   rent payable in relation to a hostel; or
    (e)   rent under the tenancy is attributable to board and attendance, and–
        (i)   the relevant authority has made an application to the rent officer in accordance with regulation 13D(10) (board and attendance determination), regulation 15 (applications to the rent officer for determinations) or regulation 17 (substitute determinations or substitute redeterminations); and
        (ii)   the rent officer has determined that a substantial part of the rent under the tenancy is fairly attributable to board and attendance and has notified the relevant authority of this in accordance with article 4C, 4D or 4E of the Rent Officers Order.
    (6)   In this regulation–
    ''the LHA date'' means the date by reference to which the local housing allowance used to determine the maximum rent (LHA) was identified;
    ''registered social landlord'' has the same meaning as in Part 1 of the Housing Act 1996 or, in Scotland, sections 57 and 59 of the Housing (Scotland) Act 2001.

Amendment
1.   Amended by reg 5(4)(a) of SI 2008 No 586 as from 7.4.08.

Determination of a maximum rent (LHA)

13D.–(1)   Subject to paragraph (3) to (11), the maximum rent (LHA) shall be the local housing allowance determined by the rent officer by virtue of article 4B(2A) or (4) of the Rent Officers Order which is applicable to–

(a)   the broad rental market area in which the dwelling to which the claim or award of housing benefit relates is situated at the relevant date; and

(b)   the category of dwelling which applies at the relevant date in accordance with paragraph (2).

(2)   The category of dwelling which applies is–

(a)   the category specified in paragraph 1(1)(a) of Schedule 3B to the Rent Officers Order (one bedroom shared accommodation) where paragraph (b) does not apply because neither sub-paragraph (b)(i) nor (ii) are satisfied in the claimant's case and–

   (i)   neither the claimant nor his partner (where he has one) is a person to whom paragraph 6 of Schedule 3 (severe disability premium) applies; or

   [¹ (ii) the claimant's partner is not a care leaver;]

(b)   the category specified in paragraph 1(1)(b) of Schedule 3B to the Rent Officers Order (one bedroom self contained accommodation) where that applies in the claimant's case at the relevant date in accordance with the size criteria ¹[as set out in paragraph (3)] and–

   (i)   the claimant (together with his partner where he has one) has the exclusive use of two or more rooms; or

   (ii)   the claimant (together with his partner where he has one) has the exclusive use of one room, a bathroom and toilet and a kitchen or facilities for cooking,

and in this sub-paragraph "room" means a bedroom or room suitable for living in except for a room which the claimant shares with any person other than a member of his household, a non-dependant of his, or a person who pays rent to him or his partner; or

(c)   in any other case, the category which corresponds with the number of bedrooms to which the claimant is entitled in accordance with paragraph (3).

(3)   The claimant shall be entitled to one bedroom for each of the following categories of occupier (and each occupier shall come within the first category only which applies to him)–

(a)   a couple (within the meaning of Part 7 of the Act);

(b)   a person who is not a child;

(c)   two children of the same sex;

(d)   two children who are less than 10 years old;

(e)   a child.

(4)   The relevant authority shall determine–

(a)   the cap rent (in accordance with the definition in paragraph (12)); and

(b)   whether the cap rent exceeds the applicable local housing allowance.

(5)   Where the applicable local housing allowance exceeds the cap rent, for the purpose of determining the appropriate maximum housing benefit, the amount of the claimant's liability shall be the amount of the applicable local housing allowance.

(6)   Where paragraph (5) applies, the maximum rent (LHA) shall be the lower of–

(a)   the applicable local housing allowance; or

(b)   the amount equal to the cap rent determined in accordance with paragraph (4)(a) plus £15.

(7)   Where no local housing allowance applicable to a claim or award of housing benefit falling within paragraph (2)(c) has been determined, the relevant authority shall–

(a)   apply to the rent officer for local housing allowance determinations for the category of dwelling applicable to the claim or award of housing benefit for each broad rental market area falling within its area, in whole or in part, at the relevant date, which shall be specified in the application; and

(b)   apply the local housing allowance so determined for the broad rental market area in which the dwelling to which the claim or award of housing benefit relates is situated at the relevant date.

(8)   Subject to paragraph (9), where–

(a)   the relevant authority receives a request from a person stating that–

(i)   he is contemplating occupying as his home a dwelling within the area of the relevant authority which contains a specified number of bedrooms, exceeding five, and

(ii)   that if he does so, he is likely to claim housing benefit; and

(b)   no local housing allowance determination is in effect for a broad rental market area falling within, in whole or in part, the area of the relevant authority for the category of dwelling containing the number of bedrooms specified in the request,

the relevant authority shall apply to the rent officer for local housing allowance determinations for each broad rental market area falling within its area, in whole or in part, for the category of dwelling containing the number of bedrooms specified in the request, and in this sub-paragraph ''bedroom'' means has the meaning specified in paragraph 1(2) of Schedule 3B to the Rent Officers Order.

(9)   The request must–

(a)   be made on a form approved by the relevant authority for the purpose of making a request under paragraph (8);

(b)   be properly completed; and

(c)   contain the following matters–

(i)   the signature of the prospective occupier;

(ii)   the signature of the person to whom the prospective occupier would incur liability to make such payments;

(iii)   a statement that the person in paragraph (ii) agrees to the application being made for that determination; and

(iv)   an indication that the prospective occupier is contemplating occupying the dwelling as his home and that if he does so, he is likely to claim housing benefit.

(10)   The relevant authority shall apply to the rent officer for a board and attendance determination to be made in accordance with article 4C of the Rent Officers Order where–

(a)   the relevant authority is required to determine a maximum rent (LHA) by virtue of regulation 13C; and

(b)   part of the rent under the tenancy appears to the relevant authority to be likely to be attributable to board and attendance.

(11)   Where an application to a rent officer is required in accordance with paragraph (10) it shall be made within the same period following the day on which the relevant authority becomes obliged to determine a maximum rent (LHA) by virtue of regulation 13C as would be required if the application were to be made under regulation 14(1).

(12)   In this regulation–

''cap rent'' means the aggregate of such payments specified in regulation 12(1) (rent) which the claimant is liable to pay, or is treated as liable to pay by virtue of regulation 8 (circumstances in which a person is treated as liable to make payments in respect of a dwelling) subject to regulation 12B(3) (mixed use accommodation),

(4) (more than one person liable to make payments) and (6) (discretion in relation to eligible rent);

"care leaver" means a person who has not attained the age of 22 and–

(a) has ceased to be the subject of a care order made pursuant to section 31(1)(a) of the Children Act 1989 which had previously been made in respect to him either–
    (i) after he attained the age of 16 years; or
    (ii) before he attained the age of 16 years, but had continued after he attained that age;

(b) was formerly provided with accommodation under section 20 of the Children Act 1989;

(c) has ceased to be subject to a supervision requirement by a children's hearing under section 70 of the Children (Scotland) Act 1995 ("the 1995 Act") made in respect of him which had continued after he attained the age of 16 years, other than a case where–
    (i) the ground of referral was based on the sole condition as to the need for compulsory measures of care specified in section 52(1)(i) of the 1995 Act (commission of offences by child); or
    (ii) he was required by virtue of the supervision requirement to reside with a parent or guardian of his within the meaning of the 1995 Act, or with a friend or relative of his or of his parent or guardian;

(d) has ceased to be a child in relation to whom the parental rights and responsibilities were transferred to a local authority under a parental responsibilities order made in accordance with section 86 of the 1995 Act or treated as so vested in accordance with paragraph 3 of Schedule 3 to that Act, either–
    (i) after he attained the age of 16 years; or
    (ii) before he attained the age of 16 years, but had continued after he attained that age; or

(e) has ceased to be provided with accommodation by a local authority under section 25 of the 1995 Act where he has previously been provided with accommodation by the authority under that provision either–
    (i) after he attained the age of 16 years; or
    (ii) before he attained the age of 16 years, but had continued to be in such accommodation after he attained that age;

"occupiers" means the persons whom the relevant authority is satisfied occupy as their home the dwelling to which the claim or award relates except for any joint tenant who is not a member of the claimant's household;

"relevant date" means, as the case may require–

(a) the date of the claim to which the claim or relevant information referred to in regulation 13C (2) (a) or (b) relates;

(b) the date of the change of dwelling, change which affects the category of dwelling, or date of death, to which a notification referred to in regulation 13C(2)(c) or (d) relates; or

(c) the date on which the anniversary of the LHA date referred to in regulation 13C(3) falls.

"tenancy" includes

(a) in Scotland, any other right of occupancy; and

(b) in any other case, a licence to occupy premises,

and reference to a tenant, landlord or any other expression appropriate to a tenancy shall be construed accordingly.

Amendment

1.   Amended by reg 5(4)(b) of SI 2008 No 586 as from 7.4.08.

Publication of local housing allowances

13E.–(1)   A relevant authority shall take such steps as appear to it to be appropriate for the purpose of securing that information in relation to broad rental market areas falling in whole or in part within its area, and local housing allowances applicable to such broad rental market areas, is brought to the attention of persons who may be entitled to housing benefit from the authority.''.

Substitution of regulation 14 of the Housing Benefit (Persons who have attained the qualifying age for state pension credit) Regulations 2006

8.   For regulation 14 (requirement to refer to rent officers), substitute–

'' Requirement to refer to rent officers

14.–(1)   Subject to the following provisions of this regulation, a relevant authority shall apply to a rent officer for a determination to be made in pursuance of the Housing Act functions where–

(a)   it has received a claim on which rent allowance may be awarded and any of the circumstances specified in regulation 13C(5)(a) to (e) (rent allowance cases for which a maximum rent (standard local rent) is not to be determined) apply;

(b)   it has received relevant information regarding a claim on which rent allowance may be awarded and any of the circumstances specified in regulation 13C(5)(a) to (e) apply;

(c)   it has received a notification of a change relating to a rent allowance and a maximum rent (LHA) does not fall to be determined under regulation 13C (determination of a maximum rent (LHA));

(d)   it has received a notification of a change of dwelling and any of the circumstances specified in regulation 13C(5)(a) to (e) apply;

(e)   it has received, except in the case where any liability to make payments in respect of a dwelling would be to a housing authority, a request from a person (''the prospective occupier''), on a properly completed form approved for the purpose by the relevant authority, which includes the specified matters and any of the circumstances specified in regulation 13C(5)(a) to (d) apply;

(f)   52 weeks have expired since it last made an application under sub-paragraph (a), (b), (c), (d) [, (e) or (h)] in relation to the claim or award in question and–

    (i)   a maximum rent (LHA) determined under regulation 13D does not apply; and

    (ii)   a maximum rent (LHA) is not to be determined under regulation 13D; [¹]

(g)   52 weeks have expired since an application was made under sub-paragraph (f) or a previous application was made under this sub-paragraph, whichever last occurred, and–

    (i)   a maximum rent (LHA) determined under regulation 13D does not apply; and

    (ii)   a maximum rent (LHA) is not to be determined under regulation 13D. [¹ or

(h)   has received notification that any of the circumstances in regulation 13C(5) apply.]

(2)   An application shall not be required under paragraph (1) where a claim, relevant information regarding a claim, notification or request relates to either–

(a) a dwelling in a hostel if, during the period of 12 months ending on the day on which that claim, relevant information regarding a claim, notification or request is received by the relevant authority–

    (i) a rent officer has already made a determination in the exercise of the Housing Act functions in respect of a dwelling in that hostel which is a similar dwelling to the dwelling to which the claim, relevant information regarding a claim, notification or request relates; and

    (ii) there has been no change relating to a rent allowance that has affected the dwelling in respect of which that determination was made; or

(b) an "excluded tenancy" within the meaning of Schedule 2 (excluded tenancies).

(3) The provision of information to the rent officer in accordance with regulation 95A(5) shall be treated as an application to the rent officer under paragraph (1).

(4) Where a relevant authority receives a request pursuant to paragraph (1)(e) (request from prospective occupier) and it is a case where, by reason of paragraph (2) (hostels or excluded tenancies), an application to a rent officer is not required, the authority shall–

(a) return it to the prospective occupier, indicating why no such application is required; and

(b) where it is not required by reason of either paragraph (2)(a) (hostels) of this regulation or paragraph 2 of Schedule 2 (cases where the rent officer has already made a determination), shall also send him a copy of that determination within 4 days of the receipt of that request by the authority.

(5) Where an application to a rent officer is required by paragraph (1) it shall be made within 3 days, or as soon as practicable after that date, of–

(a) the relevant authority receiving a claim on which rent allowance may be awarded;

(b) the relevant authority receiving relevant information regarding a claim on which rent allowance may be awarded;

(c) the relevant authority receiving a notification of a change relating to a rent allowance;

(d) the relevant authority receiving a notification of a change of dwelling; or

(e) the day on which the period mentioned in paragraph (1)(f) or (g) expired,

except that, in the case of a request to which paragraph (1)(e) (request from prospective occupier) applies, the application shall be made within 2 days of the receipt of that request by the authority.

(6) In calculating any period of days mentioned in paragraphs (4) or (5), no regard shall be had to a day on which the offices of the relevant authority are closed for the purposes of receiving or determining claims.

(7) For the purpose of this regulation a dwelling in a hostel shall be regarded as similar to another dwelling in that hostel if each dwelling provides sleeping accommodation for the same number of persons.

(8) In this regulation–

"change relating to a rent allowance" means a change or increase to which paragraph 2(3)(a), (b), (c) or (d) of Schedule 2 applies;

"prospective occupier" shall include a person currently in receipt of housing benefit in respect of a dwelling which he occupies as his home and who is contemplating entering into a new agreement to occupy that dwelling, but only where his current agreement commenced 11 months or more before the request under paragraph (1)(e);

"specified matters" means–

(a) the signature of the prospective occupier;

(b) the signature of the person to whom the prospective occupier would incur liability to make such payments;

(c)   a statement that the person in paragraph (b) agrees to the application being made for that determination; and

(d)   an indication that the prospective occupier is contemplating occupying the dwelling as his home and that if he does so, he is likely to claim housing benefit;

"tenancy" includes–

(a)   in Scotland, any other right of occupancy; and

(b)   in any other case, a licence to occupy premises,

and reference to a tenant, landlord or any other expression appropriate to a tenancy shall be construed accordingly;

[¹]

Amendment

1.   Amended by reg 5(5) of SI 2008 No 586 as from 7.4.08.

Substitution of regulations 15 to 18 of the Housing Benefit (Persons who have attained the qualifying age for state pension credit) Regulations 2006

9.   For regulations 15 (applications to the rent officer for redetermination) to 18 (application of provisions to substitute determinations or substitute redeterminations) substitute–

" Application to the rent officer for redeterminations

15.–(1)   Subject to paragraph (2) and regulation 16 (application for redetermination by rent officer), where a relevant authority has obtained from a rent officer either or both of the following–

(a)   a determination on a reference made under regulation 13D(10) (board and attendance determination) or regulation 14 (requirement to refer to rent officers);

(b)   a redetermination on a reference made under regulation 16(2) (application for redetermination by rent officer),

the authority may apply to the rent officer for a redetermination of any determination or redetermination he has made which has effect at the date of the application.

(2)   No application shall be made for a further redetermination of a redetermination made in response to an application under paragraph (1).

Application for a redetermination by a rent officer

16.–(1)   This paragraph applies where–

(a)   a person affected makes written representations which are signed by him, to a relevant authority concerning a decision which it makes in relation to him;

(b)   those representations relate, in whole or in part, to a rent officer's determination or redetermination in exercise of the Housing Act functions except for functions relating to broad rental market area determinations and local housing allowance determinations or amended determinations; and

(c)   those representations are made no later than one month after the day on which the person affected was notified of the decision by the relevant authority.

(2)   Subject to paragraphs (3) and (4), where paragraph (1) applies, the relevant authority shall, within 7 days of receiving the representations, apply to the rent officer for a redetermination or, as the case may be, a further redetermination in exercise of the Housing Act functions and a copy of those representations shall accompany the local authority's application.

(3)   Except where paragraph (4) applies, a relevant authority, in relation to any determination by a rent officer of an application under regulation 13D(10) (board

and attendance determination) or 14(1) (requirement to refer to rent officers), shall not apply for a redetermination under paragraph (2) more than once in respect of an individual claimant's dwelling to which that determination relates.

(4)   Paragraph (2) shall operate so as to require a relevant authority to make a second application where the following conditions are met in addition to those imposed by that paragraph–

(a)   the written representations made under paragraph (1) relate to a redetermination by a rent officer made in response to an application by the relevant authority under regulation 15 (application to the rent officer for redetermination);

(b)   by the time of that application, the rent officer has already provided a redetermination under this regulation of a determination made in response to an application under regulation 13D(10) or 14(1); and

(c)   both the application under this regulation referred to in sub-paragraph (b) and the second application for which this paragraph provides relate to the same claimant.

(5)   here a decision has been revised in consequence of a redetermination, substitute determination or substitute redetermination by a rent officer in exercise of the Housing Act functions (except for those relating to broad rental market area determinations and local housing allowance determinations or amended determinations) and that redetermination, substitute determination or substitute redetermination has led to–

(a)   a reduction in the maximum rent, the redetermination, substitute determination or substitute redetermination shall be a change of circumstances;

(b)   an increase in the maximum rent, the redetermination, substitute determination or substitute redetermination shall have effect in place of the original determination.

Substitute determinations or substitute redeterminations

17.–(1)   In a case where either–

(a)   the appropriate authority discovers that an application it has made to the rent officer contained an error in respect of any of the following–

(i)   the size of the dwelling;

(ii)   the number of occupiers;

(iii) the composition of the household;

(iv) the terms of the tenancy; or

(b)   the rent officer has, in accordance with article 7A(1) or (2) of the Rent Officers Order, notified an appropriate authority of an error he has made (other than in the application of his professional judgement),

the authority shall apply to the rent officer for a substitute determination, substitute redetermination, board and attendance redetermination, substitute board and attendance determination or substitute board and attendance redetermination, as the case may be.

(2)   In its application to the rent officer the relevant authority shall state the nature of the error and withdraw any previous application relating to the same case for a redetermination or substitute determination or substitute redetermination, which it has made but to which the rent officer has not yet responded.

Application of provisions to substitute determinations or substitute redeterminations

18.   Regulations 15, 16 and 17 apply to a substitute determination or substitute redetermination as they apply to the determination or redetermination it replaces.''.

Insertion of regulation 18A into the Housing Benefit (Persons who have attained the qualifying age for state pension credit) Regulations 2006

10. After regulation 18 (application of provisions to substitute determinations or substitute redeterminations) insert–

" Amended determinations

18A.–(1) This regulation applies where a decision has been revised in consequence of an amended broad rental market area determination or amended local housing allowance determination by a rent officer.

(2) Where that amended determination has led to a reduction in the maximum rent (LHA) applicable to a claimant, the amended determination shall be a change of circumstances in relation to that claimant.

(3) Where that amended determination has led to an increase in the maximum rent (LHA) applicable to a claimant, the amended determination shall have effect in place of the original determination.".

Amendment of regulation 48 of the Housing Benefit (Persons who have attained the qualifying age for state pension credit) Regulations 2006

11. In regulation 48(4)(a) (diminishing notional capital rule) for "regulation 61(4)(a)" substitute "regulation 61(3)(a)".

Substitution of regulation 50 of the Housing Benefit (Persons who have attained the qualifying age for state pension credit) Regulations 2006

12. For regulation 50 (maximum housing benefit) substitute–

" 50. The amount of a person's appropriate maximum housing benefit in any week shall be 100 per cent. of his eligible rent calculated on a weekly basis in accordance with regulations 61 and 62 (calculation of weekly amounts and rent free periods) less any deductions in respect of non-dependants which fall to be made under regulation 55 (non-dependant deductions)."

Amendment of regulation 53 of the Housing Benefit (Persons who have attained the qualifying age for state pension credit) Regulations 2006

13. In regulation 53(4) (extended payments (severe disablement allowance and incapacity benefit)) for "regulation 61(8)" substitute "regulation 61(7)".

Substitution of regulation 55 of the Housing Benefit (Persons who have attained the qualifying age for state pension credit) Regulations 2006

14. For regulation 55 (non-dependant deductions) substitute–

" 55.–(1) Subject to the following provisions of this regulation, the deductions referred to in regulation 50 (maximum housing benefit) shall be–

(a) in respect of a non-dependant aged 18 or over in remunerative work, £47.75 per week;

(b) in respect of a non-dependant aged 18 or over to whom sub-paragraph (a) does not apply, £7.40 per week.

(2) In the case of a non-dependant aged 18 or over to whom paragraph (1)(a) applies because he is in remunerative work, where it is shown to the appropriate authority that his normal weekly gross income is–

(a) less than £111.00, the deduction to be made under this regulation shall be that specified in paragraph (1)(b);

(b) not less than £111.00 but less than £164.00, the deduction to be made under this regulation shall be £17.00;

(c) not less than £164.00 but less than £213.00, the deduction to be made under this regulation shall be £23.35;

(d)   not less than £213.00 but less than £283.00, the deduction to be made under this regulation shall be £38.20;

(e)   not less than £283.00 but less than £353.00, the deduction to be made under this regulation shall be £43.50.

(3)   Only one deduction shall be made under this regulation in respect of a couple or, as the case may be, members of a polygamous marriage and, where, but for this paragraph, the amount that would fall to be deducted in respect of one member of a couple or polygamous marriage is higher than the amount (if any) that would fall to be deducted in respect of the other, or any other, member, the higher amount shall be deducted.

(4)   In applying the provisions of paragraph (2) in the case of a couple or, as the case may be, a polygamous marriage, regard shall be had, for the purpose of paragraph (2) to the couple's or, as the case may be, all members of the polygamous marriage's joint weekly gross income.

(5)   Where a person is a non-dependant in respect of more than one joint occupier of a dwelling (except where the joint occupiers are a couple or members of a polygamous marriage), the deduction in respect of that non-dependant shall be apportioned between the joint occupiers (the amount so apportioned being rounded to the nearest penny) having regard to the number of joint occupiers and the proportion of the payments in respect of the dwelling payable by each of them.

(6)   No deduction shall be made in respect of any non-dependants occupying a claimant's dwelling if the claimant or his partner is–

(a)   blind or treated as blind by virtue of paragraph 6(5) of Schedule 3 (severe disability premiums); or

(b)   receiving in respect of himself either–
         (i)   attendance allowance; or
         (ii)   the care component of the disability living allowance.

(7)   No deduction shall be made in respect of a non-dependant if–

(a)   although he resides with the claimant, it appears to the appropriate authority that his normal home is elsewhere; or

(b)   he is in receipt of a training allowance paid in connection with a Youth Training Scheme established under section 2 of the 1973 Act or section 2 of the Enterprise and New Towns (Scotland) Act 1990; or

(c)   he is a full-time student during a period of study within the meaning of regulation 53(1) of the Housing Benefit Regulations 2006 (Students); or

(d)   he is a full-time student and during a recognised summer vacation appropriate to his course he is not in remunerative work; or

(e)   he is a full-time student and the claimant or his partner has attained the age of 65; or

(f)   he is not residing with the claimant because he has been a patient for a period in excess of 52 weeks, or a prisoner, and for these purposes–
         (i)   "patient" has the meaning given in paragraph (18) of regulation 7 (circumstances in which a person is or is not to be treated as occupying a dwelling as his home);
         (ii)   where a person has been a patient for two or more distinct periods separated by one or more intervals each not exceeding 28 days, he shall be treated as having been a patient continuously for a period equal in duration to the total of those distinct periods; and
         (iii)   "prisoner" means a person who is detained in custody pending trial or sentence upon conviction or under a sentence imposed by a court other than a person who is detained in hospital under the provisions of the Mental Health Act 1983, or, in Scotland, under the provisions of the Mental Health (Care and Treatment) (Scotland) Act 2003 or the Criminal Procedure (Scotland) Act 1995.

(8)   No deduction shall be made in calculating the amount of a rent rebate or allowance in respect of a non-dependant aged less than 25 who is on income support or an income-based jobseeker's allowance.

(9)   No deduction shall be made in respect of a non-dependant who is on state pension credit.

(10)   In the case of a non-dependant to whom paragraph (2) applies because he is in remunerative work, there shall be disregarded from his weekly gross income–

(a)   any attendance allowance or disability living allowance received by him;

(b)   any payment made under the Macfarlane Trust, the Macfarlane (Special Payments) Trust, the Macfarlane (Special Payments) (No. 2) Trust, the Fund, the Eileen Trust or the Independent Living Funds which had his income fallen to be calculated under regulation 40 (calculation of income other than earnings) of the Housing Benefit Regulations 2006 would have been disregarded under paragraph 23 of Schedule 5 (income in kind) to those Regulations; and

(c)   any payment which had his income fallen to be calculated under regulation 40 of the Housing Benefit Regulations 2006 would have been disregarded under paragraph 35 of Schedule 5 (payments made under certain trusts and certain other payments) to those Regulations.''.

Amendment of regulations 59 and 60 of the Housing Benefit (Persons who have attained the qualifying age for state pension credit) Regulations 2006

15.–[¹ (1)   In regulation 59 (date of which change of circumstances is to take effect)–

(a)   in paragraph (1) for ''regulations 60 and 61(6)'' substitute ''regulations 60 and 61(5)''; and

(b)   in paragraph (3) for ''regulation 61(6)'' substitute ''regulation 61(5)''.]

(2)   In regulation 60(9) (change of circumstances where state pension credit payable) for ''regulation 61(6)'' substitute ''regulation 61(5)''.

Amendment
1.   Substituted by reg 5(6) of SI 2008 No 586 as from 7.4.08.

Substitution of regulations 61 and 62 of the Housing Benefit (Persons who have attained the qualifying age for state pension credit) Regulations 2006

16.   For regulations 61 (calculation of weekly amounts) and 62 (rent free periods) substitute–

'' Calculation of weekly amounts

61.–(1)   A person's entitlement to housing benefit in any benefit week shall be calculated in accordance with the following provisions of this regulation.

(2)   The weekly amount of a claimant's eligible rent shall be–

(a)   subject to paragraph (3), where rent is payable at intervals of one week or a multiple thereof, the amount of eligible rent payable weekly or, where it is payable at intervals of a multiple of a week, the amount determined by dividing the amount of eligible rent payable by the number equal to the number of weeks in respect of which it is payable; or

(b)   subject to paragraph (3), where the rent is payable at intervals of a calendar month or multiples thereof, the amount determined by dividing the amount payable by the number equal to the number of calendar months in respect of which it is payable, multiplying by 12 and dividing by 52;

(c)   subject to paragraph (3), where the rent is payable at intervals of a day or multiples thereof, the amount determined by dividing the amount payable by the number equal to the number of days in respect of which it is payable and multiplying by 7.

(3)   In a case–

(a)   to which regulation 57(2) (date on which entitlement is to commence) applies, his eligible rent for the benefit week in which he becomes liable to make payments in respect of a dwelling which he occupies as his home shall be calculated by multiplying his daily rent by the number equal to the number of days in that benefit week for which he is liable to make such payments;

(b)   where a change of circumstances takes effect in a benefit week under regulation 59(2A), (but is not a change described in sub-paragraph (c)(ii) of this regulation), (2B), (8) or (9) other than on the Monday of a benefit week then the claimant's eligible rent for that benefit week shall be calculated by multiplying his daily rent by the appropriate number of days in that benefit week;

(c)   where–

   (i)   the amount of eligible rent which the claimant is liable to pay in respect of a dwelling is altered and that change of circumstances takes effect under regulation 59(2); or

   (ii)   the claimant–

      (aa)   moves to a new dwelling occupied as the home,

      (bb)   he is not entitled to be treated, immediately after that move, as occupying two dwellings as his home or as occupying his former dwelling as his home, and

      (cc)   that change of circumstances takes effect under regulation 59(2A),

other than on the Monday of a benefit week, then the claimant's eligible rent for that benefit week shall be calculated by multiplying his old and new daily rent by the number equal to the number of days in that week which relate respectively to the old and new amounts which he is liable to pay.

(4)   In the case of a claimant whose weekly eligible rent falls to be calculated in accordance with paragraph (3)(a) or (b) by reference to the daily rent in his case, his weekly applicable amount, weekly income, the weekly amount of any non-dependant deductions and the minimum amount payable in his case shall be calculated in the same manner as his weekly eligible rent by reference to the amounts determined in his case in accordance with Parts 5 to 7 (applicable amounts, income and capital, and amount of benefit).

(5)   Where a change in the amount of a claimant's applicable amount, income or non-dependant deductions falls to be taken into account in the same benefit week as a change in his eligible rent to which paragraph (3)(c) applies, it shall be taken into account in that week on a daily basis in the same manner and as if it had occurred on the same day as that change in his eligible rent.

(6)   Any amount determined under these Regulations may, if it is appropriate, be rounded to the nearest whole penny by disregarding any amount less than half a penny and treating any amount of half a penny or more as a whole penny.

(7)   In any case where a claimant has received–

(a)   an extended payment under regulation 72 of the Housing Benefit Regulations 2006, his entitlement shall be adjusted in such circumstances and by such amount as are prescribed in Part 3 of Schedule 7 to those Regulations; or

(b)   an extended payment (severe disablement allowance and incapacity benefit), his entitlement shall be adjusted in such circumstances and by such amount as are prescribed in paragraph 9 of Schedule 7 to these Regulations.

(8)   In this regulation "daily rent" shall mean the amount determined by dividing by 7 the amount determined under whichever sub-paragraph of paragraph (2) is appropriate in each case.

(9)   Where a claimant is entitled to benefit in respect of two (but not more than two) dwellings in accordance with regulation 7(6) his eligible rent shall be calculated in respect of each dwelling in accordance with this regulation.

Rent free periods
62.–(1)   This regulation applies to a claimant for any period (referred to in this regulation as a rent free period) in, or in respect of, which he is not liable to pay rent except for any period to which regulation 8(1)(d) (waiver of rent by landlord in return for work done) applies.

(2)   In the case of the beginning or ending of a claimant's rent-free period, his eligible rent for the benefit week in which the rent free period begins and ends shall be calculated on a daily basis as if those benefit weeks were weeks to which regulation 61(3) applies.

(3)   For the purpose of determining the weekly applicable amount and income of a claimant to whom this regulation applies, the weekly amount of any non-dependant deductions and the minimum amount payable in his case–

(a)   in a case to which regulation 61(2)(a) applies, the amounts determined in his case in accordance with Parts 5 to 7 (applicable amounts, income and capital, and amount of benefit) shall be multiplied by 52 or 53, whichever is appropriate, and divided by the number equal to the number of weeks in that 52 or 53 week period in respect of which he is liable to pay rent;

(b)   subject to paragraph (4), in a case to which regulation 61(2)(b) or (c) applies, the amounts determined in his case in accordance with Parts 5 to 7 shall be multiplied by 365 or 366, whichever is appropriate and divided by the number of days in that 365 or 366 day period in respect of which he is liable to pay rent.

(4)   In a case to which paragraph (3)(b) applies, where either regulation 61(4) or (5) also applies or it is the beginning or end of a rent-free period, the weekly amounts referred to in paragraph (3) shall first be calculated in accordance with sub-paragraph (b) of that paragraph and then determined on a daily basis in the same manner as the claimant's eligible rent.''.

Amendment of regulations 76 and 77 of the Housing Benefit (Persons who have attained the qualifying age for state pension credit) Regulations 2006
17.–(1)   In regulation 76 (circumstances in which payment is to be made to a landlord) after paragraph (2) insert–

'' (2A)   In a case where–
(a)   a relevant authority has determined a maximum rent (LHA) in accordance with regulation 13D; and
(b)   the rent allowance exceeds the amount which the claimant is liable to pay his landlord by way of rent,
any payment of rent allowance made to a landlord pursuant to this regulation or to regulation 77 may include all or part of any amount by which the rent allowance exceeds the amount which the claimant is liable to pay his landlord as rent but shall not include any amount by which the rent allowance exceeds the amount which the claimant is liable to pay his landlord as rent and arrears of rent.''.

(2)   In regulation 77 (circumstances in which payment may be made to a landlord)–
(a)   in paragraph (1) for ''paragraph (3)'' substitute ''paragraphs (3) and (3A)'';
(b)   in paragraph (3) after ''paragraph (1)'' insert '', (3A) or (3B)'';
(c)   after paragraph (3) insert–

'' (3A)   In a case where a relevant authority has determined a maximum rent in accordance with regulation 13D–

(a)   sub-paragraphs (a) and (b) of paragraph (1) shall not apply; and
(b)   payment of a rent allowance to a person's landlord may be made where–
    (i)   the relevant authority considers that the claimant is likely to have difficulty in relation to the management of his financial affairs;
    (ii)   the relevant authority considers that it is improbable that the claimant will pay his rent; or
    (iii)   a direct payment has previously been made by the relevant authority to the landlord in accordance with regulation 76 in respect of the current award of housing benefit.

(3B)   Where the relevant authority suspects that the grounds in paragraph (3A)(b)(i) or (ii) apply and is considering whether to make payments on one of those grounds, it may make a payment of a rent allowance to the person's landlord for a period not exceeding 8 weeks.''.

Substitution of Schedule 2 to the Housing Benefit (Persons who have attained the qualifying age for state pension credit) Regulations 2006

18.   For Schedule 2 (excluded tenancies) substitute–

'' SCHEDULE 2
Regulation 14
Excluded tenancies

1. An excluded tenancy is any tenancy to which any of the following paragraphs applies.

2.–(1) Subject to sub-paragraphs (2) and (3), where a rent officer has made a determination, which relates to the tenancy in question or any other tenancy of the same dwelling this paragraph applies to–
(a)   the tenancy in respect of which that determination was made; and
(b)   any other tenancy of the same dwelling on terms which are substantially the same, other than the term relating to the amount of rent, as those terms were at the time of that determination or, if earlier, at the end of the tenancy.

(2)   For the purposes of any claim, notification, request or application under regulation 14(1) (''the later application''), a tenancy shall not be an excluded tenancy by virtue of sub-paragraph (1) by reference to a rent officer's determination made in consequence of an earlier claim, notification, request or application (''the earlier application'') where–
(a)   the earlier and later applications were made in respect of the same claimant or different claimants; and
(b)   the earlier application was made more than 52 weeks before the later application was made.

(3)   Sub-paragraph (1) shall not apply where subsequent to the making of the determination mentioned in that sub-paragraph–
(a)   the number of occupiers of the dwelling has changed and that dwelling is not in a hostel;
(b)   there has been a substantial change in the condition of the dwelling (including the making of improvements) or the terms of the tenancy other than a term relating to rent;
(c)   there has been a rent increase under a term of the tenancy and the term under which that increase was made was either included in the tenancy at the time when the application for that determination was made (or was a term substantially the same as such a term) and that determination was not made under paragraph 1(2), 2(2) or 3(3) of Schedule 1 to the Rent Officers Order;
(d)   in a case where the rent officer has made a determination under paragraph 2(2) of Schedule 1 to the Rent Officers Order (size and rent determinations), but since the date of the application for that determination–
    (i)   a child, who is a member of the household occupying the dwelling, has attained the age of 10 years;
    (ii)   a young person, who is a member of the household occupying that dwelling, has attained the age of 16 years; or
    (iii)   there is a change in the composition of the household occupying the dwelling.

3.–(1)   This paragraph applies where the landlord is a registered housing association, except in a case where the local authority considers that–
(a)   the claimant occupies a dwelling larger than is reasonably required by him and any others who occupy that dwelling (including any non-dependants of his and any person paying rent to him); or
(b)   the rent payable for that dwelling is unreasonably high.

(2)   Where the circumstances set out in head (a) or (b) of sub-paragraph (1) above exist, the authority shall so state in their application for a determination.

4. This paragraph applies to a tenancy entered into before–
- (a) in Scotland, 2nd January 1989; and
- (b) in any other case, 15th January 1989.

5. This paragraph applies to a regulated tenancy within the meaning of–
- (a) in Scotland, the Rent (Scotland) Act 1984; and
- (b) in any other case, the Rent Act 1977.

6. This paragraph applies to a housing association tenancy which–
- (a) in Scotland, is a tenancy to which Part 6 of the Rent (Scotland) Act 1984 applies; and
- (b) in any other case, is a housing association tenancy to which Part 6 of the Rent Act 1977 applies.

7. This paragraph applies to a protected occupancy or statutory tenancy within the meaning of the Rent (Agriculture) Act 1976.

8. This paragraph applies to a tenancy at a low rent within the meaning of Part 1 of the Landlord and Tenant Act 1954 or Schedule 10 to the Local Government and Housing Act 1989.

9. This paragraph applies to a tenancy of any dwelling which is a bail hostel or probation hostel approved by the Secretary of State under section 9(1) of the Criminal Justice and Court Services Act 2000.

10. This paragraph applies to a tenancy of a housing action trust established under Part 3 of the Housing Act 1988.

11.–(1) Subject to sub-paragraphs (2) and (3) this paragraph applies to a tenancy–
- (a) in respect of a dwelling comprised in land which has been disposed of under section 32 of the Housing Act 1985 or section 12 of the Housing (Scotland) Act 1987;
- (b) in respect of a dwelling comprised in land which has been disposed of with the consent required by section 43 of the Housing Act 1985 or section 12 of the Housing (Scotland) Act 1987;
- (c) in respect of which the fee simple estate has been acquired, under the right conferred by Chapter 2 of Part 1 of the Housing Act 1996, otherwise than from a housing action trust within the meaning of Part 3 of the Housing Act 1988, or in respect of which the house has been acquired under the right conferred by Part 3 of the Housing (Scotland) Act 1988; or
- (d) in respect of a dwelling disposed of under the New Towns (Transfer of Housing Stock) Regulations 1990 to a person who is an approved person for the purposes of disposal under those Regulations or in respect of a dwelling disposed of pursuant to powers contained in the New Towns (Scotland) Act 1968 to a housing association.

- (2) This paragraph shall not apply to a tenancy to which sub-paragraph (1) refers if–
- (a) there has been an increase in rent since the disposal or acquisition, as the case may be, occurred; and
- (b) the local authority stated in the application for determination that–
  - (i) the claimant occupies a dwelling larger than is reasonably required by him and any others who occupy that dwelling (including any non-dependant of his and any person paying rent to him); or
  - (ii) the rent payable for that dwelling is unreasonably high.

- (3) Where the disposal or acquisition, as the case may be, took place on or after 7th October 2002, sub-paragraph (2)(b) shall apply to a tenancy to which sub-paragraph (1) refers as if head (i) were omitted.

12. This paragraph applies to a shared ownership tenancy.

13. In this Schedule, "rent" shall be construed in accordance with paragraph (8) of regulation 14 (interpretation of "tenancy" and other expressions appropriate to a tenancy) and, subject to that paragraph, has the same meaning–
- (a) in Scotland, as in section 25 of the Housing (Scotland) Act 1988, except that the reference to the house in subsection (3) shall be construed as a reference to the dwelling;
- (b) in any other case, as in section 14 of the Housing Act 1988, except that the reference to the dwelling-house in subsection (4) shall be construed as a reference to the dwelling,

and–
  - (i) other expressions have the same meanings as in regulation 14(8);
  - (ii) in the case of a determination by a rent officer pursuant to a request for such a determination under regulation 14(1)(e), any reference to a "tenancy" shall be taken as a reference to a prospective tenancy and any reference to an "occupier" or any person "occupying" a dwelling shall, in the case of such a determination, be taken to be a reference to a potential occupier or potential occupation of that dwelling.".

Amendment of Schedule 7 to the Housing Benefit (Persons who have attained the qualifying age for state pension credit) Regulations 2006

19. In paragraph 2(3) of Schedule 7 (extended payments (severe disablement allowance and incapacity benefit) of housing benefit) for "regulation 61(4)(c)" substitute "regulation 61(3)(c)".

Substitution of Part 14 of and Schedule 9 to the Housing Benefit (Persons who have attained the qualifying age for state pension credit) Regulations 2006
    20.   For Part 14 substitute–

'' PART 14

Former pathfinder authorities

Modifications in respect of former pathfinder authorities
    103.–(1)   In this regulation and in Schedule 9, "former pathfinder authority" means a relevant authority specified in Part 1 of that Schedule.
    (2)   The provisions of Part 2 of Schedule 9 apply in relation to the area of a former pathfinder authority.''.

    (1)   For Schedule 9 (pathfinder authorities) substitute–

'' SCHEDULE 9
Regulation 103

Former pathfinder authorities

PART 1

Former pathfinder authorities
    Argyll and Bute
    Blackpool
    Brighton and Hove
    Conwy
    Coventry
    East Riding of Yorkshire
    Edinburgh
    Guildford
    Leeds
    Lewisham
    North East Lincolnshire
    Norwich
    Pembrokeshire
    St Helens
    Salford
    South Norfolk
    Teignbridge
    Wandsworth

PART 2

Application of the Regulations
    1.   These Regulations shall apply to former pathfinder authorities subject to the provisions of this Part of this Schedule.

Amendment of regulation 2
    2.   In regulation 2(1) (interpretation)–
    (a)   in the definition of "eligible rent", in sub-paragraph (a) for "or 12D (eligible rent and maximum rent (LHA))" substitute ", 12D (eligible rent and maximum rent (LHA)) or any of regulations 12E to 12K (transitional protection for pathfinder cases)";
    (b)   after the definition of "maximum rent (LHA)" insert–

'' "maximum rent (standard local rent)" means a maximum rent (standard local rate) determined in accordance with regulation 13A;''.

Amendment of regulation 11
    3.   In regulation 11(1) (eligible housing costs)–
    (a)   in paragraph (c) omit "or"; and

(b) after sub-paragraph (d) insert–

" ; or
(e) any of regulations 12E to 12K (transitional protection for pathfinder cases), and regulations 13C (when a maximum rent (LHA) is to be determined) and 13D (determination of a maximum rent (LHA)),".

Amendment of regulation 12B

4. In regulation 12B(1) (eligible rent) for "or 12D (eligible rent and maximum rent (LHA))" substitute ", 12D (eligible rent and maximum rent (LHA)) or any of regulations 12E to 12K (transitional protection for pathfinder cases)".

Amendment of regulation 12D

5. In regulation 12D (eligible rent and maximum rent (LHA)) before paragraph (1) insert–

" (A1) This regulation shall not apply where any of regulations 12E to 12K (transitional protection for pathfinder cases) apply."

Insertion of regulations 12E to 12K

6. After regulation 12D (eligible rent and maximum rent (LHA)) insert–

" Basic transitional protection for pathfinder cases

12E.–(1) This regulation applies where–
(a) reference was made to a maximum rent (standard local rate) in determining the amount of the eligible rent which applied immediately before 7th April 2008;
(b) on 7th April 2008 the local authority determines a maximum rent (LHA) by virtue of regulation 13C(4A)(a); and
(c) regulations 12F (cases where the claimant enjoyed protection on death before 7th April 2008) and 12G (cases where the claimant enjoyed 13 week protection before 7th April 2008) do not apply.
(2) Where this regulation applies, the claimant's eligible rent is–
(a) the maximum rent (LHA) where that is higher than the eligible rent which applied immediately before 7th April 2008; or
(b) the amount of the eligible rent which applied immediately before 7th April 2008.
(3) Where the eligible rent is the amount of the eligible rent which applied immediately before 7th April 2008, it will continue to apply until, on or after 7th April 2008, the first of the following events occurs–
(a) the relevant authority is required to determine a maximum rent (LHA) by virtue of regulation 13C(2)(d)(i) (change of category of dwelling) because the claimant has become entitled to a larger category of dwelling and the maximum rent (LHA) is higher than that eligible rent;
(b) the relevant authority is required to determine a maximum rent (LHA) by virtue of regulation 13C(2)(d)(i) (change of category of dwelling) because the claimant has become entitled to a smaller category of dwelling;
(c) the relevant authority is required to determine an eligible rent following a change of dwelling;
(d) the relevant authority is required to determine an eligible rent in accordance with regulation 12H (cases where a death occurs in the first year on or after 7th April 2008) following the death of a linked person;
(e) the relevant authority determines a maximum rent (LHA) on 7th April 2009 by virtue of regulation 13C(4A)(b).
(4) Where the eligible rent is the maximum rent (LHA), it shall be treated as if it had been determined in accordance with regulation 12D(2)(a) (eligible rent is maximum rent (LHA)) and shall apply according to the provisions of regulation 12D (eligible rent and maximum rent (LHA)).

Cases where the claimant enjoyed protection on death before 7th April 2008

12F.–(1) This regulation applies where–
(a) immediately before 7th April 2008 the claimant enjoyed protection on death in accordance with regulation 12A(4)(a)(ii) (pathfinder protection on death based on reckonable rent); and
(b) on 7th April 2008 the local authority determines a maximum rent (LHA) by virtue of regulation 13C(4A)(a).
(2) Where this regulation applies, the claimant's eligible rent is–
(a) the maximum rent (LHA) where that is higher than the eligible rent which applied immediately before 7th April 2008; or
(b) the amount of the eligible rent which applied immediately before 7th April 2008.
(3) Where the eligible rent is the amount of the eligible rent which applied immediately before 7th April 2008, it will continue to apply until, on or after 7th April 2008, the first of the following events occurs–

(a)   the end of 12 months after the death to which the protection relates;

(b)   the relevant authority is required to determine a maximum rent (LHA) by virtue of regulation 13C(2)(d)(i) (change of category of dwelling) and it is higher than that eligible rent;

(c)   the relevant authority is required to determine an eligible rent following a change of dwelling;

(d)   the relevant authority is required to determine an eligible rent in accordance with regulation 12H (cases where a death occurs in the first year on or after 7th April 2008) following the death of a linked person;

(4)   Where the eligible rent ceases to apply because of paragraph (3)(a), the eligible rent will be the maximum rent (LHA) which would have applied but for the transitional protection.

(5)   Where the eligible rent is the maximum rent (LHA), it shall be treated as if it had been determined in accordance with regulation 12D(2)(a) (eligible rent is maximum rent (LHA)) and shall apply according to the provisions of regulation 12D (eligible rent and maximum rent (LHA)).

Cases where the claimant enjoyed 13 week protection before 7th April 2008

12G.–(1)   This regulation applies where–

(a)   immediately before 7th April 2008 the claimant enjoyed 13 week protection in accordance with regulation 12A(6)(a) (lo cal housing allowance pathfinder 13 week protection); and

(b)   on 7th April 2008 the local authority determines a maximum rent (LHA) by virtue of regulation 13C(4A)(a).

(2)   Where this regulation applies, the claimant's eligible rent is–

(a)   the maximum rent (LHA) where that is higher than the eligible rent which applied immediately before 7th April 2008; or

(b)   the amount of the eligible rent which applied immediately before 7th April 2008.

(3)   Where the eligible rent is the amount of the eligible rent which applied immediately before 7th April 2008, it will continue to apply until, on or after 7th April 2008, the first of the following events occurs –

(a)   the end of the day when the protection expires, namely 13 weeks after the date of the claim;

(b)   the relevant authority is required to determine a maximum rent (LHA) by virtue of regulation 13C(2)(d)(i) (change of category of dwelling) and it is higher than that eligible rent;

(c)   the relevant authority is required to determine an eligible rent following a change of dwelling;

(d)   the relevant authority is required to determine an eligible rent in accordance with regulation 12H (cases where a death occurs in the first year on or after 7th April 2008) following the death of a linked person.

(4)   Where the eligible rent ceases to apply because of paragraph (3)(a), the eligible rent will be the maximum rent (LHA) which would have applied but for the transitional protection.

(5)   Where the eligible rent is the maximum rent (LHA), it shall be treated as if it had been determined in accordance with regulation 12D(2)(a) (eligible rent is maximum rent (LHA)) and shall apply according to the provisions of regulation 12D (eligible rent and maximum rent (LHA)).

Cases where a death occurs in the first year on or after 7th April 2008

12H.–(1)   This regulation applies where–

(a)   the eligible rent is that specified in regulation 12E(2)(b) (basic transitional protection for pathfinder cases), 12F(2)(b) (transitional protection where the claimant enjoyed protection on death before 7th April 2008), 12G(2)(b) (transitional protection where the claimant enjoyed 13 week protection before 7th April 2008) or paragraph (2)(b) of this regulation;

(b)   a linked person dies on or after 7th April 2008 and before 7th April 2009;

(c)   the claimant occupies the same dwelling as the linked person at the date of death; and

(d)   the relevant authority determines a maximum rent (LHA) by virtue of regulation 13C(2)(d)(i) or (ii) (change of category of dwelling or death of a linked person).

(2)   Where this regulation applies, the claimant's eligible rent is–

(a)   the maximum rent (LHA) where that is higher than the eligible rent which applied immediately before the date of the death; or

(b)   the amount of the eligible rent which applied immediately before the date of the death.

(3)   Where the eligible rent is the amount of the eligible rent which applied immediately before the date of death, it will continue to apply until, on or after the date of the death, the first of the following events occurs–

(a)   the end of 12 months from the date of the death;

(b)   the relevant authority is required to determine a maximum rent (LHA) by virtue of regulation 13C(2)(d)(i) (change of category of dwelling) and it is higher than that eligible rent;

(c)   the relevant authority is required to determine an eligible rent following a change of dwelling;

(d)   the relevant authority is required to determine an eligible rent in accordance with this regulation following the death of another linked person.

(4)   Where the eligible rent is the maximum rent (LHA), it shall be treated as if it had been determined in accordance with regulation 12D(2)(a) (eligible rent is maximum rent (LHA)) and shall apply according to the provisions of regulation 12D (eligible rent and maximum rent (LHA)).

(5)   For the purposes of paragraph (1)(c), a claimant shall be treated as occupying the dwelling if regulation 7(13) is satisfied and for that purpose paragraph (13) of regulation 7 shall have effect as if sub-paragraph (b) were omitted.

Basic transitional protection in the second year and subsequent years after 7th April 2008
12I.–(1)   This regulation applies where–
(a)   immediately before 7th April 2009 the claimant was enjoying basic transitional protection under regulation 12E; and
(b)   the local authority determines a maximum rent (LHA) by virtue of 13C(4A)(b) on 7th April 2009.
(2)   Where this regulation applies, the claimant's eligible rent is–
(a)   the maximum rent (LHA) where it is higher than the eligible rent applying immediately before 7th April 2008; or
(b)   in any other case, the lower of–
    (i)   the amount of the eligible rent applying immediately before 7th April 2008; or
    (ii)   the amount of the cap rent by reference to which the maximum rent (LHA) was determined, plus £15.
(3)   Where the claimant's eligible rent is determined in accordance with paragraph (2)(b), it continues to apply until, on or after 7th April 2009, the first of the following events occurs–
(a)   the relevant authority is required to determine a maximum rent (LHA) by virtue of regulation 13C(2)(d)(i) (change of category of dwelling) because the claimant has become entitled to a larger category of dwelling or 13C(3) (anniversary of the LHA date) and the maximum rent (LHA) is higher than that eligible rent;
(b)   the relevant authority is required to determine a maximum rent (LHA) by virtue of regulation 13C(2)(d)(i) (change of category of dwelling) because the claimant has become entitled to a smaller category of dwelling;
(c)   the relevant authority is required to determine an eligible rent following a change of dwelling;
(d)   the relevant authority is required to determine an eligible rent in accordance with regulation 12K (protection on death in the second and subsequent years after 7th April 2008) following the death of a linked person.
(4)   Where the eligible rent is the maximum rent (LHA), it shall be treated as if it had been determined in accordance with regulation 12D(2)(a) (eligible rent is maximum rent (LHA)) and shall apply according to the provisions of regulation 12D (eligible rent and maximum rent (LHA)).

Transitional protection in the second year after 7th April 2008 where the claimant is already enjoying protection on death
12J.–(1)   This regulation applies where–
(a)   immediately before 7th April 2009 the claimant was enjoying transitional protection on death under regulation 12H (cases where a death occurs in the first year on or after 7th April 2008); and
(b)   the local authority determines a maximum rent (LHA) by virtue of regulation 13C(4A)(b) on 7th April 2009 .
(2)   Where this regulation applies, the claimant's eligible rent is–
(a)   the maximum rent (LHA) where that is higher than the eligible rent which applied immediately before the date of the death to which the protection relates; or
(b)   the amount of the eligible rent which applied immediately before the date of the death.
(3)   Where the eligible rent which applies is the one that applied immediately before the date of the death, it continues to apply until, on or after the date of the death, the first of the following events occurs–
(a)   the end of 12 months after the date of the death to which the protection relates;
(b)   the relevant authority is required to determine a maximum rent (LHA) by virtue of regulation 13C(2)(d)(i) (change of category of dwelling) and it is higher than that eligible rent;
(c)   the relevant authority is required to determine an eligible rent following a change of dwelling;
(d)   the relevant authority is required to determine an eligible rent in accordance with regulation 12K (protection on death in the second and subsequent years after 7th April 2008) following the death of a linked person.
(4)   Where the eligible rent ceases to apply because of paragraph (3)(a) the eligible rent is the one that would have applied if the relevant authority not determined an eligible rent in accordance with regulation 12H(2)(b) (transitional protection where a death occurs in the first year on or after 7th April 2008).
(5)   Where the eligible rent is the maximum rent (LHA), it shall be treated as if it had been determined in accordance with regulation 12D(2)(a) (eligible rent is maximum rent (LHA)) and shall apply according to the provisions of regulation 12D (eligible rent and maximum rent (LHA)).

Protection on death in the second and subsequent years after 7th April 2008
12K.–(1)   This regulation applies where–

    (a)   the claimant's eligible rent is that specified in regulation 12I(2)(b) (basic transitional protection in the second and subsequent years after 7th April 2008), 12J(2)(b) (transitional protection in the second year after 7th April 2008 where the claimant is already enjoying protection on death) or paragraph (2)(b) of this regulation; and

    (b)   a linked person dies on or after 7th April 2009;

    (c)   the claimant occupies the same dwelling as the linked person at the date of death; and

    (d)   the relevant authority determines a maximum rent (LHA) by virtue of regulation 13C(2)(d)(i) or (ii) (change of category of dwelling or death of a linked person).

    (2)   Where this regulation applies, the claimant's eligible rent is–

    (a)   the maximum rent (LHA) where that is higher than the eligible rent which applied immediately before the date of the death; or

    (b)   the amount of eligible rent which applied immediately before the death.

    (3)   Where the eligible rent which applies is the one that applied immediately before the date of the death, it will continue to apply until, on or after the date of the death, the first of the following events occurs–

    (a)   the end of 12 months from the date of the death;

    (b)   the relevant authority is required to determine a maximum rent (LHA) by virtue of regulation 13C(2)(d)(i) or (3) (change of category of dwelling or anniversary of the LHA date) and it is higher than that eligible rent;

    (c)   the relevant authority is required to determine an eligible rent following a change of dwelling;

    (d)   the relevant authority is required to determine an eligible rent in accordance with this regulation following the death of another linked person.

    (4)   Where the eligible rent ceases to apply because of paragraph (3)(a) the eligible rent is the one that would have applied but had the relevant authority not determined an eligible rent in accordance with this regulation.

    (5)   Where the eligible rent is the maximum rent (LHA), it shall be treated as if it had been determined in accordance with regulation 12D(2)(a) (eligible rent is maximum rent (LHA)) and shall apply according to the provisions of regulation 12D (eligible rent and maximum rent (LHA)).

    (6)   For the purposes of paragraph (1)(c), a claimant shall be treated as occupying the dwelling if regulation 7(13) is satisfied and for that purpose paragraph (13) of regulation 7 shall have effect as if sub-paragraph (b) were omitted.''.

Amendment of regulation 13C

7.   In regulation 13C (when a maximum rent (LHA) is to be determined)–

    (a)   in paragraph (1) for "paragraphs (2) or (3)" substitute "paragraphs (2), (3) or (4A)";

    (b)   in paragraph (3) after "LHA date" insert "except where paragraph (4A)(b) applies";

    (c)   after paragraph (4) insert–

'' (4A)   This paragraph applies where it is–

    (a)   7th April 2008 and reference was made to a maximum rent (standard local rate) in determining the amount of the eligible rent which applied immediately before 7th April 2008; or

    (b)   7th April 2009 and the eligible rent which applies on that date was determined in accordance with regulation 12E(2)(b) (basic transitional protection for pathfinder cases) or 12H(2)(b) (transitional protection where a death occurs in the first year on or after 7th April 2008).''.

Amendment of regulation 13D

8.   In regulation 13D(12) (determination of a maximum rent (LHA)) in the definition of "relevant date" after sub-paragraph (c) insert–

'' (d)   7th April 2008;

    (e)   7th April 2009.''.''

The Housing Benefit (Local Housing Allowance, Miscellaneous and Consequential) Amendment Regulations 2007

(SI 2007 No.2870)

Made   *2nd October 2007*
Laid before Parliament   *8th October 2007*
Coming into force in accordance with regulation 1

The Secretary of State for Work and Pensions makes the following Regulations in exercise of the powers conferred on him by sections 130A(2) and (3), 137(1) and 175(3) and (4) of the Social Security Contributions and Benefits Act 1992 and paragraph 4(4A) of Schedule 7 to the Child Support, Pensions and Social Security Act 2000.

This instrument contains only regulations made by virtue of, or consequential upon, section 30 of the Welfare Reform Act 2007 and is made before the end of the period of six months beginning with the coming into force of that section.

In accordance with section 176(1) of the Social Security Administration Act 1992, the Secretary of State has consulted with organisations appearing to him to be representative of the authorities concerned.

Citation, commencement and interpretation

1.–(1) These Regulations may be cited as the Housing Benefit (Local Housing Allowance, Miscellaneous and Consequential) Amendment Regulations 2007.

(2) This regulation and, subject to paragraph (4) (which relates to non-local housing allowance cases), regulations 2 to 6, shall come into force on 7th April 2008.

(3) This paragraph applies to a case where no reference was made to a maximum rent (standard local rate) in determining the amount of the eligible rent which applied immediately before 7th April 2008 and in this paragraph–

"eligible rent" shall be construed in accordance with–

(i) regulations 12 or 12A of the Housing Benefit Regulations 2006 or the Housing Benefit (Persons who have attained the qualifying age for state pension credit) Regulations 2006 as in force immediately before 7th April 2008; or

(ii) in a case to which paragraph 4 of Schedule 3 to the Housing Benefit and Council Tax Benefit (Consequential Provisions) Regulations 2006 applies, regulations 12 and 13 of the Housing Benefit Regulations 2006 or the Housing Benefit (Persons who have attained the qualifying age for state pension credit) Regulations 2006 as set out in paragraph 5 of that Schedule as in force immediately before 7th April 2007.

"maximum rent (standard local rate)" means a maximum rent (standard local rate) determined in accordance with regulation 13A of the Housing Benefit Regulations 2006 or the Housing Benefit (persons who have attained the qualifying age for state pension credit) Regulations 2006 as in force immediately before 7th April 2008.

(4) In a case to which paragraph (3) applies, these Regulations shall come into force on the day when, on or after 7th April 2008, the first of the following sub-paragraphs applies–

(a) a relevant authority is required to apply to a rent officer by virtue of regulation 14 of the Housing Benefit Regulations or the Housing Benefit (State Pension Credit) Regulations;

(b) sub-paragraph (a) would apply but for the case falling within regulation 14(4)(a) of, or regulations 14(4)(b) of and paragraph 2 of Schedule 2 to, the Housing Benefit Regulations or the Housing Benefit (State Pension Credit) Regulations (no application to rent officer required as an existing rent officer determination may be used);

    (c)   a relevant authority is required to determine an eligible rent in accordance with regulation 12(3)(b) of the Housing Benefit Regulations or the Housing Benefit (State Pension Credit) Regulations; or

    (d)   a relevant authority is required to determine an eligible rent in accordance with regulation 12(3) of the Housing Benefit Regulations 2006 or regulation 12(3) of the Housing Benefit (Persons who have attained the qualifying age for state pension credit) Regulations 2006 as set out in paragraph 5 of Schedule 3 to the Consequential Provisions Regulations,

and in this paragraph "relevant authority" means an authority administering housing benefit.

    (5)   Where paragraph (4) does not apply before 6th April 2009, these Regulations shall come into force on that date.

    (6)   In paragraph (4) of this regulation–

"the Housing Benefit Regulations" means the Housing Benefit Regulations 2006 as in force immediately before the coming into force of regulations 4 to 19 of the Housing Benefit (Local Housing Allowance and Information Sharing) Amendment Regulations 2007 in that case;

"the Housing Benefit (State Pension Credit) Regulations" means the Housing Benefit (persons who have attained the qualifying age for state pension credit) Regulations 2006 as in force immediately before the coming into force of regulations 4 to 19 of the Housing Benefit (State Pension Credit) (Local Housing Allowance and Information Sharing) Amendment Regulations 2007 in that case;

"the Consequential Provisions Regulations" means the Housing Benefit and Council Tax Benefit (Consequential Provisions) Regulations 2006 as in force immediately before the coming into force of regulations 2 to 6 of these regulations in that case.

Amendment of the Housing Benefit and Council Tax Benefit (Decisions and Appeals) Regulations 2001

4.–(1)   The Housing Benefit and Council Tax Benefit (Decisions and Appeals) Regulations 2001 shall be amended as follows.

    (2)   In regulation 7 (decisions superseding earlier decisions)–

    (a)   omit paragraphs (2ZA), (2B) and (2C);

    (b)   in paragraph (3) omit "regulation 88(3) of the Housing Benefit Regulations, regulation 69(3) of the Housing Benefit (State Pension Credit) Regulations".

    (3)   After regulation 7 (decisions superseding earlier decisions) insert–

"Decisions superseding earlier decisions in accordance with paragraph 4(4A) of Schedule 7 to the Act

7A.–(1)   The prescribed cases and circumstances in which a decision must be made under paragraph 4 of Schedule 7 to the Act (decisions superseding earlier decisions) are set out in paragraphs (2) to (4).

    (2)   The appropriate relevant authority must make a decision superseding an earlier decision where it is required to determine a maximum rent (LHA) in accordance with [¹ regulation 13C(3)] of the Housing Benefit Regulations and [¹ regulation 13C(3)] of the Housing Benefit (State Pension Credit) Regulations (when a maximum rent (LHA) is to be determined).

    (3)   The appropriate relevant authority must make a decision superseding an earlier decision in any case to which regulation 14(1)(f) or (g) or the Housing Benefit Regulations or regulation 14(1)(f) or (g) of the Housing Benefit (State Pension Credit) Regulations (requirement to refer to rent officers) applies.

    (4)   The appropriate relevant authority must make a decision superseding an earlier decision where a change of circumstances specified in regulation 88(3) of the Housing Benefit Regulations or regulation 69(3) of the Housing Benefit (State

Pension Credit) Regulations (changes of circumstances which do not need to be notified) occurs.''.

(4)   In regulation 8 (date from which a decision superseding an earlier decision takes effect)–
(a)   in paragraph (6A) for ''regulation 7(2ZA)'' substitute ''regulation 7A(3)'';
(b)   for paragraph (15) substitute–

[¹ ''(15)   A decision to which regulation 7A(2) applies shall take effect–
(a)   on the day of decision, where the determination in accordance with regulation 13C(3) of the Housing Benefit Regulations or regulation 13C(3) of the Housing Benefit (State Pension Credit) Regulations (when maximum rent (LHA) is to be determined) was made on the first day of the benefit week; and
(b)   in any other case, on the first day of the benefit week following the week in which the determination in accordance with regulation 13C(3) of the Housing Benefit Regulations or regulation 13C(3) of the Housing Benefit (State Pension Credit) Regulations (when maximum rent (LHA) is to be determined) was made.'']

Amendment
1.   Amended by reg 6(2) of SI 2008 No 586 as from 7.4.08.

Amendment of the Discretionary Financial Assistance Regulations 2001
5.   For regulation 4(a) (limit on the amount of the discretionary housing payment that may be made) of the Discretionary Financial Assistance Regulations 2001 substitute–

''(a)   periodical payments in respect of the dwelling which a person occupies as his home, other than payments in respect of council tax, an amount equal to the aggregate of the payments specified in–
(i)   regulation 12(1) of the Housing Benefit Regulations less the aggregate of the amounts referred to in regulation 12B(2) of those Regulations calculated on a weekly basis in accordance with regulations 80 and 81 of those Regulations; or
(ii)   regulation 12(1) of the Housing Benefit (State Pension Credit) Regulations less the aggregate of the amounts referred to in regulation 12B(2) of those Regulations, calculated on a weekly basis in accordance with regulations 61 and 62 of those Regulations; or''.

Amendment of Housing Benefit and Council Tax Benefit (Consequential Provisions) Regulations 2006
6.–(1)   Schedules 3 and 4 to the Housing Benefit and Council Tax Benefit (Consequential Provisions) Regulations 2006 shall be amended as follows.
(2)   For paragraphs 4 and 5 of Schedule 3 substitute–

''Eligible rent
4.–(1)   Subject to the following provisions of this paragraph, the eligible rent of a person–
(a)   who was entitled to housing benefit on both the first date and the second date; or
(b)   who is liable to make payments in respect of a dwelling occupied by him as his home, which is exempt accommodation, shall be determined in accordance with–
(i)   regulations 12 (rent) and 13 (maximum rent) of the Housing Benefit Regulations, or, as the case may be,

(ii)   regulations 12 (rent) and 13 (maximum rent) of the Housing Benefit (State Pension Credit) Regulations,

as set out in paragraph 5.

(2)   Sub-paragraph (1)(a) shall not apply to–

(a)   any determination of a person's eligible rent in a case where a relevant authority is required to determine a maximum rent (LHA) by virtue of regulation 13C of the Housing Benefit Regulations or, as the case may be, regulation 13C of the Housing Benefit (State Pension Credit) Regulations; or

(b)   any subsequent determination of his eligible rent.

(3)   Sub-paragraph (1)(a) shall only apply in a case where–

(a)   either–

(i)   the dwelling occupied as his home by a person to whom sub-paragraph (1)(a) refers is the same on both the first date and the second date; or

(ii)   the dwelling so occupied was not the same by reason only that the change was caused by a fire, flood, explosion or natural catastrophe rendering the dwelling occupied as the home on the first date uninhabitable; and

(b)   the person–

(i)   was continuously entitled to and in receipt of housing benefit between the first date and the second date in respect of the dwelling to which head (a) above applies; or

(ii)   was not entitled to or receiving housing benefit for a period not exceeding 4 weeks, but was in continuous occupation of the dwelling to which head (a) above refers between the first date and the second date; or

(iii)   is a person to whom sub-paragraph (4) applies.

(4)   This sub-paragraph applies in the case of a person (''the claimant'') who becomes, or whose partner becomes, a welfare to work beneficiary, and–

(a)   the claimant ceases to be entitled to housing benefit in respect of his residence in the dwelling he occupies as his home;

(b)   the claimant subsequently becomes re-entitled to housing benefit–

(i)   in respect of the same dwelling, or

(ii)   in respect of a different dwelling in a case to which sub-paragraph (3)(a)(ii) applies; and

(c)   the first day of that entitlement is within 52 weeks of the claimant or his partner becoming a welfare to work beneficiary.

(5)   A person shall be deemed to fulfil the requirements of sub-paragraphs (1)(a) and (3), where–

(a)   he occupies the dwelling which he occupied on the relevant date;

(b)   this paragraph applied to the previous beneficiary on the relevant date; and

(c)   the requirements of sub-paragraphs (6) and (7) are satisfied in his case.

(6)   The requirements of this sub-paragraph are that the person was, on the relevant date–

(a)   the partner of the previous beneficiary; or

(b)   in a case where the previous beneficiary died on the relevant date, was a person to whom sub-paragraph (10)(b), (c) or (d) of regulation 13 (restrictions on unreasonable payments), as specified in paragraph 5, applied and for the purposes of this sub-paragraph ''claimant'' in that paragraph of that regulation shall be taken to be a reference to the previous beneficiary.

(7)   The requirements of this sub-paragraph are that a claim for housing benefit is made within 4 weeks of the relevant date and where such a claim is made it shall be treated as having been made on the relevant date.

(8)   The eligible rent of a person to whom–

(a) regulation 10A of and Schedule A1 to the Housing Benefit Regulations (entitlement to housing benefit by refugees), or, as the case may be,

(b) regulation 10A of and Schedule A1 to the Housing Benefit (State Pension Credit) Regulations (entitlement to housing benefit by refugees)

apply, shall be determined in accordance with–

    (i) regulations 12 (rent) and 13 (maximum rent) of the Housing Benefit Regulations, or, as the case may be,

    (ii) regulations 12 (rent) and 13 (maximum rent) of the Housing Benefit (State Pension Credit) Regulations,

as set out in paragraph 5.

(9) Sub-paragraphs (1) to (8) above shall continue to have effect in the case of a claimant who has ceased to be a welfare to work beneficiary or whose partner has ceased to be such a beneficiary where the claimant is entitled to housing benefit at the end of the 52 week period to which sub-paragraph (4)(c) refers.

(10) In this paragraph–

"the first date" means 1st January 1996, except in a case to which sub-paragraph (5) applies, when it shall be the relevant date;

"the second date" means any day after the first date for which a claimant's entitlement to housing benefit is to be determined;

"eligible rent" means as the case may require, an eligible rent determined in accordance with–

(a) regulations 12B (eligible rent), 12C (eligible rent and maximum rent), 12D (eligible rent and maximum rent (LHA)) or any of regulations 12E to 12K (transitional protection for pathfinder cases); or

(b) regulations 12 (rent) and 13 (restrictions on unreasonable payments) as set out in paragraph 5 of Schedule 3 to the Consequential Provisions Regulations in a case to which paragraph 4 of that Schedule applies;

"exempt accommodation" means accommodation which is–

(a) a resettlement place provided by persons to whom the Secretary of State has given assistance by way of grant pursuant to section 30 of the Jobseekers Act 1995 (grants for resettlement places); and for this purpose "resettlement place" shall have the same meaning as it has in that section; or

(b) provided by a non-metropolitan county council in England within the meaning of section 1 of the Local Government Act 1972, a housing association, a registered charity or voluntary organisation where that body or a person acting on its behalf also provides the claimant with care, support or supervision;

"imprisoned" means detained in custody pending sentence upon conviction or under a sentence imposed by a court;

"previous beneficiary" means a person–

(a) who died, left the dwelling or was imprisoned, as the case may be;

(b) who was on that date in receipt of housing benefit or was on that date within 52 weeks of having become a welfare to work beneficiary; and

(c) to whom this regulation applied on that date;

and, in this paragraph, a reference to a person occupying a dwelling as his home shall be taken to include a person who is treated as occupying a dwelling as his home by virtue of regulation 7 of the Housing Benefit Regulations or, as the case may be, regulation 7 of the Housing Benefit (State Pension Credit) Regulations;

"the qualifying age for state pension credit" means (in accordance with section 1(2)(b) and (6) of the State Pension Credit Act 2002)–

(a) in the case of a woman, pensionable age; or

(b) in the case of a man, the age which is pensionable age in the case of a woman born on the same day as the man;

"relevant authority" means an authority administering housing benefit;

"the relevant date" means the date–

(a)   of the death of a previous beneficiary;

(b)   on which a previous beneficiary who was the claimant's partner left the dwelling so that he and the claimant ceased to be living together as husband and wife; or

(c)   on which a previous beneficiary, other than a beneficiary to whom regulation 7(13) of the Housing Benefit Regulations or, as the case may be, regulation 7(13) of the Housing Benefit (State Pension Credit) Regulations applied, was imprisoned, but only where on that date he was the partner of the claimant,

as the case may be;

"state pension credit" means state pension credit under the State Pension Credit Act 2002;

"welfare to work beneficiary" means a person to whom regulation 13A(1) of the Social Security (Incapacity for Work) (General) Regulations 1995 applies.

5.–(1)   For the purposes of paragraph 4(1), regulation 12 of both the Housing Benefit Regulations and the Housing Benefit (State Pension Credit) Regulations is as follows–

"Rent

12.–(1)   Subject to the following provision of this regulation, the payments in respect of which housing benefit is payable in the form of a rent rebate or allowance are the following periodical payments which a person is liable to make in respect of the dwelling which he occupies as his home–

(a)   payments of, or by way of, rent;

(b)   payments in respect of a licence or permission to occupy the dwelling;

(c)   payments by way of mesne profits or, in Scotland, violent profits;

(d)   payments in respect of, or in consequence of, use and occupation of the dwelling;

(e)   payments of, or by way of, service charges payment of which is a condition on which the right to occupy the dwelling depends;

(f)   mooring charges payable for a houseboat;

(g)   where the home is a caravan or a mobile home, payments in respect of the site on which it stands;

(h)   any contribution payable by a person resident in an almshouse provided by a housing association which is either a charity of which particulars are entered in the register of charities established under section 3 of the Charities Act 1993 (register of charities) or an exempt charity within the meaning of that Act, which is a contribution towards the cost of maintaining that association's almshouses and essential services in them;

(i)   payments under a rental purchase agreement, that is to say an agreement for the purchase of a dwelling which is a building or part of one under which the whole or part of the purchase price is to be paid in more than one instalment and the completion of the purchase is deferred until the whole or a specified part of the purchase price has been paid; and

(j)   where, in Scotland, the dwelling is situated on or pertains to a croft within the meaning of section 3(1) of the Crofters (Scotland) Act 1993, the payment in respect of the croft land.

(2)   A rent rebate or, as the case may be, a rent allowance shall not be payable in respect of the following periodical payments–

(a)   payments under a long tenancy except a shared ownership tenancy granted by a housing association or a housing authority;

(b)   payments under a co-ownership scheme;

(c)   payments by an owner;

(d)   payments under a hire purchase, credit sale or conditional sale agreement except to the extent the conditional sale agreement is in respect of land; and

(e)   payments by a Crown tenant.

(3)   Subject to any apportionment in accordance with paragraphs (4) and (5) and to regulations 13 and 13ZA (restrictions on unreasonable payments and rent increases), the amount of a person's eligible rent shall be the aggregate of such payments specified in paragraph (1) as he is liable to pay less–

(a)   except where he is separately liable for charges for water, sewerage or allied environmental services, an amount determined in accordance with paragraph (6);

(b)   where payments include service charges which are wholly or partly ineligible, an amount in respect of the ineligible charges determined in accordance with Schedule 1; and

(c)   where he is liable to make payments in respect of any service charges to which paragraph (1)(e) does not apply, but to which paragraph 3(2) of Schedule 1 (unreasonably low service charges) applies in the particular circumstances, an amount in respect of such charges determined in accordance with paragraph 3(2) of Schedule 1.

(4)   Where the payments specified in paragraph (1) are payable in respect of accommodation which consists partly of residential accommodation and partly of other accommodation, only such proportion thereof as is referable to the residential accommodation shall count as eligible rent for the purposes of these Regulations.

(5)   Where more than one person is liable to make payments in respect of a dwelling, the payments specified in paragraph (1) shall be apportioned for the purpose of calculating the eligible rent for each such person having regard to all the circumstances, in particular, the number of such persons and the proportion of rent paid by each such person.

(6)   The amount of the deduction referred to in paragraph (3) shall be–

(a)   except in a case to which sub-paragraph (c) applies, if the dwelling occupied by the claimant is a self-contained unit, the amount of the charges;

(b)   in any other case except one to which sub-paragraph (c) applies, the proportion of those charges in respect of the self-contained unit, which is obtained by dividing the area of the dwelling occupied by the claimant by the area of the self-contained unit of which it forms part; or

(c)   where the charges vary in accordance with the amount of water actually used, the amount which the appropriate authority considers to be fairly attributable to water and sewerage services, having regard to the actual or estimated consumption of the claimant.

(7)   In this regulation and Schedule 1–

"service charges" means periodical payments for services, whether or not under the same agreement as that under which the dwelling is occupied, or whether or not such a charge is specified as separate from or separately identified within other payments made by the occupier in respect of the dwelling; and

"services" means services performed or facilities (including the use of furniture) provided for, or rights made available to, the occupier of a dwelling.''.

(2)   For the purposes of paragraph 4(1), regulation 13 of both the Housing Benefit Regulations and the Housing Benefit (State Pension Credit) Regulations is as follows–

"Restrictions on unreasonable payments

13.–(1)   Where a rent is registered in respect of a dwelling under Part 4 or 5 of the Rent Act 1977 or Part 4 or 7 of the Rent (Scotland) Act 1984 and the rent recoverable from a claimant is limited to the rent so registered, his eligible rent determined in accordance with regulation 12 (rent) shall not exceed the rent so registered.

(2)   Where a rent has been determined by a rent assessment committee or a private rented housing committee in respect of a dwelling under Part 1 of the Housing

Act 1988 or Part 2 of the Housing (Scotland) Act 1988, the claimant's eligible rent determined in accordance with regulation 12 shall not exceed the rent determined by the committee during the twelve months beginning with the first day on which that determination had effect.

(3)   The relevant authority shall consider–

(a)   whether by reference to a determination or re-determination made by a rent officer in exercise of a function conferred on him by an order under section 122 of the Housing Act 1996 or otherwise, whether a claimant occupies a dwelling larger than is reasonably required by him and others who also occupy that dwelling (including any non-dependants of his and any person paying rent to him) having regard in particular to suitable alternative accommodation occupied by a household of the same size; or

(b)   whether by reference to a determination or re-determination made by a rent officer in exercise of a function conferred on him by an order under section 122 of the Housing Act 1996 or otherwise, whether the rent payable for his dwelling is unreasonably high by comparison with the rent payable in respect of suitable alternative accommodation elsewhere,

and, where it appears to the authority that the dwelling is larger than is reasonably required or that the rent is unreasonably high, the authority shall, subject to paragraphs (4) to (7), treat the claimant's eligible rent, as reduced by such amount as it considers appropriate having regard in particular to the cost of suitable alternative accommodation elsewhere and the claimant's maximum housing benefit shall be calculated by reference to the eligible rent as so reduced.

(4)   If any person to whom paragraph (10) applies–

(a)   is aged 60 or over;

(b)   is incapable of work for the purposes of one or more of the provisions of the Social Security Act, or Part 2 of the Act;

(c)   is treated as capable of work in accordance with regulations made under section 171E of the Act; or

(d)   is a member of the same household as a child or young person for whom he or his partner is responsible,

no deduction shall be made under paragraph (3) unless suitable cheaper alternative accommodation is available and the authority considers that, taking into account the relevant factors, it is reasonable to expect the claimant to move from his present accommodation.

(5)   No deduction shall be made under paragraph (3) for a period of 12 months from the date of death of any person to whom paragraph (10) applied or, had a claim been made, would have applied, if the dwelling which the claimant occupies is the same as that occupied by him at that date except where the deduction began before the death occurred.

(6)   For the purposes of paragraph (5), a claimant shall be treated as occupying the dwelling if paragraph (13) of regulation 7 (circumstances in which a person is to be treated as occupying a dwelling) is satisfied and for that purpose sub-paragraph (b) of that paragraph shall be treated as if it were omitted.

(7)   Without prejudice to the operation of paragraph (4), but subject to paragraph (8), where the relevant authority is satisfied that a person to whom paragraph (10) applies was able to meet the financial commitments for his dwelling when they were entered into, no deduction shall be made under paragraph (3) during the first 13 benefit weeks of the claimant's award of housing benefit.

(8)   Paragraph (7) shall not apply where a claimant was previously entitled to benefit in respect of an award of housing benefit which fell wholly or partly less than 52 weeks before the commencement of his current award of housing benefit.

(9)   For the purposes of this regulation–

(a)   in deciding what is suitable alternative accommodation, the relevant authority shall take account of the nature of the alternative accommodation and the facilities provided having regard to the age and state of health of all the persons to whom paragraph (10) applies and, in particular, where a claimant's present dwelling is occupied with security of tenure, accommodation shall not be treated as suitable alternative accommodation unless that accommodation will be occupied on terms which will afford security of tenure reasonably equivalent to that presently enjoyed by the claimant; and

(b)   the relevant factors in paragraph (4) are the effects of a move to alternative accommodation on–
    (i)   the claimant's prospects of retaining his employment; and
    (ii)   the education of any child or young person referred to in paragraph (4)(d) if such a move were to result in a change of school.

(10)   This paragraph applies to the following persons–
(a)   the claimant;
(b)   any member of his family;
(c)   if the claimant is a member of a polygamous marriage, any partners of his and any child or young person for whom he or a partner is responsible and who is a member of the same household;
(d)   subject to paragraph (11), any relative of the claimant or his partner who occupies the same dwelling as the claimant, whether or not they reside with him.

(11)   Paragraph (10)(d) shall only apply to a relative who has no separate right of occupation of the dwelling which would enable him to continue to occupy it even if the claimant ceased his occupation of it.''.

(3)   For the purposes of regulation 12(3) of both the Housing Benefit Regulations and the Housing Benefit (State Pension Credit) Regulations, as inserted by paragraph (1) above, regulation 13ZA of both those Regulations is as follows–

"Restrictions on rent increases
13ZA.–(1)   Subject to paragraph (2), where a claimant's eligible rent is increased during an award of housing benefit, the relevant authority shall, if it considers, whether by reference to a determination or re-determination made by a rent officer in exercise of a function conferred on him by an order under section 122 of the Housing Act 1996, or otherwise, either–
(a)   that the increase is unreasonably high having regard in particular to the level of increases for suitable alternative accommodation, or
(b)   in the case of an increase which takes place less than 12 months after the date of the previous increase, that the increase is unreasonable having regard to the length of time since that previous increase,
treat the eligible rent as reduced either by the full amount of the increase or, if it considers that a lesser increase was reasonable in all the circumstances, by the difference between the full amount of the increase and the increase that is reasonable having regard in particular to the level of increases for suitable alternative accommodation, and the claimant's maximum housing benefit shall be calculated by reference to the eligible rent as so reduced.

(2)   No deduction shall be made under this regulation for a period of 12 months from the date of death of any person to whom paragraph (11) of regulation 13 (restrictions on unreasonable payments) applied or, had a claim been made, would have applied, if the dwelling which the claimant occupies is the same as that occupied by him at that date except where the deduction began before the death occurred.

(3)   For the purposes of paragraph (2), a claimant shall be treated as occupying the dwelling if paragraph (13) of regulation 7 (circumstances in which a person is to be treated as occupying a dwelling) is satisfied and for that purpose sub-paragraph (b) of that paragraph shall be treated as if it were omitted.''.''.

(3)   For paragraph 8 of Schedule 3 substitute–

"Local reference rent taper
8.–(1)   Regulation 13 of both the Housing Benefit Regulations and the Housing Benefit (State Pension Credit) Regulations (maximum rent) shall have effect in the case of a claimant to whom any of sub-paragraphs (3) to (6) applies subject to the amendment specified in sub-paragraph (2).
(2)   In paragraph (3) of regulation 13 at the end, add "plus 50 per cent. of the amount by which the claim related rent exceeds the local reference rent."
(3)   This sub-paragraph applies to a claimant who has been continuously entitled to and in receipt of housing benefit–
(a)   in respect of the same dwelling for a period which includes 5th October 1997; and
(b)   which included an addition by virtue of paragraph (3) or (4) of regulation 11 of the 1987 Regulations as they had effect on 5th October 1997.
(4)   Sub-paragraph (3) above shall continue to have effect in the case of a person who has ceased to be a welfare to work beneficiary or whose partner has ceased to be such a beneficiary where the person is entitled to housing benefit at the end of the 52 week period to which sub-paragraph (5) refers.
(5)   This sub-paragraph applies in the case of a person–
(a) · who was entitled to housing benefit in respect of the dwelling he occupied as his home on or before 5th October 1997;
(b)   whose entitlement to housing benefit in respect of that dwelling was continuous from that date until it ceased because either the person or his partner became a welfare to work beneficiary;
(c)   who on the day before entitlement to housing benefit ceased, was in receipt of an addition to benefit by virtue of paragraph (4) or (5) of regulation 11 of the 1987 Regulations as they had effect on 5th October 1997; and
(d).   who subsequently becomes re-entitled to housing benefit in respect of that dwelling within 52 weeks of him or his partner becoming a welfare to work beneficiary.
(6)   In this paragraph, "welfare to work beneficiary" means a person to whom regulation 13A(1) of the Social Security (Incapacity for Work) (General) Regulations 1995 applies.".

(4)   In Schedule 4–
(a)   for regulation 10A(1), substitute–

"10A.–(1)   Where a person, who has made a claim for asylum, is notified that he has been recorded by the Secretary of State as a refugee, these Regulations shall have effect with respect to his entitlement to housing benefit for the relevant period which applies in his case in accordance with Schedule A1(treatment of claims for housing benefit by refugees), but that entitlement is–
(a)   subject to the provisions of Schedule A1; and
(b)   with respect to regulations 12 (rent) and 13 (maximum rent), subject to paragraph 4(8) of Schedule 3 to the Housing Benefit and Council Tax Benefit (Consequential Provisions) Regulations 2006.";

(b)   for paragraph 3 of Schedule A1 as inserted by paragraph 2(2), substitute–

"Eligible rent
3.–(1)   Subject to sub-paragraph (2), for the purpose of determining a claimant's eligible rent–
(a)   regulations 12 and 13 have effect as they were in force on 1st January 1996;
(b)   in paragraph (1) of regulation 12 of the former Regulations (restrictions on rent increases) as saved by paragraph 5 of Schedule 3 to the Housing Benefit

and Council Tax Benefit (Consequential Provisions) Regulations 2006 the words from "whether by reference" to "or otherwise" shall be omitted; and

(c)   regulation 14 (requirement to refer to a rent officer) shall not have effect.

(2)   In determining a claimant's eligible rent for the relevant period, the relevant authority may have regard to information in their possession or which they may obtain, as to the level of rents which had effect in that period in respect of any area in which the claimant occupied a dwelling as his home and in respect of which his claim for housing benefit is made."; and

(c)   for paragraph 7 of Schedule 1A, substitute–

"Calculation of amount of benefit
7.   The appropriate maximum housing benefit to which a claimant is entitled under regulation 10A and this Schedule shall be calculated on a weekly basis in accordance with Part 8 as it had effect for the relevant period.".

The Rent Officers (Housing Benefit Functions) Amendment Order 2007
(SI 2007 No.2871)

Made   *2nd October 2007*
Laid before Parliament   *8th October 2007*
Coming into force in accordance with article 1

The Secretary of State for Work and Pensions, makes the following Order in exercise of the powers conferred by section 122(1) and (6) of the Housing Act 1996.

Citation, commencement and interpretation
1.–(1)   This Order may be cited as the Rent Officers (Housing Benefit Functions) Amendment Order 2007.

(2)   This article and articles 2 (application of the Rent Officers Order), 3 (amendment of the Rent Officers Order), 11 (application of the Rent Officers (Scotland) Order) and 12 (amendment of the Rent Officers (Scotland) Order) shall come into force on 20th March 2008.

(3)   Articles 4 and 13 shall come into force on 20th March immediately after the coming into force of articles 2, 3, 11 and 12.

(4)   Articles 5 to 10 and 14 to 19 shall come into force on 7th April 2008.

(5)   In this Order–
"local authority" has the same meaning as in the Social Security Administration Act 1992;
"the Rent Officers Order" means the Rent Officers (Housing Benefit Functions) Order 1997; and
"the Rent Officers (Scotland) Order" means Rent Officers (Housing Benefit Functions) (Scotland) Order 1997.

Application of the Rent Officers Order
2.   Those provisions of the Rent Officers Order which on 19th March 2008 apply only in relation to the area of a local authority listed in the Schedule, shall apply in the same way to the area of every other local authority in England and Wales.

Amendment of the Rent Officers Order
3.   The Rent Officers Order shall be amended in accordance with the following provisions of this Order.

Amendments to the Rent Officers Order relating to the local housing allowance coming into force on 20th March 2008

4.–(1) In article 2(interpretation)–

(a) in the definition of "broad rental market area" after "paragraph 4 of Part 1 of Schedule 3A" insert "or paragraph 4 of Schedule 3B, as the case may be,";

(b) in the definition for "broad rental market area determination" after "article 4B(1)" insert "or 4B(1A), as the case may be";

(c) in the definition of "local housing allowance determination" after "article 4B(2)" insert "or article 4B(2A), as the case may be";

(d) after the definition of "tenancy" add–

"working day" means any day other than a Saturday, a Sunday, Christmas Day, Good Friday or a day which is a bank holiday in England and Wales under the Banking and Financial Dealings Act 1971.".

(2) In article 4B (broad rental market area determinations and local housing allowance determinations)–

(a) in paragraph (1) for "local authority" in the first place in which it occurs substitute "pathfinder authority";

(b) after paragraph (1) insert–

"(1A) On 20th March 2008 and so often thereafter as a rent officer considers appropriate, a rent officer shall, in relation to each local authority,–

(a) determine one or more broad rental market areas which will (during the month which next begins after the determination is made) fall, in whole or in part, within the area of the local authority so that every part of the area of that local authority falls within a broad rental market area and no part of the area of that authority falls within more than one broad rental market area; and

(b) give to that local authority a notice which–

(i) specifies the area contained within each broad rental market area as falls, in whole or in part, within the area of that authority, by reference to the postcodes for each such broad rental market area; and

(ii) identifies such of those postcodes as fall within the area of that authority.";

(c) after paragraph (2) insert–

"(2A) No more than 10 and not less than 8 working days before the end of each month a rent officer shall–

(a) for each broad rental market area determine, in accordance with the provisions of Schedule 3B–

(i) a local housing allowance for each of the categories of dwelling set out in paragraph 1 of Schedule 3B; and

(ii) local housing allowances for such other categories of dwelling of more than five bedrooms as a rent officer believes are likely to be required for the purpose of calculating housing benefit; and

(b) give to each local authority notice of the local housing allowance determination made in accordance with paragraph (a) for each broad rental market area falling within, in whole or in part, the area of that authority.";

(d) after paragraph (3) insert–

"(3A) Any broad rental market area determination made in accordance with paragraph (1A), or local housing allowance determination made in accordance with paragraph (2A) before 7th April 2008, shall take effect on 7th April 2008 and any subsequent determination shall take effect on the first [¹] day of the month which begins after the day on which the determination is made.";

(e)   after paragraph (5) insert–

"(6)   Where a rent officer has made a local housing allowance determination in accordance with paragraph (2A) he shall–
  (a)   make an approximate monthly allowance determination in relation to that local housing allowance determination; and
  (b)   give notice of the approximate monthly allowance determination to each authority to which he is required to give notice of the local housing allowance determination when he gives notice of that determination.".

(3)   In article 7A(errors)–
(a)   in paragraph (3)–
       (i)   after "broad rental market area determination" insert "determined in accordance with article 4B(1)"";
       (ii)   after "local housing allowance determination" insert "determined in accordance with article 4B(2)"";
(b)   after paragraph (3) insert–

"(4)   If a rent officer is of the opinion that he has made an error (other than in the application of his professional judgement) in relation to a broad rental market area determination determined in accordance with article 4B(1A) or a local housing allowance determination determined in accordance with article 4B(2A), he shall notify any local authority to which notification of that determination was sent of the error, and the amended determination, as soon as practicable after he becomes aware of it.".

(4)   After Schedule 3A insert–

"SCHEDULE 3B
Broad rental market area determinations and local housing allowance determinations

Categories of dwelling
  1.–(1)   The categories of dwelling for which a rent officer is required to determine a local housing allowance in accordance with article 4B(2A)(a)(i) are–
  (a)   a dwelling where the tenant has the exclusive use of only one bedroom and where the tenancy provides for him to share the use of one or more of–
       (i)   a kitchen;
       (ii)   a bathroom;
       (iii) a toilet; or
       (iv)   a room suitable for living in;
  (b)   a dwelling where the tenant (together with his partner where he has one) has the exclusive use of only one bedroom and exclusive use of a kitchen, a bathroom, a toilet and a room suitable for living in;
  (c)   a dwelling where the tenant has the use of only two bedrooms;
  (d)   a dwelling where the tenant has the use of only three bedrooms;
  (e)   a dwelling where the tenant has the use of only four bedrooms;
  (f)   a dwelling where the tenant has the use of only five bedrooms.
  2.   In–
  (a)   sub-paragraph (1)(b) "partner" has the same meaning as in regulation 2 of the Housing Benefit Regulations or, as the case may be, regulation 2 of the Housing Benefit (State Pension Credit) Regulations;
  (b)   sub-paragraph (1)(c) to (f) "bedroom" means a bedroom, except for a bedroom which the tenant shares with any person other than–
       (i)   a member of his household;
       (ii)   a non-dependant of the tenant (within the meaning of regulation 3 of the Housing Benefit Regulations or, as the case may be, regulation 3 of the Housing Benefit (State Pension Credit) Regulations); or
       (iii) a person who pays rent to the tenant.

Local housing allowance for category of dwelling in paragraph 1

2.–(1) Subject to paragraph 3 (anomalous local housing allowances), the rent officer must determine a local housing allowance for each category of dwelling in paragraph 1 in accordance with the following sub-paragraphs.

(2) The rent officer must compile a list of rents.

(3) A list of rents means a list in ascending order of the rents which, in the rent officer's opinion, are payable at the date of the determination for a dwelling let under an assured tenancy which meets the criteria specified in sub-paragraph (5).

(4) The list must include any rents which are of the same amount.

(5) The criteria for including an assured tenancy on the list of rents in relation to each category of dwelling specified in paragraph 1 are–

(a) that the dwelling let under the assured tenancy is in the broad rental market area for which the local housing allowance for that category of dwelling is being determined;

(b) that the dwelling is in a reasonable state of repair; and

(c) that the assured tenancy permits the tenant to use exclusively or share the use of, as the case may be, the same number and type of rooms as the category of dwelling in relation to which the list of rents is being compiled.

(6) Where rent is payable other than weekly the rent officer must use the figure which would be payable if the rent were to be payable weekly by–

(a) multiplying the rent by an appropriate figure to obtain the rent for a year;

(b) dividing the total in (a) by 365; and

(c) multiplying the total in (b) by 7.

(7) When compiling the list of rents for each category of dwelling, the rent officer must–

(a) assume that no one who would have been entitled to housing benefit had sought or is seeking the tenancy; and

(b) exclude the amount of any rent which, in the rent officer's opinion, is fairly attributable to the provision of services performed for, or facilities (including the use of furniture) provided for, or rights made available to, the tenant which are ineligible to be met by housing benefit.

(8) When compiling the list of rents, the rent officer may include rents in other similar areas in which he believes a comparable market exists where he is not satisfied that the broad rental market area contains a sufficient number of dwellings that accord with the relevant category of dwelling set out in paragraph 1 to enable him to make a local housing allowance determination.

(9) The local housing allowance for each category of dwelling specified in paragraph 1 is the amount of the median rent in the list of rents for that category of dwelling.

(10) The median rent is determined as follows–

(a) where there is an even number of rents on the list, the formula is–

$$\frac{\text{The amount of the rent at } P + \text{the amount of the rent at P1}}{2} = \text{the local housing allowance}$$

where

P is the position on the list defined by dividing the number of rents on the list by 2 and P1 is the following position on the list.

(b) where there is an odd number of rents on the list, the formula is–

$$\frac{\text{the number of rents on the list} + 1}{2} = L$$

where

L is the position on the list in which the rent used to identify the local housing allowance lies.

(11) Where the median rent is not a whole number of pence, the rent must be rounded to the nearest whole penny by disregarding any amount less than half a penny and treating any amount of half a penny or more as a whole penny.

Anomalous local housing allowances

3.–(1) Where–

(a) the rent officer has determined the local housing allowance for each of the categories of dwelling in paragraph 1(1) in accordance with the preceding paragraphs of this Schedule; and

(b) the local housing allowance for a category of dwelling in paragraph 1(1)(b) to (f) is lower than the local housing allowance for any of the categories of dwelling which precede it,

that local housing allowance shall be the same as the highest local housing allowance which precedes it.

(2) Where–

(a) the rent officer has determined a local housing allowance following an application made under article 4B(4); and

(b)   that local housing allowance is lower than the local housing allowance for the category of dwelling in paragraph 1(1)(f),

that local housing allowance shall be the same as the local housing allowance for the category of dwelling in paragraph 1(1)(f).

Broad rental market area

4.   In this Schedule "broad rental market area" means an area–

(a)   comprising two or more distinct areas of residential accommodation, each distinct area of residential accommodation adjoining at least one other in the area;

(b)   within which a person could reasonably be expected to live having regard to facilities and services for the purposes of health, education, recreation, personal banking and shopping, taking account of the distance of travel, by public and private transport, to and from facilities and services of the same type and similar standard; and

(c)   containing residential premises of a variety of types, and including such premises held on a variety of tenancies.".

Amendment

1.   Amended by Art 2(2) of SI 2008 No 587 as from 7.4.08.

Amendments to the Rent Officers Order relating to the local housing allowance coming into force on 7th April 2008

5.–(1)   In article 3(2)(a) (determinations) omit ", except for a local authority which is a pathfinder authority,".

(2)   In article 4B(6) (broad rental market area determinations and local housing allowance determinations) after "paragraph (2A)" insert ", (4) or (4A)".

Amendments to the Rent Officers Order relating to the local housing allowance coming into force on 7th April 2008 save for certain purposes

6.–(1)   This article shall not apply where–

(a)   a board and attendance determination, board and attendance redetermination, substitute board and attendance determination or substitute board and attendance redetermination is to be made and the application for the board and attendance determination or original board and attendance determination was made by virtue of regulation 13A(6) of the Housing Benefit Regulations 2006 or, as the case may be, regulation 13A(6) of the Housing Benefit (Persons who have attained the qualifying age for state pension credit) Regulations 2006 as in force immediately before 7th April 2008;

(b)   a local housing allowance determination is to be made and the application was made by virtue of regulation 13A(4) or (5) of the Housing Benefit Regulations 2006 or, as the case may be, regulation 13A(4) or (5) of the Housing Benefit (Persons who have attained the qualifying age for state pension credit) Regulations 2006 as in force immediately before 7th April 2008; or

(c)   an error in relation to a broad rental market area determination, local housing allowance determination, board and attendance determination or a board and attendance redetermination is to be corrected and the original determination was made in accordance with the Rent Officers Order as in force immediately before 7th April 2008.

(2)   For the purpose of sub-paragraph (1)(c) "original determination" means the broad rental market area determination, local housing allowance determination, board and attendance determination or board and attendance redetermination to which the correction of an error relates.

(3)   In article 2–

(a)   for the definition of "broad rental market area" substitute–

" "broad rental market area" has the meaning specified in paragraph 4 of Schedule 3B;";

(b)   for the definition of "broad rental market area determination" substitute–
" "broad rental market area determination" means a determination made in accordance with article 4B(1A);'';
(c)   for the definition of "local housing allowance determination" substitute–
" "local housing allowance determination" means a determination made in accordance with article 4B(2A);'';
(d)   omit the definition of "pathfinder authority".
(e)   for the definition of "relevant date" substitute–
" "relevant date" means the date specified by a local authority in an application for a local housing allowance determination made in accordance with regulation 13D(7)(a) of the Housing Benefit Regulations or, as the case may be, regulation 13D(7)(a) of the Housing Benefit (State Pension Credit) Regulations;''.
(4)   In article 4B (broad rental market area determinations and local housing allowance determinations)–
(a)   omit paragraphs (1), (2) and (3);
(b)   for paragraph (4) substitute–

"(4)   Where a local authority makes an application in accordance with regulation 13D(7)(a) of the Housing Benefit Regulations or, as the case may be, regulation 13D(7)(a) of the Housing Benefit (State Pension Credit) Regulations, a rent officer shall determine, in accordance with the provisions of Schedule 3B and as soon as is reasonably practicable, the local housing allowance for that category of dwelling at the relevant date, for each broad rental market area falling within, in whole or in part, the area of the local authority that made the application, at the relevant date.

(4A)   Where a local authority makes an application in accordance with regulation 13D(8) of the Housing Benefit Regulations or, as the case may be, regulation 13D(8) of the Housing Benefit (State Pension Credit) Regulations, a rent officer shall determine in accordance with the provisions of Schedule 3B and as soon as is reasonably practicable, the local housing allowance for that category of dwelling for each broad rental market area falling within, in whole or in part, the areas of the local authority.''.

(c)   in paragraph (5)–
(i)   in sub-paragraph (a) for "pathfinder authority" substitute "local authority";
[¹ (ii) for sub-paragraphs (b) and (c) substitute–

"(b)   any local housing allowance determination made in accordance with paragraph (4) shall take effect for the month in which the relevant date falls, except that no such determination can have effect before 7th April 2008; and
(c)   any local housing allowance determination made in accordance with paragraph (4A) shall take effect for the month in which notice is given in accordance with sub-paragraph (a), except that no such determination can have effect before 7th April 2008."]
[¹ (iii)]
(5)   For article 4C(1) and (2) (board and attendance determinations and notifications) substitute–

"4C.–(1)   Where a relevant authority makes an application to a rent officer in accordance with regulation 13D(10) of the Housing Benefit Regulations or, as the case may be, regulation 13D(10) of the Housing Benefit (State Pension Credit) Regulations, a rent officer shall determine whether or not a substantial part of the rent under the tenancy at the relevant time is fairly attributable to board and attendance.

(2)   Where a rent officer determines that a substantial part of the rent under the tenancy at the relevant time is fairly attributable to board and attendance, he shall–
(a)   notify the relevant authority accordingly; and
(b)   treat the application as if it had been made in accordance with regulation 14(1) of the Housing Benefit Regulations or, as the case may be regulation 14(1) of the Housing Benefit (State Pension Credit) Regulations.''.

(6)   In articles 4D (board and attendance redeterminations) and 4E (substitute board and attendance determinations and substitute board and attendance redeterminations) for ''pathfinder authority'' in both places in which it occurs substitute ''local authority''.
(7)   In article 7A (errors)–
(a)   in paragraph (2) for ''pathfinder authority'' substitute ''local authority'';
(b)   omit paragraph (3).
(8)   Omit Schedule 3A.

Amendment
1.   Amended by Art 2(3) of SI 2008 No 587 as from 7.4.08.

Amendments to the Rent Officers Order relating to information sharing coming into force on 7th April 2008 save for certain purposes

7.–(1)   This article shall not apply where information is provided to the rent officer by virtue of regulation 14 or 114 of the Housing Benefit Regulations 2006 or, as the case may be, regulation 14 or 95 of the Housing Benefit (Persons who have attained the qualifying age for state pension credit) Regulations 2006 as in force immediately before 7th April 2008.
(2)   For Article 4C(4) (board and attendance determinations and notifications) substitute–

''(4)   Where an application for a board and attendance determination is treated as if it had been made in accordance with regulation 14(1) of the Housing Benefit Regulations or, as the case may be, regulation 14(1) of the Housing Benefit (State Pension Credit) Regulations, then, for the purposes of paragraph (a)(ii) of the definition of ''relevant period'' in article 2(1), it shall be treated as having been received on the day on which the further information provided in accordance with regulation 114A(4) of the Housing Benefit Regulations or regulation 95A(4) of the Housing Benefit (State Pension Credit) Regulations is received.''.

(3)   In article 5 (insufficient information) for '', he shall serve notice on the local authority requesting that information'' substitute ''where the information supplied under regulation 114A of the Housing Benefit Regulations or regulation 95A of the Housing Benefit (State Pension Credit) Regulations was incomplete or incorrect, he shall serve notice on the local authority requesting it to supply the further information required under regulation 114A or regulation 95A, as the case may be, or to confirm whether the information already supplied is correct and, if it is not, to supply the correct information''.
(4)   For paragraph 7(3) of Part 2 of Schedule 1 substitute–

''(3)   For the purposes of paragraphs 1, 2, 3, and 6 of Part 1 of this Schedule, the rent officer shall assume that the rent payable under the tenancy at the relevant time is–
(a)   where an amount is notified to the rent officer under regulation 114A(4)(b) of the Housing Benefit Regulations or, as the case may be, regulations 95A(4)(b) of the Housing Benefit (State Pension Credit) Regulations in respect of that tenancy, that notified amount less the total of any ineligible charges included in that amount; or

(b)   in any other case, the total amount stated under regulation 114A(3)(d) of the Housing Benefit Regulations or, as the case may be regulation 95A(3)(d) of the Housing Benefit (State Pension Credit) Regulations less the total of any ineligible charges included in that stated amount.''.

Amendments to the Rent Officers Order relating to ineligible service charges coming into force on 7th April 2008 save for certain purposes

8.–(1)   This article shall not apply where the rent officer is required to make a determination under paragraphs 1, 2, 3, or 6 of Part 1 of Schedule 1 to the Rent Officers Order by virtue of–

(a)   an application made under–

    (i)   regulation 14 of the Housing Benefit Regulations 2006 as in force before the substitution of regulation 14 by virtue of regulation 8 of the Housing Benefit (Local Housing Allowance and Information Sharing) Amendment Regulations 2007; or

    (ii)   regulation 14 of the Housing Benefit (Persons who have attained the qualifying age for state pension credit) Regulations 2006 as in force before the substitution of regulation 14 by virtue of regulation 8 of the Housing Benefit (State Pension Credit) (Local Housing Allowance and Information Sharing) Amendment Regulations 2007; or

(b)   an application for a redetermination, substitute determination or substitute redetermination relating to a determination to which sub-paragraph (a) applies made under regulation 15, 16 or 17 of the Regulations referred to in sub-paragraph (a)(i) or (ii).

(2)   For paragraph 7(1) (ineligible charges and support charges) of Part 2 of Schedule 1 substitute–

''(1)   ''ineligible charges'' means service charges which are ineligible to be met by housing benefit by virtue of regulation 12B(2) (rent) of and Schedule 1 (ineligible service charges) to the Housing Benefit Regulations or, as the case may be, regulation 12B(2) of and Schedule 1 to the Housing Benefit (State Pension Credit) Regulations except in the case of a tenancy where the rent includes payments for board and attendance, and the rent officer considers that a substantial part of the rent under the tenancy is fairly attributable to board and attendance, charges specified in paragraph 1(a)(i) of Schedule 1 to the Housing Benefit Regulations or, as the case may be, in paragraph 1(a)(i) of Schedule 1 to the Housing Benefit (State Pension Credit) Regulations (charges for meals).''.

Amendments to the Rent Officers Order relating to claim-related rent coming into force on 7th April 2008 save for certain purposes

9.–(1)   This article shall not apply where the rent officer has made a determination under paragraphs 1, 2, 3, 4 or 5 of Part 1 of Schedule 1 to the Rent Officers Order and that determination was made in relation to–

(a)   an application under–

    (i)   regulation 14 of the Housing Benefit Regulations 2006 as in force before the substitution of regulation 14 by virtue of regulation 8 of the Housing Benefit (Local Housing Allowance and Information Sharing) Amendment Regulations 2007; or

    (ii)   regulation 14 of the Housing Benefit (Persons who have attained the qualifying age for state pension credit) Regulations 2006 as in force before the substitution of regulation 14 by virtue of regulation 8 of the Housing Benefit (State Pension Credit) (Local Housing Allowance and Information Sharing) Amendment Regulations 2007; or

(b)   an application for a redetermination, substitute determination or substitute redetermination relating to a determination to which sub-paragraph (a) applies made under regulation 15, 16 or 17 of the Regulations referred to in sub-paragraph (a)(i) or (ii).

(2) In paragraph 6 of Part 1 of Schedule 1–

(a) for sub-paragraph (1) substitute–

"(1)   In this paragraph, and in paragraph 9, "claim-related rent" means the claim-related rent determined by the rent officer in accordance with paragraph (2A).";

(b) after sub-paragraph (1) insert–

"(2A)   The rent officer shall determine that the claim-related rent is–

(a) where he makes a determination under sub-paragraph (2) of paragraph 1, sub-paragraph (2) of paragraph 2 and sub-paragraph (3) of paragraph 3, the lowest of the three rents determined under those sub-paragraphs;

(b) where he makes a determination under only two of the sub-paragraphs referred to in paragraph (a), the lower of the two rents determined under those sub-paragraphs;

(c) where he makes a determination under only one of the sub-paragraphs referred to in paragraph (a), the rent determined under that sub-paragraph;

(d) where he does not make a determination under any of the sub-paragraphs referred to in sub-paragraph (a), the rent payable under the tenancy of the dwelling at the relevant time.".

(c) omit sub-paragraph (2); and

(d) in sub-paragraph (3) omit "Where the dwelling is not in a hostel,".

(3) In paragraph 9(1) of Part 3 of Schedule 1–

(a) for sub-paragraph (1)(c) substitute–

"(c)   where that claim-related rent includes an amount which would be ineligible for housing benefit under paragraph 1(a)(i) of Schedule 1 to the Housing Benefit Regulations or, as the case may be, paragraph 1(a)(i) of Schedule 1 to the Housing Benefit (State Pension Credit) Regulations (charges for meals), the inclusion of an ineligible amount in respect of meals;";

(b) after sub-paragraph (1)(d) insert–

"(da)   where any rent determined under paragraph 4 includes an amount which would be ineligible for housing benefit under the provisions referred to in sub-paragraph (c), the inclusion of an ineligible amount in respect of meals; and".

Amendments to the Rent Officers Order which remake amendments made by the Housing Benefit and Council Tax Benefit (Consequential Provisions) Regulations 2006

10.–(1)   In article 2 (interpretation)–

(a)   for the definition of "hostel" substitute–

" "hostel" has the same meaning as in regulation 2(1) of the Housing Benefit Regulations or, as the case may be, regulation 2(1) of the Housing Benefit (State Pension Credit) Regulations;";

(b)   after that definition insert–

" "the Housing Benefit Regulations" means the Housing Benefit Regulations 2006;

"the Housing Benefit (State Pension Credit) Regulations" means the Housing Benefit (Persons who have attained the qualifying age for state pension credit) Regulations 2006;";

(c)   for the definition of "rent" substitute–

"rent" means any of the periodical payments referred to in regulation 12(1) of the Housing Benefit Regulations or, as the case may be, regulation 12(1) of the Housing Benefit (State Pension Credit) Regulations;";

(d)   omit the definition of the "1987 Regulations".

(2)   In article 3A (transitional arrangements for determination of single room rents with effect from 2nd July 2001), for "regulation 12A of the 1987 Regulations" substitute "regulation 14 of the Housing Benefit Regulations or, as the case may be, regulation 14 of the Housing Benefit (State Pension Credit) Regulations".

(3)   In article 4A (substitute determinations and substitute redeterminations), for "regulation 12C of the 1987 Regulations" substitute "regulation 17 of the Housing Benefit Regulations or, as the case may be, regulation 17 of the Housing Benefit (State Pension Credit) Regulations".

(4)   In article 4E (substitute board and attendance determinations and substitute board and attendance redeterminations), wherever "regulation 12C of the 1987 Regulations" occurs, substitute "regulation 17 of the Housing Benefit Regulations or, as the case may be, regulation 17 of the Housing Benefit (State Pension Credit) Regulations".

(5)   In article 6 (exceptions)–

(a)   in paragraph (2) for "regulation 7(3) of the 1987 Regulations" substitute "regulation 9(4) of the Housing Benefit Regulations or, as the case may be, regulation 9(4) of the Housing Benefit (State Pension Credit) Regulations"; and

(b)   in paragraph (3), for "the 1987 Regulations" substitute "the Housing Benefit Regulations and the Housing Benefit (State Pension Credit) Regulations".

(6)   In article 7 (special cases), for "regulation 10(1) of the 1987 Regulations" substitute "regulation 12(1) of the Housing Benefit Regulations or, as the case may be, regulation 12(1) of the Housing Benefit (State Pension Credit) Regulations".

(7)   In Schedule 1–

(a)   in Part 1, in paragraph 4(4) (local reference rents), for the definition of "non-dependant" substitute–

" "non-dependant" means a non-dependant of the tenant within the meaning of regulation 3 of the Housing Benefit Regulations or, as the case may be, regulation 3 of the Housing Benefit (State Pension Credit) Regulations;";

(b)   in Part 4, in paragraph 11(5)(b) (indicative rent levels), for "regulation 3 of the 1987 Regulations" substitute "regulation 3 of the Housing Benefit Regulations or, as the case may be, regulation 3 of the Housing Benefit (State Pension Credit) Regulations".

(8)   In Schedule 3A (categories of dwelling), in Part 1, in paragraph 1(2)(b), for "regulation 3 of the 1987 Regulations" substitute "regulation 3 of the Housing Benefit Regulations or, as the case may be, regulation 3 of the Housing Benefit (State Pension Credit) Regulations.".

Application of the Rent Officers (Scotland) Order

11.   Those provisions of the Rent Officers (Scotland) Order which on 19th March 2008 apply only in relation to the areas of the local authority of Argyll and Bute and the local authority of Edinburgh, shall apply in the same way to the area of every other local authority in Scotland.

Amendments to the Rent Officers (Scotland) Order

12.   The Rent Officers (Scotland) Order shall be amended in accordance with the following provisions of this Order.

Amendments to the Rent Officers (Scotland) Order relating to the local housing allowance coming into force on 20th March 2008

13.–(1) In article 2 (interpretation)–

(a) in the definition of ''broad rental market area'' after ''paragraph 4 of Part 1 of Schedule 3A'' insert ''or paragraph 4 of Schedule 3B, as the case may be,'';

(b) in the definition for ''broad rental market area determination'' after ''article 4B(1)'' insert ''or 4B(1A), as the case may be'';

(c) in the definition of ''local housing allowance determination'' after ''article 4B(2)'' insert ''or article 4B(2A), as the case may be'';

(d) after the definition of ''tenancy'' add–
''working day'' means any day other than a Saturday, a Sunday or a day which is a bank holiday in Scotland under the Banking and Financial Dealings Act 1971.''.

(2) In article 4B (broad rental market area determinations and local housing allowance determinations)–

(a) in paragraph (1) for ''local authority'' in the first place in which it occurs substitute ''pathfinder authority'';

(b) after paragraph (1) insert–

''(1A) On 20th March 2008 and so often thereafter as a rent officer considers appropriate, a rent officer shall, in relation to each local authority,–

(a) determine one or more broad rental market areas which will (during the month which next begins after the determination is made) fall, in whole or in part, within the area of the local authority so that every part of the area of that local authority falls within a broad rental market area and no part of the area of that authority falls within more than one broad rental market area; and

(b) give to that local authority a notice which–

(i) specifies the area contained within each broad rental market area as falls, in whole or in part, within the area of that authority, by reference to the postcodes for each such broad rental market area; and

(ii) identifies such of those postcodes as fall within the area of that authority.'';

(c) after paragraph (2) insert–

''(2A) No more than 10 and not less than 8 working days before the end of each month a rent officer shall–

(a) for each broad rental market area determine, in accordance with the provisions of Schedule 3B–

(i) a local housing allowance for each of the categories of dwelling set out in paragraph 1 of Schedule 3B; and

(ii) local housing allowances for such other categories of dwelling of more than five bedrooms as a rent officer believes are likely to be required for the purpose of calculating housing benefit; and

(b) give to each local authority notice of the local housing allowance determination made in accordance with paragraph (a) for each broad rental market area falling within, in whole or in part, the area of that authority.'';

(d) after paragraph (3) insert–

''(3A) Any broad rental market area determination made in accordance with paragraph (1A), or local housing allowance determination made in accordance with paragraph (2A) before 7th April 2008, shall take effect on 7th April 2008 and any subsequent determination shall take effect on the first [¹] day of the month which begins after the day on which the determination is made.'';

(e)   after paragraph (5) insert–

''(6)   Where a rent officer has made a local housing allowance determination in accordance with paragraph (2A) he shall–
(a)   make an approximate monthly allowance determination in relation to that local housing allowance determination; and
(b)   give notice of the approximate monthly allowance determination to each authority to which he is required to give notice of the local housing allowance determination when he gives notice of that determination.''.

(3)   In article 7A (errors)–
(a)   in paragraph (3)–
(i)   after ''broad rental market area determination'' insert ''determined in accordance with article 4B(1)'';
(ii)   after ''local housing allowance determination'' insert ''determined in accordance with article 4B(2)'';
(b)   after paragraph (3) insert–

''(4)   If a rent officer is of the opinion that he has made an error (other than in the application of his professional judgement) in relation to a broad rental market area determination determined in accordance with article 4B(1A) or a local housing allowance determination determined in accordance with article 4B(2A), he shall notify any local authority to which notification of that determination was sent of the error, and the amended determination, as soon as practicable after he becomes aware of it.''.

(4)   After Schedule 3A insert–

Article 4B
''SCHEDULE 3B

Broad rental market area determinations and local housing allowance determinations

Categories of dwelling
   1.–(1)   The categories of dwelling for which a rent officer is required to determine a local housing allowance in accordance with article 4B(2A)(a)(i) are–
(a)   a dwelling where the tenant has the exclusive use of only one bedroom and where the tenancy provides for him to share the use of one or more of–
(i)   a kitchen;
(ii)   a bathroom;
(iii)   a toilet; or
(iv)   a room suitable for living in;
(b)   a dwelling where the tenant (together with his partner where he has one) has the exclusive use of only one bedroom and exclusive use of a kitchen, a bathroom, a toilet and a room suitable for living in;
(c)   a dwelling where the tenant has the use of only two bedrooms;
(d)   a dwelling where the tenant has the use of only three bedrooms;
(e)   a dwelling where the tenant has the use of only four bedrooms;
(f)   a dwelling where the tenant has the use of only five bedrooms.
   (2)   In–
(a)   sub-paragraph (1)(b) ''partner'' has the same meaning as in regulation 2 of the Housing Benefit Regulations or, as the case may be, regulation 2 of the Housing Benefit (State Pension Credit) Regulations;
(b)   sub-paragraph (1)(c) to (f) ''bedroom'' means a bedroom, except for a bedroom which the tenant shares with any person other than–
(i)   a member of his household;

     (ii)   a non-dependant of the tenant (within the meaning of regulation 3 of the Housing Benefit Regulations or, as the case may be, regulation 3 of the Housing Benefit (State Pension Credit) Regulations); or

     (iii)   a person who pays rent to the tenant.

Local housing allowance for category of dwelling in paragraph 1

2.–(1)   Subject to paragraph 3 (anomalous local housing allowances), the rent officer must determine a local housing allowance for each category of dwelling in paragraph 1 in accordance with the following sub-paragraphs.

(2)   The rent officer must compile a list of rents.

(3)   A list of rents means a list in ascending order of the rents which, in the rent officer's opinion, are payable at the date of the determination for a dwelling let under an assured tenancy which meets the criteria specified in sub-paragraph (5).

(4)   The list must include any rents which are of the same amount.

(5)   The criteria for including an assured tenancy on the list of rents in relation to each category of dwelling specified in paragraph 1 are–

     (a)   that the dwelling let under the assured tenancy is in the broad rental market area for which the local housing allowance for that category of dwelling is being determined;

     (b)   that the dwelling is in a reasonable state of repair; and

     (c)   that the assured tenancy permits the tenant to use exclusively or share the use of, as the case may be, the same number and type of rooms as the category of dwelling in relation to which the list of rents is being compiled.

(6)   Where rent is payable other than weekly the rent officer must use the figure which would be payable if the rent were to be payable weekly by–

     (a)   multiplying the rent by an appropriate figure to obtain the rent for a year;

     (b)   dividing the total in (a) by 365; and

     (c)   multiplying the total in (b) by 7.

(7)   When compiling the list of rents for each category of dwelling, the rent officer must–

     (a)   assume that no one who would have been entitled to housing benefit had sought or is seeking the tenancy; and

     (b)   exclude the amount of any rent which, in the rent officer's opinion, is fairly attributable to the provision of services performed for, or facilities (including the use of furniture) provided for, or rights made available to, the tenant which are ineligible to be met by housing benefit.

(8)   When compiling the list of rents, the rent officer may include rents in other similar areas in which he believes a comparable market exists where he is not satisfied that the broad rental market area contains a sufficient number of dwellings that accord with the relevant category of dwelling set out in paragraph 1 to enable him to make a local housing allowance determination.

(9)   The local housing allowance for each category of dwelling specified in paragraph 1 is the amount of the median rent in the list of rents for that category of dwelling.

(10)   The median rent is determined as follows–

     (a)   where there is an even number of rents on the list, the formula is–

$$\frac{\text{The amount of the rent at P} + \text{the amount of the rent at P1}}{2} = \text{the local housing allowance}$$

where
P is the position on the list defined by dividing the number of rents on the list by 2 and P1 is the following position on the list.

     (b)   where there is an odd number of rents on the list, the formula is–

$$\frac{\text{the number of rents on the list} + 1}{2} = \text{L}$$

where
L is the position on the list in which the rent used to identify the local housing allowance lies.

(11)   Where the median rent is not a whole number of pence, the rent must be rounded to the nearest whole penny by disregarding any amount less than half a penny and treating any amount of half a penny or more as a whole penny.

Anomalous local housing allowances

3.–(1)   Where–

     (a)   the rent officer has determined the local housing allowance for each of the categories of dwelling in paragraph 1(1) in accordance with the preceding paragraphs of this Schedule; and

     (b)   the local housing allowance for a category of dwelling in paragraph 1(1)(b) to (f) is lower than the local housing allowance for any of the categories of dwelling which precede it,

that local housing allowance shall be the same as the highest local housing allowance which precedes it.

(2)   Where–

(a)   the rent officer has determined a local housing allowance following an application made under article 4B(4); and

(b)   that local housing allowance is lower than the local housing allowance for the category of dwelling in paragraph 1(1)(f),

that local housing allowance shall be the same as the local housing allowance for the category of dwelling in paragraph 1(1)(f).

Broad rental market area

4.   In this Schedule "broad rental market area" means an area–

(a)   comprising two or more distinct areas of residential accommodation, each distinct area of residential accommodation adjoining at least one other in the area;

(b)   within which a person could reasonably be expected to live having regard to facilities and services for the purposes of health, education, recreation, personal banking and shopping, taking account of the distance of travel, by public and private transport, to and from facilities and services of the same type and similar standard; and

(c)   containing residential premises of a variety of types, and including such premises held on a variety of tenancies.".

Amendment

1.   Amended by Art 2(4) of SI 2008 No 587 as from 7.4.08.

Amendments to the Rent Officers (Scotland) Order relating the to local housing allowance coming into force on 7th April 2008

14.–(1)   In article 3(2)(a) (determinations) omit "except in relation to the area of a local authority which is a pathfinder authority".

(2)   In article 4B(6) (broad rental market area determinations and local housing allowance determinations) after "paragraph (2A)" insert ", (4) or (4A)".

Amendments to the Rent Officers (Scotland) Order relating to the local housing allowance coming into force on 7th April 2008 save for certain purposes

15.–(1)   This article shall not apply where–

(a)   a board and attendance determination, board and attendance redetermination, substitute board and attendance determination or substitute board and attendance redetermination is to be made and the application for the board and attendance determination or original board and attendance determination was made by virtue of regulation 13A(6) of the Housing Benefit Regulations 2006 or, as the case may be, regulation 13A(6) of the Housing Benefit (Persons who have attained the qualifying age for state pension credit) Regulations 2006 as in force immediately before 7th April 2008;

(b)   a local housing allowance determination is to be made and the application was made by virtue of regulation 13A(4) or (5) of the Housing Benefit Regulations 2006 or, as the case may be, regulation 13A(4) or (5) of the Housing Benefit (Persons who have attained the qualifying age for state pension credit) Regulations 2006 as in force immediately before 7th April 2008; or

(c)   an error in relation to a broad rental market area determination, local housing allowance determination, board and attendance determination or a board and attendance redetermination is to be corrected and the original determination was made in accordance with the Rent Officers (Scotland) Order as in force immediately before 7th April 2008.

(2)   For the purpose of sub-paragraph (1)(c) "original determination" means the broad rental market area determination, local housing allowance determination, board and attendance determination or board and attendance redetermination to which the correction of an error relates.

(3)   In article 2–

(a)   for the definition of "broad rental market area" substitute–
" "broad rental market area" has the meaning specified in paragraph 4 of Schedule 3B;'';
(b)   for the definition of "broad rental market area determination" substitute–
" "broad rental market area determination" means a determination made in accordance with article 4B(1A);'';
(c)   for the definition of "local housing allowance determination" substitute–
" "local housing allowance determination" means a determination made in accordance with article 4B(2A);'';
(d)   omit the definition of "pathfinder authority".
(e)   for the definition of "relevant date" substitute–
" "relevant date" means the date specified by a local authority in an application for a local housing allowance determination made in accordance with regulation 13D(7)(a) of the Housing Benefit Regulations or, as the case may be, regulation 13D(7)(a) of the Housing Benefit (State Pension Credit) Regulations;''.
(4)   In article 4B (broad rental market area determinations and local housing allowance determinations)–
(a)   omit paragraphs (1), (2) and (3);
(b)   for paragraph (4) substitute–

"(4)   Where a local authority makes an application in accordance with regulation 13D(7)(a) of the Housing Benefit Regulations or, as the case may be, regulation 13D(7)(a) of the Housing Benefit (State Pension Credit) Regulations, a rent officer shall determine, in accordance with the provisions of Schedule 3B and as soon as is reasonably practicable, the local housing allowance for that category of dwelling at the relevant date, for each broad rental market area falling within, in whole or in part, the area of the local authority that made the application, at the relevant date.
(4A)   Where a local authority makes an application in accordance with regulation 13D(8) of the Housing Benefit Regulations or, as the case may be, regulation 13D(8) of the Housing Benefit (State Pension Credit) Regulations, a rent officer shall determine in accordance with the provisions of Schedule 3B and as soon as is reasonably practicable, the local housing allowance for that category of dwelling for each broad rental market area falling within, in whole or in part, the areas of the local authority.''.

(c)   in paragraph (5)–
  (i)   in sub-paragraph (a) for "pathfinder authority" substitute "local authority";
  [¹ (ii) for sub-paragraphs (b) and (c) substitute–

"(b)   any local housing allowance determination made in accordance with paragraph (4) shall take effect for the month in which the relevant date falls, except that no such determination can have effect before 7th April 2008; and
(c)   any local housing allowance determination made in accordance with paragraph (4A) shall take effect for the month in which notice is given in accordance with sub-paragraph (a), except that no such determination can have effect before 7th April 2008.'']
  [¹ (iii)]
(5)   For article 4C(1) and (2) (board and attendance determinations and notifications) substitute–

"4C.–(1)   Where a relevant authority makes an application to a rent officer in accordance with regulation 13D(10) of the Housing Benefit Regulations or, as the case may be, regulation 13D(10) of the Housing Benefit (State Pension Credit) Regulations, a rent officer shall determine whether or not a substantial part of the rent under the tenancy at the relevant time is fairly attributable to board and attendance.

(2)   Where a rent officer determines that a substantial part of the rent under the tenancy at the relevant time is fairly attributable to board and attendance, he shall–

(a)   notify the relevant authority accordingly; and

(b)   treat the application as if it had been made in accordance with regulation 14(1) of the Housing Benefit Regulations or, as the case may be regulation 14(1) of the Housing Benefit (State Pension Credit) Regulations.''.

(6)   In articles 4D (board and attendance redeterminations) and 4E (substitute board and attendance determinations and substitute board and attendance redeterminations) for ''pathfinder authority'' in both places in which it occurs substitute ''local authority''.

(7)   In article 7A (errors)–

(a)   in paragraph (2) for ''pathfinder authority'' substitute ''local authority'';

(b)   omit paragraph (3).

(8)   Omit Schedule 3A.

Amendment

1.   Amended by Art 2(5) of SI 2008 No 587 as from 7.4.08.

Amendments to the Rent Officers (Scotland) Order relating to information sharing coming into force on 7th April 2008

16.–(1)   This article shall not apply where information is provided to the rent officer by virtue of regulation 14 or 114 of the Housing Benefit Regulations 2006 or, as the case may be, regulation 14 or 95 of the Housing Benefit (Persons who have attained the qualifying age for state pension credit) Regulations 2006 as in force immediately before 7th April 2008.

(2)   For Article 4C(4) (board and attendance determinations and notifications) substitute–

''(4)   Where an application for a board and attendance determination is treated as if it had been made in accordance with regulation 14(1) of the Housing Benefit Regulations or, as the case may be, regulation 14(1) of the Housing Benefit (State Pension Credit) Regulations, then, for the purposes of paragraph (a)(ii) of the definition of ''relevant period'' in article 2(1), it shall be treated as having been received on the day on which the further information provided in accordance with regulation 114A(4) of the Housing Benefit Regulations or regulation 95A(4) of the Housing Benefit (State Pension Credit) Regulations is received.''.

(3)   In article 5 (insufficient information) for '', he shall serve notice on the local authority requesting that information'' substitute ''where the information supplied under regulation 114A of the Housing Benefit Regulations or regulation 95A of the Housing Benefit (State Pension Credit) Regulations was incomplete or incorrect, he shall serve notice on the local authority requesting it to supply the further information required under regulation 114A or regulation 95A, as the case may be, or to confirm whether the information already supplied is correct and, if it is not, to supply the correct information''.

(4)   For paragraph 7(3) of Part 2 of Schedule 1 substitute–

''(3)   For the purposes of paragraphs 1, 2, 3, and 6 of Part 1 of this Schedule, the rent officer shall assume that the rent payable under the tenancy at the relevant time is–

(a)   where an amount is notified to the rent officer under regulation 114A(4)(b) of the Housing Benefit Regulations or, as the case may be, regulations 95A(4)(b) of the Housing Benefit (State Pension Credit) Regulations in respect of that tenancy, that notified amount less the total of any ineligible charges included in that amount; or

(b)   in any other case, the total amount stated under regulation 114A(3)(d) of the Housing Benefit Regulations or, as the case may be regulation 95A(3)(d) of the Housing Benefit (State Pension Credit) Regulations less the total of any ineligible charges included in that stated amount.''.

Amendments to the Rent Officers (Scotland) Order relating to ineligible service charges coming into force on 7th April 2008 save for certain purposes

17.–(1)   This article shall not apply where the rent officer is required to make a determination under paragraphs 1, 2, 3, or 6 of Part 1 of Schedule 1 to the Rent Officers (Scotland) Order by virtue of–

(a)   an application made under–

    (i)   regulation 14 of the Housing Benefit Regulations 2006 as in force before the substitution of regulation 14 by virtue of regulation 8 of the Housing Benefit (Local Housing Allowance and Information Sharing) Amendment Regulations 2007; or

    (ii)   regulation 14 of the Housing Benefit (Persons who have attained the qualifying age for state pension credit) Regulations 2006 as in force before the substitution of regulation 14 by virtue of regulation 8 of the Housing Benefit (State Pension Credit) (Local Housing Allowance and Information Sharing) Amendment Regulations 2007; or

(b)   an application for a redetermination, substitute determination or substitute redetermination relating to a determination to which sub-paragraph (a) applies made under regulation 15, 16 or 17 of the Regulations referred to in sub-paragraph (a)(i) or (ii).

(2)   For paragraph 7(1) (ineligible charges and support charges) of Part 2 of Schedule 1 substitute–

''(1)   ''ineligible charges'' means service charges which are ineligible to be met by housing benefit by virtue of regulation 12B(2) (rent) of and Schedule 1 (ineligible service charges) to the Housing Benefit Regulations or, as the case may be, regulation 12B(2) of and Schedule 1 to the Housing Benefit (State Pension Credit) Regulations except in the case of a tenancy where the rent includes payments for board and attendance, and the rent officer considers that a substantial part of the rent under the tenancy is fairly attributable to board and attendance, charges specified in paragraph 1(a)(i) of Schedule 1 to the Housing Benefit Regulations or, as the case may be, in paragraph 1(a)(i) of Schedule 1 to the Housing Benefit (State Pension Credit) Regulations (charges for meals).''.

Amendments to the Rent Officers (Scotland) Order relating to claim-related rent coming into force on 7th April 2008 save for certain purposes

18.–(1)   This article shall not apply where the rent officer has made a determination under paragraphs 1, 2, 3, 4 or 5 of Part 1 of Schedule 1 to the Rent Officers (Scotland) Order and that determination was made in relation to–

(a)   an application under–

    (i)   regulation 14 of the Housing Benefit Regulations 2006 as in force before the substitution of regulation 14 by virtue of regulation 8 of the Housing Benefit (Local Housing Allowance and Information Sharing) Amendment Regulations 2007; or

    (ii)   regulation 14 of the as in force before the substitution of regulation 14 by virtue of regulation 8 of the Housing Benefit (State Pension Credit) (Local Housing Allowance and Information Sharing) Amendment Regulations 2007; or

(b)   an application for a redetermination, substitute determination or substitute redetermination relating to a determination to which sub-paragraph (a) applies made under regulation 15, 16 or 17 of the Regulations referred to in sub-paragraph (a)(i) or (ii).

(2)   In paragraph 6 of Part 1 of Schedule 1–

(a)   for sub-paragraph (1) substitute–

"(1)   In this paragraph, and in paragraph 9, "claim-related rent" means the claim-related rent determined by the rent officer in accordance with paragraph (2A).";

(b)   after sub-paragraph (1) insert–

"(2A)   The rent officer shall determine that the claim-related rent is–

(a)   where he makes a determination under sub-paragraph (2) of paragraph 1, sub-paragraph (2) of paragraph 2 and sub-paragraph (3) of paragraph 3, the lowest of the three rents determined under those sub-paragraphs;

(b)   where he makes a determination under only two of the sub-paragraphs referred to in paragraph (a), the lower of the two rents determined under those sub-paragraphs;

(c)   where he makes a determination under only one of the sub-paragraphs referred to in paragraph (a), the rent determined under that sub-paragraph;

(d)   where he does not make a determination under any of the sub-paragraphs referred to in sub-paragraph (a), the rent payable under the tenancy of the dwelling at the relevant time.".

(c)   omit sub-paragraph (2); and

(d)   in sub-paragraph (3) omit "Where the dwelling is not in a hostel,".

(3)   in paragraph 9(1) of Part 3 of Schedule 1–

(a)   for sub-paragraph (1)(c) substitute–

"(c)   where that claim-related rent includes an amount which would be ineligible for housing benefit under paragraph 1(a)(i) of Schedule 1 to the Housing Benefit Regulations or, as the case may be, paragraph 1(a)(i) of Schedule 1 to the Housing Benefit (State Pension Credit) Regulations (charges for meals), the inclusion of an ineligible amount in respect of meals;";

(b)   after sub-paragraph (1)(d) insert–

"(da)   where any rent determined under paragraph 4 includes an amount which would be ineligible for housing benefit under the provisions referred to in sub-paragraph (c), the inclusion of an ineligible amount in respect of meals; and".

Amendments to the Rent Officers (Scotland) Order which remake amendments made by the Housing Benefit and Council Tax Benefit (Consequential Provisions) Regulations 2006

19.–(1) In article 2 (interpretation)–

(a)   for the definition of "hostel" substitute–

" "hostel" has the same meaning as in regulation 2(1) of the Housing Benefit Regulations or, as the case may be, regulation 2(1) of the Housing Benefit (State Pension Credit) Regulations;";

(b)   after that definition insert–

" "the Housing Benefit Regulations" means the Housing Benefit Regulations 2006;

"the Housing Benefit (State Pension Credit) Regulations" means the Housing Benefit (Persons who have attained the qualifying age for state pension credit) Regulations 2006;'';

(c)   for the definition of "rent" substitute–

" "rent" means any of the periodical payments referred to in regulation 12(1) of the Housing Benefit Regulations or, as the case may be, regulation 12(1) of the Housing Benefit (State Pension Credit) Regulations;'';

(d)   omit the definition of the "1987 Regulations".

(2)   In article 3A (transitional arrangements for determination of single room rents with effect from 2nd July 2001), for "regulation 12A of the 1987 Regulations" substitute "regulation 14 of the Housing Benefit Regulations or, as the case may be, regulation 14 of the Housing Benefit (State Pension Credit) Regulations".

(3)   In article 4A (substitute determinations and substitute redeterminations), for "regulation 12C of the 1987 Regulations" substitute "regulation 17 of the Housing Benefit Regulations or, as the case may be, regulation 17 of the Housing Benefit (State Pension Credit) Regulations".

(4)   In article 4E (substitute board and attendance determinations and substitute board and attendance redeterminations), wherever "regulation 12C of the 1987 Regulations" occurs, substitute "regulation 17 of the Housing Benefit Regulations or, as the case may be, regulation 17 of the Housing Benefit (State Pension Credit) Regulations".

(5)   In article 6 (exceptions)–

(a)   in paragraph (2) for "regulation 7(3) of the 1987 Regulations" substitute "regulation 9(4) of the Housing Benefit Regulations or, as the case may be, regulation 9(4) of the Housing Benefit (State Pension Credit) Regulations"; and

(b)   in paragraph (3), for "the 1987 Regulations", substitute "the Housing Benefit Regulations and the Housing Benefit (State Pension Credit) Regulations".

(6)   In article 7 (special cases), for "regulation 10(1) of the 1987 Regulations" substitute "regulation 12(1) of the Housing Benefit Regulations or, as the case may be, regulation 12(1) of the Housing Benefit (State Pension Credit) Regulations".

(7)   In Schedule 1–

(a)   in Part 1, in paragraph 4(4) (local reference rents), for the definition of "non-dependant" substitute–

" "non-dependant" means a non-dependant of the tenant within the meaning of regulation 3 of the Housing Benefit Regulations or, as the case may be, regulation 3 of the Housing Benefit (State Pension Credit) Regulations;'';

(b)   in Part 4, in paragraph 11(5)(b) (indicative rent levels), for "regulation 3 of the 1987 Regulations" substitute "regulation 3 of the Housing Benefit Regulations or, as the case may be, regulation 3 of the Housing Benefit (State Pension Credit) Regulations".

(8)   In Schedule 3A (categories of dwelling), in Part 1, in paragraph 1(2)(b), for "regulation 3 of the 1987 Regulations" substitute "regulation 3 of the Housing Benefit Regulations or, as the case may be, regulation 3 of the Housing Benefit (State Pension Credit) Regulations.".

SCHEDULE
LISTED AUTHORITIES

Blackpool
Brighton and Hove
Conwy
Coventry
East Riding of Yorkshire
Guildford
Leeds

Lewisham
North East Lincolnshire
Norwich
Pembrokeshire
St Helens
Salford
South Norfolk
Teignbridge
Wandsworth

The Welfare Reform Act 2007 (Commencement No.4, and Savings and Transitional Provisions) Order 2007

(SI 2007 No.2872)

Made   *30th September 2007*

The Secretary of State for Work and Pensions makes the following Order in exercise of the powers conferred by sections 68 and 70(2) of the Welfare Reform Act 2007

Citation and interpretation

1.–(1) This Order may be cited as the Welfare Reform Act 2007 (Commencement No.4, and Savings and Transitional Provisions) Order 2007.

(2) In this Order–

"the Act" means the Welfare Reform Act 2007;

"the Administration Act" means the Social Security Administration Act 1992;

"the Contributions and Benefits Act" means the Social Security Contributions and Benefits Act 1992;

"the Consequential Provisions Regulations" means the Housing Benefit and Council Tax Benefit (Consequential Provisions) Regulations 2006;

"the Housing Act" means the Housing Act 1996;

"the Housing Benefit (State Pension Credit) Regulations" means the Housing Benefit (Persons who have attained the qualifying age for state pension credit) Regulations 2006;

"the Regulations" means the Housing Benefit Regulations 2006.

Appointed days

2.–(1) 7th April 2008 is the appointed day for the coming into force of–

(a) *omitted*;

(b) *omitted*;

(c) Schedule 8 to the Act (repeals), in so far as it relates to the repeal of–

    (i) section 130(4) of the Contributions and Benefits Act (housing benefit);

    (ii) section 5(3) of the Administration Act (power to make regulations about information or evidence required by rent officer);

    (iii) section 122(3) of the Housing Act (functions of rent officers in connection with housing benefit and rent allowance subsidy);

    (iv) in section 122(5)(b) of the Housing Act, the words "or regulations"; and

    (v) paragraph 3(2) of Schedule 13 to the Housing Act (housing benefit and related matters: consequential amendments);

and section 67 of the Act (repeals) in so far as it relates to those repeals; and

(d) paragraph 12 of Schedule 5 to the Act (minor and consequential amendments relating to Part 2) so far as it relates to the amendment of section 122(5) of the Housing Act and section 40 of the Act in so far as it relates to that consequential amendment.

(2) *Omitted*

(3)   *Omitted*
(4)   This article is subject to the savings and transitional provisions in articles 3 to 5.

Transitional provisions and savings in relation to section 130(4) of the Contributions and Benefits Act and section 122(3) and (5) of the Housing Act

3.–(1)   Notwithstanding article 2 and subject to article 4–

(a)   section 130(4) of the Contributions and Benefits Act and section 122(3) and (5) of the Housing Act shall continue to have effect as they were in force immediately before 7th April 2008 so far as is required for the purpose of conferring power to amend or revoke the regulations referred to in paragraph (2), until 7th April 2009; and

(b)   any regulations made under any of the provisions referred to in sub-paragraph (a) shall continue to have effect in relation to the period ending on the date specified in paragraph (3), (4), (5) or (6) except for paragraphs 11 and 12 of Schedule 2 to the Consequential Provisions Regulations.

(2)   The regulations are–
(a)   the Regulations;
(b)   the Housing Benefit (State Pension Credit) Regulations; and
(c)   the Consequential Provisions Regulations.

(3)   In relation to a case in which reference was made to a maximum rent (standard local rate) in determining the eligible rent which applied immediately before 7th April 2008, the date is 7th April 2008.

(4)   In relation to a case where–
(a)   either–
   (i)   a claim for housing benefit is made, delivered or received on or after 7th April 2008 but the date the claim is made or is treated as being made is a date before 7th April 2008 by virtue of regulations 83, 83A, 84 or 85 of the Regulations or regulations 64, 64A, 65 or 66 of the Housing Benefit (State Pension Credit) Regulations; or
   (ii)   a claim was made or was treated as made before 7th April 2008 but the decision on the claim was not made by that date; and
(b)   reference to a maximum rent (standard local rate) would have been made in determining the eligible rent which applied immediately before 7th April 2008 had the decision on the claim been made before that date,
the date is 7th April 2008.

(5)   In relation to a non-local housing allowance case the date is the relevant date for that case.

(6)   In relation to a case where–
(a)   either–
   (i)   a claim for housing benefit is made, delivered or received on or after the 7th April 2008 but the date the claim is made or is treated as being made is a date before that date by virtue of regulations 83, 83A, 84 or 85 of the Regulations or regulations 64, 64A, 65 or 66 of the Housing Benefit (State Pension Credit) Regulations; or
   (ii)   a claim was made or was treated as made before 7th April 2008 but the decision on the claim was not made by that date; and
(b)   the case would have been a non-local housing allowance case had the decision on the claim been made before 7th April 2008,
the date is the relevant date for that case.

(7)   In this article–
"eligible rent" shall be construed, except in the definition of "the relevant date", in accordance with–

(a)   regulations 12 or 12A of the Regulations or the Housing Benefit (State Pension Credit) Regulations as in force immediately before the 7th April 2008; or

(b)   in a case to which paragraph 4 of Schedule 3 to the Consequential Provisions Regulations applies, regulations 12 and 13 of the Housing Benefit Regulations 2006 or the Housing Benefit (Persons who have attained the qualifying age for state pension credit) Regulations 2006 as set out in paragraph 5 of that Schedule as in force immediately before the 7th April 2008;

"maximum rent (standard local rate)" means a maximum rent (standard local rate) determined in accordance with regulation 13A of the Regulations or the Housing Benefit (State Pension Credit) Regulations as in force immediately before 7th April 2008;

"non-local housing allowance case" means a case where no reference was made to a maximum rent (standard local rate) in determining the amount of the eligible rent which applied immediately before 7th April 2008;

"the relevant date" means, in relation to a non-local housing allowance case–

(a)   the day on or after 7th April 2008 when any of the following sub-paragraphs first applies–

    (i)   a relevant authority is required to apply to a rent officer by virtue of regulation 14 of the Regulations or the Housing Benefit (State Pension Credit) Regulations as in force immediately before that day;

    (ii)   sub-paragraph (i) would apply but for the case falling within regulation 14(4)(a) of, or 14(4)(b) of and paragraph 2 of Schedule 2 to, the Regulations or the Housing Benefit (State Pension Credit) Regulations as in force immediately before that day;

    (iii)   a relevant authority is required to determine an eligible rent in accordance with regulation 12(3)(b) of the Regulations or the Housing Benefit (State Pension Credit) Regulations as in force immediately before that day;

    (iv)   a relevant authority is required to determine an eligible rent in accordance with regulation 12(3) of the Housing Benefit Regulations 2006 or the Housing Benefit (Persons who have attained the qualifying age for state pension credit) Regulations 2006 as set out in paragraph 5 of Schedule 3 to the Consequential Provisions Regulations as in force immediately before that day; or

(b)   6th April 2009 in any case where paragraph (a) does not apply before that date;

"relevant authority" means an authority administering housing benefit.

Transitional provisions and savings in relation to section 130(4) of the Contributions and Benefits Act and extended payments

4.–(1)   Notwithstanding article 2, regulations 72 and 73 of, and Schedules 7 and 8 to, the Regulations, and regulation 53 of, and Schedule 7 to, the Housing Benefit (State Pension Credit) Regulations shall continue to have effect in relation to the period ending on 6th October 2008 or such later date as is provided by paragraphs (2) or (3).

(2)   Where an extended payment award is determined before 6th October 2008 and the extended payment period will end after that date, the date shall be the end of that extended payment period.

(3)   Where a claim for an extended payment is made or treated as made on a date before 6th October 2008 but the extended payment award was not determined by that date, the date shall be the end of that extended payment period.

(4)   In this Article–

"extended payment" means a payment of housing benefit pursuant to–

(a)   regulation 72 of the Regulations (extended payments);

(b)   regulation 73 of the Regulations (extended payments (severe disablement allowance and incapacity benefit)); or

(c)   regulation 53 of the Housing Benefit (State Pension Credit) Regulations (extended payments severe disablement allowance and incapacity benefit),

where the date on which the claimant ceased to be entitled to housing benefit in accordance with regulation 77 or 78 of the Regulations or regulation 58 of the Housing Benefit (State Pension Credit) Regulations was before 6th October 2008; and

"extended payment period" means the period during which a person is entitled to housing benefit in accordance with regulation 72(6) or 73(6) of the Regulations or regulation 53(6) of the Housing Benefit (State Pension Credit) Regulations.

Transitional provisions and savings in relation to section 5(3) of the Administration Act

5.   Notwithstanding article 2, any regulations made under both section 5(1)(h) and 5(3) of the Administration Act shall continue to have effect for all purposes relating to the furnishing of information or evidence required by a rent officer under section 122 of the Housing Act 1996 in relation to a claim for or an award of housing benefit which relates to any period before 7th April 2008.

The Income-related Benefits (Subsidy to Authorities) Amendment Order 2008
(SI 2008 No.196)

Made	*28th January 2008*
Laid before Parliament	*6th February 2008*
Coming into force	*28th February 2008*

The Secretary of State for Work and Pensions makes the following Order in exercise of the powers conferred by sections 140B, 140C(1) and (4), 140F(2) and 189(1), (4), (5) and (7) of the Social Security Administration Act 1992.

In accordance with section 189(8) of that Act he has sought the consent of the Treasury. In accordance with section 176(1) of that Act he has consulted with organisations appearing to him to be representative of the authorities concerned.

Citation, commencement and interpretation

1.–(1)   This Order may be cited as the Income-related Benefits (Subsidy to Authorities) Amendment Order 2008 and shall come into force on 28th February 2008.

(2)   This Order shall have effect from 1st April 2006.

(3)   In this Order, "the principal Order" means the Income-related Benefits (Subsidy to Authorities) Order 1998.

Amendment of Part III of the principal Order

2.–(1)   Part III of the principal Order (calculation of subsidy) shall be amended in accordance with the following paragraphs.

(2)   In article 13 (relevant benefit) for "articles 18 and 21" substitute "article 18".

(3)   In article 18 (additions to subsidy)–

(a)   in paragraph (1) for "paragraphs (8), (9) and (10)" substitute "paragraphs (8) and (9)"; and

(b)   omit paragraphs (10) and (11).

(4)   Omit article 21 (additions to subsidy in respect of security against fraud and error).

Amendment of Schedule 1 to the principal Order

3.   For Schedule 1 to the principal Order (sums used in the calculation of subsidy) substitute the Schedule set out in the Schedule to this Order.

SCHEDULE
SCHEDULE TO BE SUBSTITUTED FOR SCHEDULE 1 TO THE PRINCIPAL
ORDER
"SCHEDULE 1
Articles 12(1)(b) and 17(1) and (8)

SUMS TO BE USED IN THE CALCUALTION OF SUBSIDY

RELEVANT YEAR 2006-2007

Local authority	Administration subsidy (£)	Non-HRA Rent Rebates Threshold (£)	Cap (£)
Adur	474,798	117.63	208.18
Allerdale	1,099,537	94.42	166.78
Alnwick	246,020	81.85	145.23
Amber Valley	1,440,889	94.89	167.80
Arun	1,119,127	123.12	217.48
Ashfield	884,292	89.10	157.56
Ashford	695,507	116.91	206.73
Aylesbury Vale	766,303	113.05	200.37
Babergh	521,463	108.20	191.31
Barking	2,938,869	223.51	355.32
Barnet	2,926,508	223.51	355.32
Barnsley	2,411,933	79.15	140.95
Barrow in Furness	819,973	98.76	174.63
Basildon	1,571,112	114.95	203.26
Basingstoke and Deane	967,560	117.07	206.80
Bassetlaw	859,394	99.33	175.65
Bath and NE Somerset	1,781,980	100.71	177.90
Bedford	1,299,391	93.24	165.29
Berwick upon Tweed	286,511	88.60	156.65
Bexley	1,745,432	223.51	355.32
Birmingham	13,749,369	95.47	169.29
Blaby	328,544	85.08	150.76
Blackburn with Darwen	1,792,140	108.94	192.43
Blackpool	2,874,572	90.73	164.69
Blyth Valley	1,040,064	75.02	133.00
Bolsover	702,096	77.36	139.66
Bolton	2,904,157	81.72	145.82
Boston	516,218	85.21	150.85
Bournemouth	1,723,844	102.41	192.46
Bracknell Forest	857,743	127.20	228.58
Bradford	5,045,062	86.20	161.99
Braintree	939,885	104.64	185.03
Breckland	1,013,228	107.01	189.70
Brent	4,013,244	223.51	375.78
Brentwood	351,021	118.62	209.76
Bridgnorth	794,402	96.45	171.82
Brighton and Hove	3,444,442	105.84	207.96

Local authority	Administration subsidy (£)	Non-HRA Rent Rebates Threshold (£)	Cap (£)
Bristol	4,136,619	93.23	184.32
Broadland	638,765	107.01	189.70
Bromley	2,341,620	223.51	355.32
Bromsgrove	439,854	99.45	183.77
Broxbourne	756,281	126.48	223.65
Broxtowe	919,429	81.36	145.09
Burnley	1,217,644	96.75	170.90
Bury	1,396,125	94.23	166.63
Calderdale	1,921,135	83.75	148.18
Cambridge	861,033	111.41	197.00
Camden	3,953,396	223.51	374.07
Cannock Chase	653,682	99.89	182.66
Canterbury	1,415,721	112.34	198.63
Caradon	657,976	94.69	167.43
Carlisle	1,005,039	92.14	162.92
Carrick	799,852	107.83	190.67
Castle Morpeth	284,358	88.89	157.18
Castle Point	552,665	122.30	216.25
Charnwood	759,681	85.61	151.40
Chelmsford	908,480	119.70	212.44
Cheltenham	947,870	121.58	214.97
Cherwell	1,057,051	117.87	208.71
Chester	956,974	89.00	157.20
Chester le Street	491,553	82.28	145.95
Chesterfield	1,170,589	81.69	144.45
Chichester	1,017,546	118.48	209.27
Chiltern	481,532	117.07	206.80
Chorley	726,694	83.82	149.03
Christchurch	373,358	100.71	189.07
City of London	130,041	223.51	355.32
Colchester	1,072,497	110.25	196.54
Congleton	587,614	94.42	166.78
Copeland	675,338	88.71	168.53
Corby	486,080	91.42	167.05
Cotswold	570,370	100.71	177.90
Coventry	4,898,482	81.21	159.38
Craven	398,717	100.12	177.04
Crawley	819,798	126.74	224.91
Crewe and Nantwich	855,346	99.90	184.00
Croydon	3,574,580	223.51	369.09
Dacorum	877,167	110.97	198.70
Darlington	970,273	86.96	153.76
Dartford	584,640	114.85	203.08
Daventry	400,887	91.32	161.47
Derby	2,398,576	90.19	159.50
Derbyshire Dales	392,332	91.57	162.27
Derwentside	1,393,775	89.71	158.63
Doncaster	2,802,700	82.28	147.95
Dover	1,064,534	116.94	206.78
Dudley	3,004,566	95.78	171.85
Durham City	701,891	84.71	151.79
Ealing	3,088,321	223.51	359.62
Easington	1,181,415	87.21	154.20
East Cambridgeshire	474,922	107.01	189.70
East Devon	844,757	91.41	171.78
East Dorset	526,189	100.71	189.07
East Hampshire	643,613	117.07	206.80
East Hertfordshire	707,366	127.90	226.97
East Lindsey	1,249,863	87.82	155.45
East Northamptonshire	542,911	98.10	173.67
East Riding of Yorkshire	2,283,011	87.66	159.14

Local authority	Administration subsidy (£)	Non-HRA Rent Rebates Threshold (£)	Cap (£)
East Staffordshire	866,008	85.52	151.06
Eastbourne	1,033,093	105.32	197.95
Eastleigh	691,194	117.07	206.80
Eden	313,746	94.42	166.78
Ellesmere Port and Neston	832,836	73.57	149.46
Elmbridge	717,819	133.53	235.85
Enfield	3,047,331	223.51	355.32
Epping Forest	788,860	113.34	200.97
Epsom and Ewell	342,404	117.07	206.80
Erewash	1,548,192	83.97	148.80
Exeter	927,681	88.54	166.40
Fareham	471,565	110.95	200.14
Fenland	793,582	100.56	177.83
Forest Heath	323,870	99.04	175.13
Forest of Dean	845,742	96.52	170.67
Fylde	569,810	82.51	145.73
Gateshead	3,857,741	87.29	154.36
Gedling	691,744	83.14	147.64
Gloucester	1,007,393	105.41	186.39
Gosport	612,066	108.81	192.41
Gravesham	796,103	111.04	196.36
Great Yarmouth	1,352,948	83.55	157.02
Greenwich	4,355,483	223.51	355.32
Guildford	760,113	134.07	237.08
Hackney	4,960,192	223.51	355.82
Halton	1,515,477	86.83	159.06
Hambleton	479,880	83.08	156.20
Hammersmith and Fulham	3,260,858	223.51	355.32
Harborough	308,453	103.09	182.28
Haringey	3,988,001	223.51	355.32
Harlow	792,890	109.42	193.47
Harrogate	786,423	106.57	188.46
Harrow	1,911,419	223.51	390.44
Hart	408,682	117.07	206.80
Hartlepool	1,440,144	90.16	159.43
Hastings	1,330,158	117.07	206.80
Havant	899,168	117.07	206.80
Havering	1,633,288	223.51	355.32
Herefordshire	1,570,533	89.64	158.52
Hertsmere	795,873	107.01	189.70
High Peak	629,871	96.94	171.41
Hillingdon	2,258,065	223.51	392.59
Hinckley and Bosworth	524,775	93.60	165.52
Horsham	785,688	138.41	244.47
Hounslow	2,000,420	223.51	355.32
Huntingdonshire	996,102	115.92	205.50
Hyndburn	1,062,417	93.45	165.07
Ipswich	2,228,598	99.72	176.32
Isle of Wight	1,464,942	117.07	206.80
Isles of Scilly	10,251	104.08	184.04
Islington	4,212,357	223.51	368.15
Kennet	480,154	100.71	177.90
Kensington and Chelsea	2,690,065	223.51	405.66
Kerrier	947,063	100.71	177.90
Kettering	528,662	90.21	160.83
Kings Lynn and West Norfolk	1,318,359	87.62	163.25
Kingston upon Hull	3,575,337	90.63	166.28
Kingston upon Thames	986,179	223.51	381.54
Kirklees	3,613,752	91.86	162.45
Knowsley	2,504,176	102.02	180.40
Lambeth	5,757,721	223.51	355.32

Local authority	Administration subsidy (£)	Non-HRA Rent Rebates Threshold (£)	Cap (£)
Lancaster	1,201,235	90.85	160.63
Leeds	7,523,174	83.41	157.14
Leicester	3,117,616	92.52	163.44
Lewes	653,550	113.59	202.24
Lewisham	5,020,695	223.51	355.32
Lichfield	691,937	92.82	163.96
Lincoln	1,031,860	87.56	154.83
Liverpool	8,226,762	93.12	164.69
Luton	1,583,092	114.55	202.56
Macclesfield	812,532	103.10	197.84
Maidstone	967,587	116.30	205.64
Maldon	569,990	107.01	189.70
Malvern Hills	541,882	92.82	163.96
Manchester	7,626,793	109.17	193.03
Mansfield	997,354	93.71	165.53
Medway	2,225,582	114.85	203.08
Melton	241,719	84.14	152.81
Mendip	827,882	99.23	175.29
Merton	1,485,044	223.51	355.32
Mid Bedfordshire	724,500	106.32	188.68
Mid Devon	466,519	94.27	166.71
Mid Suffolk	415,646	100.56	177.83
Mid Sussex	1,540,983	117.07	206.80
Middlesbrough	2,074,866	98.66	174.46
Milton Keynes	1,741,690	114.35	203.06
Mole Valley	415,629	113.82	201.26
New Forest	1,035,764	126.10	222.99
Newark and Sherwood	722,959	87.56	154.82
Newcastle under Lyme	940,581	78.70	154.48
Newcastle upon Tyne	4,028,659	85.76	151.64
Newham	4,356,826	223.51	355.32
North Cornwall	1,120,411	95.06	168.08
North Devon	984,885	109.95	194.21
North Dorset	527,537	100.71	177.90
North East Derby	637,896	79.87	144.84
North East Lincoln	1,953,804	85.81	157.04
North Hertfordshire	960,531	115.06	209.56
North Kesteven	975,551	87.53	154.76
North Lincolnshire	1,319,194	83.07	147.43
North Norfolk	920,331	92.45	163.68
North Shropshire	388,232	86.90	154.64
North Somerset	1,393,347	115.92	204.97
North Tyneside	2,467,630	80.25	142.68
North Warwickshire	524,655	91.58	164.56
North West Leicester	583,539	86.63	153.18
North Wiltshire	670,088	100.71	177.90
Northampton	2,274,666	113.90	201.39
Norwich	1,696,552	90.26	160.15
Nottingham	3,525,918	83.96	148.47
Nuneaton and Bedworth	986,330	88.81	158.64
Oadby and Wigston	301,809	85.39	151.83
Oldham	2,653,120	83.75	156.81
Oswestry	274,849	89.56	158.36
Oxford	1,228,342	122.71	219.06
Pendle	1,026,708	87.23	154.26
Penwith	791,935	94.58	177.56
Peterborough	1,692,593	114.08	201.73
Plymouth	2,645,527	92.07	162.79
Poole	1,509,757	104.52	196.22
Portsmouth	1,853,841	111.09	196.41
Preston	1,331,752	94.99	167.95

Local authority	Administration subsidy (£)	Non-HRA Rent Rebates Threshold (£)	Cap (£)
Purbeck	302,203	116.19	205.43
Reading	1,580,663	135.67	239.89
Redbridge	2,258,501	223.51	361.23
Redcar and Cleveland	1,644,402	94.34	166.81
Redditch	989,952	100.51	177.74
Reigate and Banstead	689,402	131.92	233.26
Restormel	924,965	108.16	191.05
Ribble Valley	248,379	81.96	144.92
Richmond upon Thames	1,229,465	223.51	355.32
Richmondshire	287,010	97.21	171.88
Rochdale	2,802,637	87.10	154.02
Rochford	440,315	103.82	183.56
Rossendale	824,167	88.21	155.81
Rother	893,660	117.07	206.80
Rotherham	2,424,981	73.64	135.70
Rugby	599,031	94.15	167.55
Runnymede	539,293	138.57	245.03
Rushcliffe	500,350	96.48	172.21
Rushmoor	576,257	117.07	206.80
Rutland	133,560	102.90	181.96
Ryedale	780,789	83.08	156.20
Salford	3,161,396	96.36	170.38
Salisbury	680,873	121.97	221.28
Sandwell	3,585,943	103.71	184.98
Scarborough	1,142,319	98.94	174.94
Sedgefield	1,133,757	85.26	151.18
Sedgemoor	760,878	106.66	188.60
Sefton	2,930,488	98.01	173.56
Selby	399,963	92.79	164.09
Sevenoaks	768,650	117.07	206.80
Sheffield	5,295,086	83.75	148.21
Shepway	1,095,594	107.33	189.78
Shrewsbury and Atcham	758,711	95.11	168.18
Slough	1,140,095	122.26	218.49
Solihull	1,508,168	99.57	176.07
South Bedfordshire	672,310	119.67	212.85
South Bucks	320,668	117.07	206.80
South Cambridgeshire	558,174	119.89	212.00
South Derbyshire	1,854,881	94.21	166.57
South Gloucestershire	2,985,626	102.68	185.15
South Hams	779,520	100.71	177.90
South Holland	546,377	89.35	158.00
South Kesteven	681,616	92.28	165.21
South Lakeland	590,862	106.13	193.24
South Norfolk	769,615	97.21	171.88
South Northants	271,923	106.08	189.05
South Oxfordshire	730,192	117.07	206.80
South Ribble	660,992	94.42	166.78
South Shropshire	313,314	92.82	163.96
South Somerset	1,144,862	100.71	177.90
South Staffordshire	719,028	92.82	163.96
South Tyneside	2,658,850	78.12	139.95
Southampton	2,809,487	98.03	192.58
Southend on Sea	1,981,774	106.44	188.21
Southwark	5,241,758	223.51	355.32
Spelthorne	614,324	117.07	206.80
St Albans	652,738	118.06	210.28
St Edmundsbury	703,740	106.04	188.19
St Helens	2,516,332	100.64	177.95
Stafford	755,358	92.82	163.96
Staffordshire Moorlands	542,469	90.27	159.45

Local authority	Administration subsidy (£)	Non-HRA Rent Rebates Threshold (£)	Cap (£)
Stevenage	829,341	116.92	206.74
Stockport	2,034,774	85.47	168.28
Stockton on Tees	1,674,181	89.51	159.71
Stoke on Trent	3,060,875	89.33	157.94
Stratford on Avon	702,802	92.82	163.96
Stroud	820,860	107.03	189.25
Suffolk Coastal	867,772	97.13	172.18
Sunderland	4,563,641	97.04	171.42
Surrey Heath	348,929	117.07	206.80
Sutton	1,360,895	223.51	355.32
Swale	1,079,274	117.07	206.80
Swindon	1,260,063	95.38	170.55
Tameside	2,812,575	99.17	175.17
Tamworth	537,370	97.36	173.35
Tandridge	353,577	116.83	208.32
Taunton Deane	833,976	94.94	167.87
Teesdale	661,567	87.05	153.92
Teignbridge	1,067,529	112.26	198.51
Telford and Wrekin	1,711,278	92.82	163.96
Tendring	1,393,077	98.00	184.18
Test Valley	626,155	113.80	201.00
Tewkesbury	496,873	92.87	164.04
Thanet	1,969,339	106.35	188.05
Three Rivers	518,110	120.56	214.80
Thurrock	1,270,977	113.49	200.65
Tonbridge and Malling	813,111	117.07	206.80
Torbay	1,596,604	103.66	183.10
Torridge	495,365	102.57	181.36
Tower Hamlets	4,842,057	223.51	383.37
Trafford	1,711,525	95.94	169.64
Tunbridge Wells	854,025	117.07	206.80
Tynedale	387,486	93.57	165.28
Uttlesford	448,463	117.32	207.52
Vale of White Horse	665,282	117.07	206.80
Vale Royal	1,068,795	94.94	167.88
Wakefield	2,805,923	83.83	160.09
Walsall	3,629,912	95.48	168.85
Waltham Forest	2,930,557	223.51	376.70
Wandsworth	3,573,769	223.51	399.94
Wansbeck	698,492	74.07	130.97
Warrington	1,658,787	95.33	168.56
Warwick	860,250	101.13	181.21
Watford	704,314	117.41	207.59
Waveney	1,847,298	92.30	163.21
Waverley	548,201	127.22	224.72
Wealden	708,880	99.81	196.09
Wear Valley	741,774	86.22	152.44
Wellingborough	584,038	93.99	166.18
Welwyn Hatfield	769,565	110.25	198.02
West Berkshire	1,015,643	117.07	206.80
West Devon	663,711	100.71	177.90
West Dorset	736,526	100.71	177.90
West Lancashire	1,030,779	89.13	158.95
West Lindsey	661,281	86.71	153.51
West Oxfordshire	589,677	112.22	198.24
West Somerset	382,671	100.71	177.90
West Wiltshire	820,783	115.04	203.20
Westminster	3,008,961	223.51	439.11
Weymouth and Portland	861,313	104.29	184.22
Wigan	2,718,992	89.41	158.10
Winchester	540,799	117.53	207.82

Local authority	Administration subsidy (£)	Non-HRA Rent Rebates Threshold (£)	Cap (£)
Windsor and Maidenhead	1,005,534	117.07	206.80
Wirral	3,742,354	104.37	184.54
Woking	473,428	151.40	267.72
Wokingham	464,192	118.29	215.05
Wolverhampton	3,031,617	86.71	163.97
Worcester	953,099	89.41	159.80
Worthing	844,284	117.07	206.80
Wychavon	737,784	116.85	206.38
Wycombe	938,090	134.52	237.86
Wyre	918,594	94.80	167.44
Wyre Forest	898,173	96.56	170.56
York	1,125,145	98.23	173.68
Blaenau Gwent	904,503	91.65	162.04
Bridgend	1,239,070	93.01	164.47
Caerphilly	1,789,294	98.31	173.83
Cardiff	3,108,342	103.42	183.90
Carmarthenshire	1,573,857	89.75	158.70
Ceredigion	963,020	98.37	173.94
Conwy	1,345,488	86.52	159.95
Denbighshire	1,084,489	84.15	150.24
Flintshire	1,145,293	89.49	158.44
Gwynedd	1,056,456	89.13	157.59
Isle of Anglesey	591,798	87.88	155.38
Merthyr Tydfil	682,118	89.17	157.68
Monmouthshire	599,896	103.25	183.82
Neath Port Talbot	1,551,379	90.39	159.84
Newport	1,255,513	97.89	175.29
Pembrokeshire	1,111,842	87.86	155.34
Powys	876,903	92.14	163.17
Rhondda Cynon Taff	3,148,023	87.70	155.07
Swansea	2,402,081	93.70	165.69
Torfaen	858,727	101.74	181.56
Vale of Glamorgan	923,348	105.59	186.72
Wrexham	1,607,662	83.92	148.86
Aberdeen	1,918,403	79.65	142.36
Aberdeenshire	1,320,877	75.09	136.60
Angus	998,993	70.27	129.79
Argyll and Bute	963,184	85.63	151.43
Clackmannanshire	555,646	75.46	142.58
Comhairle Nan Eilean Siar	218,386	88.56	158.58
Dumfries and Galloway	1,482,458	80.33	144.62
Dundee	2,305,511	87.31	155.96
East Ayrshire	1,452,625	76.85	136.01
East Dunbartonshire	587,678	82.14	148.94
East Lothian	9,285,742	73.87	130.62
East Renfrewshire	454,444	78.82	148.06
Edinburgh	5,359,612	100.39	177.51
Falkirk	1,426,305	80.03	150.62
Fife	3,686,528	76.13	139.65
Glasgow	13,609,900	101.72	179.87
Highland	1,978,789	93.42	165.17
Inverclyde	1,261,788	99.55	170.56
Midlothian	662,177	66.98	118.45
Moray	605,372	67.74	119.77
North Ayrshire	1,710,530	71.99	130.52
North Lanarkshire	3,986,080	83.85	150.12
Orkney	134,668	78.51	138.81
Perth and Kinross	1,014,107	71.28	126.04
Renfrewshire	2,223,173	87.13	162.71
Scottish Borders	1,191,667	75.83	134.07
Shetland	119,970	102.20	180.71

Local authority	Administration subsidy (£)	Non-HRA Rent Rebates Threshold (£)	Cap (£)
South Ayrshire	1,104,578	78.20	138.25
South Lanarkshire	3,207,252	85.82	151.75
Stirling	686,031	80.89	143.01
West Dunbartonshire	1,473,983	80.57	142.48
West Lothian	2,064,220	82.78	173.49"

The Social Security (Local Authority Investigations and Prosecutions) Regulations 2008
(SI 2008 No.463)

Made	*20th February 2008*
Laid before Parliament	*27th February 2008*
Coming into force	*7th April 2008*

The Secretary of State for Work and Pensions makes the following Regulations in exercise of the powers conferred by sections 110A(1B) and (1C)(a), 116A(2)(a), 189(4) and (5) and 191 of the Social Security Administration Act 1992.

In accordance with section 176(1) of that Act, he has consulted with the organisations appearing to him to be representative of the authorities concerned.

This instrument contains only regulations made by virtue of, or consequential upon, sections 46 and 47 of the Welfare Reform Act 2007 and is made before the end of the period of 6 months beginning with the coming into force of those sections.

Citation, commencement and interpretation
1.–(1)   These Regulations may be cited as the Social Security (Local Authority Investigations and Prosecutions) Regulations 2008.

(2)   These Regulations shall come into force on 7th April 2008.

(3)   In these Regulations, "the Act" means the Social Security Administration Act 1992.

Authorisations by local authorities
2.–(1)   An authority must not proceed for a purpose mentioned in section 109A(2)(a)(authorisations for investigators) of the Act unless the authorisation concerns one or more of the benefits listed in paragraph (5).

(2)   An authority must not proceed for a purpose mentioned in section 109A(2)(c) of the Act unless the authorisation concerns relevant social security legislation relating to one or more of the benefits listed in paragraph (5).

(3)   An authority must not proceed for a purpose mentioned in section 109A(2)(d) of the Act unless the authorisation concerns a benefit offence relating to one or more of the benefits listed in paragraph (5).

(4)   An authorisation made for a purpose mentioned in section 109A(2)(a), (c) or (d) of the Act has effect in relation to a particular case only if in relation to that case an authorised officer has commenced an investigation for a purpose mentioned in section 110A(2) of that Act.

(5)   The benefits are–
(a)   income support;
(b)   a jobseeker's allowance;
(c)   incapacity benefit;
(d)   state pension credit;
(e)   an employment and support allowance.

Exercise of powers by local authorities to prosecute benefit fraud
   3.   For the purposes of paragraph (2)(a) of section 116A of the Act (local authority powers to prosecute benefit fraud), the benefits prescribed are all relevant social security benefits except for–
  (a)   income support;
  (b)   a jobseeker's allowance;
  (c)   incapacity benefit;
  (d)   state pension credit;
  (e)   an employment and support allowance.

The Housing Benefit (Local Housing Allowance, Information Sharing and Miscellaneous) Amendment Regulations 2008
(SI 2008 No.586)

Made	*3rd March 2008*
Laid before Parliament	*10th March 2008*
Coming into force	*7th April 2008*

The Secretary of State makes the following Regulations in exercise of the powers conferred by sections 123(1)(d), 130A(2) to (4), 137(1) and 175(1) and (3), (4) and (6) of the Social Security Contributions and Benefits Act 1992, sections 5(2A) to (2C), 75(3)(b), 189(1) and (3) to (6) and 191 of the Social Security Administration Act 1992 and paragraph 4(4A) and (6) of Schedule 7 to the Child Support, Pensions and Social Security Act 2000.
This instrument contains only regulations made by virtue of, or consequential upon, sections 30 and 35 of the Welfare Reform Act 2007 and is made before the end of the period of six months beginning with the coming into force of those sections.

Citation and commencement
   1.   These Regulations may be cited as the Housing Benefit (Local Housing Allowance, Information Sharing and Miscellaneous) Amendment Regulations 2008 and shall come into force on 7th April 2008.

Amendment of the Housing Benefit Regulations 2006
   2.–(1)   The Housing Benefit Regulations 2006 shall be amended as follows.
  (2)   In regulation 101 (persons from whom recovery may be sought)–
  (a)   after paragraph (2) insert–

   ''(2A)   Where an overpayment is made in a case where a relevant authority has determined a maximum rent (LHA) in accordance with regulation 13D (determination of a maximum rent (LHA)), and the housing benefit payable exceeds the amount which the claimant is liable to pay his landlord by way of rent, the relevant authority must not recover from the landlord more than the landlord has received.''; and

  (b)   in paragraph (3) for ''paragraph (1)'' substitute ''paragraphs (1) and (2A)''.

Amendment of the Housing Benefit (Persons who have attained the qualifying age for state pension credit) Regulations 2006
   3.–(1)   The Housing Benefit (Persons who have attained the qualifying age for state pension credit) Regulations 2006 shall be amended as follows.
  (2)   In regulation 82 (persons from whom recovery may be sought)–
  (a)   after paragraph (2) insert–

"(2A)   Where an overpayment is made in a case where a relevant authority has determined a maximum rent (LHA) in accordance with regulation 13D (determination of a maximum rent (LHA)), and the housing benefit payable exceeds the amount which the claimant is liable to pay his landlord by way of rent, the relevant authority must not recover from the landlord more than the landlord has received."; and

(b)   in paragraph (3) for "paragraph (1)" substitute "paragraphs (1) and (2A)".

Amendment of the Housing Benefit (Local Housing Allowance and Information Sharing) Amendment Regulations 2007

4.–(1)   The Housing Benefit (Local Housing Allowance and Information Sharing) Amendment Regulations 2007 shall be amended as follows.

(2)   In regulation 3 (amendment of the Housing Benefit Regulations 2006 relating to information sharing)–

(a)   in paragraph (1)(b), in the inserted paragraph (4A) for "regulation 114A(6)" substitute "regulation 114A(5)"; and

(b)   in paragraph (2), in paragraph (1)(b) of the inserted regulation 114A for "regulation 12A" substitute "regulation 12D".

(3)   In regulation 4(1)(g) (amendments to regulation 2 of the Housing Benefit Regulations 2006) for the inserted definition of "registered housing association" substitute–

"registered housing association" means a housing association which–

(a)   is registered in a register maintained by the Corporation or the National Assembly for Wales under Chapter 1 of Part 1 of the Housing Act 1996; or

(b)   in Scotland, is registered by Scottish Ministers by virtue of section 57(3)(b) of the Housing (Scotland) Act 2001,

and "the Corporation" has the same meaning as in section 56 of the Housing Act 1996;".

(4)   In regulation 7 (insertion of regulations 13C, 13D and 13E into the Housing Benefit Regulations 2006)–

(a)   in the inserted regulation 13C(5) for "falling within any of paragraphs 4 to 10" substitute "mentioned in any of paragraphs 4 to 11"; and

(b)   in the inserted regulation 13D(2)(b) after "size criteria" insert "as set out in paragraph (3)".

(5)   In regulation 8 (substitution of regulation 14 of the Housing Benefit Regulations 2006), in the substituted paragraph 14–

(a)   in paragraph (1)(f)–

(i)   for "or (e)" substitute ", (e) or (h)"; and

(ii)   in paragraph (ii) omit "or"; and

(b)   after paragraph (1)(g) add–

"or

(h) has received notification that any of the circumstances in regulation 13C(5) apply."; and

(c)   in paragraph (8) omit the definition of "the Corporation".

(6)   In regulation 19 (amendment of Schedules 7 and 8 to the Housing Benefit Regulations 2006) for "paragraph 3(2)" substitute "paragraph 3(3)".

Amendment of the Housing Benefit (State Pension Credit) (Local Housing Allowance and Information Sharing) Amendment Regulations 2007

5.–(1)   The Housing Benefit (State Pension Credit) (Local Housing Allowance and Information Sharing) Amendment Regulations 2007 shall be amended as follows.

(2)   In regulation 3 (amendment of the Housing Benefit (Persons who have attained the qualifying age for state pension credit) Regulations 2006 relating to information sharing)–
   (a)   in paragraph (1)(b), in the inserted paragraph (4A) for "regulation 95A(6)" substitute "regulation 95A(5)"; and
   (b)   in paragraph (2), in paragraph (1)(b) of the inserted regulation 114A for "regulation 12A" substitute "regulation 12D".

(3)   In regulation 4(1)(f) (amendments to regulation 2 of the Housing Benefit (Persons who have attained the qualifying age for state pension credit) Regulations 2006) for the inserted definition of "registered housing association" substitute–

"registered housing association" means a housing association which–
   (a)   is registered in a register maintained by the Corporation or the National Assembly for Wales under Chapter 1 of Part 1 of the Housing Act 1996; or
   (b)   in Scotland, is registered by Scottish Ministers by virtue of section 57(3)(b) of the Housing (Scotland) Act 2001,
and "the Corporation" has the same meaning as in section 56 of the Housing Act 1996;".

(4)   In regulation 7 (insertion of regulations 13C, 13D and 13E into the Housing Benefit (Persons who have attained the qualifying age for state pension credit) Regulations 2006)–
   (a)   in the inserted regulation 13C(5)(c) in the inserted regulation 13C(5) for "falling within any of paragraphs 4 to 10" substitute "mentioned in any of paragraphs 4 to 11"; and
   (b)   in the inserted regulation 13D–
      (i)   in paragraph (2)(a) for paragraph (ii) substitute–

"(ii)   the claimant's partner is not a care leaver;"; and

      (ii)   in paragraph (2)(b) after "size criteria" insert "as set out in paragraph (3)".

(5)   In regulation 8 (substitution of regulation 14 of the Housing Benefit (Persons who have attained the qualifying age for state pension credit) Regulations 2006), in the substituted paragraph 14–
   (a)   in paragraph (1)(f)–
      (i)   for "or (e)" substitute ", (e) or (h)"; and
      (ii)   in paragraph (ii) omit "or"; and
   (b)   after paragraph (1)(g) add–

"or
(h) has received notification that any of the circumstances in regulation 13C(5) apply."; and

   (c)   in paragraph (8) omit the definition of "the Corporation".

(6)   In regulation 15 (amendment of regulations 59 and 60 of the Housing Benefit (Persons who have attained the qualifying age for state pension credit) Regulations 2006) for paragraph (1) substitute–

"(1)   In regulation 59 (date of which change of circumstances is to take effect)–
   (a)   in paragraph (1) for "regulations 60 and 61(6)" substitute "regulations 60 and 61(5)"; and
   (b)   in paragraph (3) for "regulation 61(6)" substitute "regulation 61(5)".".

Amendment of the Housing Benefit (Local Housing Allowance, Miscellaneous and Consequential) Amendment Regulations 2007

6.–(1) The Housing Benefit (Local Housing Allowance, Miscellaneous and Consequential) Amendment Regulations 2007 shall be amended as follows.

(2) In regulation 4 (amendment of the Housing Benefit and Council Tax Benefit (Decisions and Appeals) Regulations 2001)–

(a) in paragraph (3), in the inserted regulation 7A(2) for "regulation 13C" in both places in which it occurs substitute "regulation 13C(3)"; and

(b) in paragraph (4)(b), for the substituted paragraph (15) substitute–

"(15) A decision to which regulation 7A(2) applies shall take effect–

(a) on the day of decision, where the determination in accordance with regulation 13C(3) of the Housing Benefit Regulations or regulation 13C(3) of the Housing Benefit (State Pension Credit) Regulations (when maximum rent (LHA) is to be determined) was made on the first day of the benefit week; and

(b) in any other case, on the first day of the benefit week following the week in which the determination in accordance with regulation 13C(3) of the Housing Benefit Regulations or regulation 13C(3) of the Housing Benefit (State Pension Credit) Regulations (when maximum rent (LHA) is to be determined) was made.".

The Rent Officers (Housing Benefit Functions) Amendment Order 2008
(SI 2008 No.587)

Made	*28th February 2008*
Laid before Parliament	*10th March 2008*
Coming into force	*7th April 2008*

The Secretary of State for Work and Pensions makes the following Order in exercise of the powers conferred by section 122(1) and (6) of the Housing Act 1996.

Citation and commencement

1. This Order may be cited as The Rent Officers (Housing Benefit Functions) Amendment Order 2008 and shall come into force on 7th April 2008.

Amendment of the Rent Officers (Housing Benefit Functions) Amendment Order 2007

2.–(1) The Rent Officers (Housing Benefit Functions) Amendment Order 2007 shall be amended as follows.

(2) In article 4 (amendments to the Rent Officers Order relating to the local housing allowance coming into force on 20th March 2008), in paragraph (2)(d) in the inserted paragraph (3A) omit "working".

(3) In article 6 (amendments to the Rent Officers Order relating to the local housing allowance coming into force on 7th April 2008 save for certain purposes), in paragraph (4)(c)–

(a) for paragraph (ii) substitute–

"(ii) for sub-paragraphs (b) and (c) substitute–

"(b) any local housing allowance determination made in accordance with paragraph (4) shall take effect for the month in which the relevant date falls, except that no such determination can have effect before 7th April 2008; and

(c) any local housing allowance determination made in accordance with paragraph (4A) shall take effect for the month in which notice is given in accordance with sub-paragraph (a), except that no such determination can have effect before 7th April 2008.'' ''

(b) omit paragraph (iii).

(4) In article 13 (amendments to the Rent Officers (Scotland) Order relating to the local housing allowance coming into force on 20th March 2008) in paragraph (2)(d) in the inserted paragraph (3A) omit ''working''.

(5) In article 15 (amendments to the Rent Officers (Scotland) Order relating to the local housing allowance coming into force on 7th April 2008 save for certain purposes) in paragraph (4)(c)–

(a) for paragraph (ii) substitute–

''(ii) for sub-paragraphs (b) and (c) substitute–

''(b) any local housing allowance determination made in accordance with paragraph (4) shall take effect for the month in which the relevant date falls, except that no such determination can have effect before 7th April 2008; and

(c) any local housing allowance determination made in accordance with paragraph (4A) shall take effect for the month in which notice is given in accordance with sub-paragraph (a), except that no such determination can have effect before 7th April 2008.'' ''

(b) omit paragraph (iii).

The Discretionary Financial Assistance (Amendment) Regulations 2008
(SI 2008 No.637)

Made	*6th March 2008*
Laid before Parliament	*12th March 2008*
Coming into force	*7th April 2008*

The Secretary of State for Work and Pensions makes the following Regulations in exercise of the powers conferred by section 69(1), (2) and (7) of the Child Support, Pensions and Social Security Act 2000 and section 189(4) to (6) of the Social Security Administration Act 1992.

In accordance with section 176(1) of the Social Security Administration Act 1992, the Secretary of State has consulted with organisations appearing to be representative of the authorities concerned.

The Social Security Advisory Committee has agreed that the proposals in respect of these Regulations should not be referred to it.

Citation and commencement

1.–(1) These Regulations may be cited as the Discretionary Financial Assistance (Amendment) Regulations 2008 and shall come into force on 7th April 2008.

(2) In these Regulations, ''the Regulations'' means the Discretionary Financial Assistance Regulations 2001.

Amendment of regulation 3

2. Regulation 3 of the Regulations (circumstances in which discretionary housing payments may be made) shall be amended as follows–

(a) in paragraph (d) for ''regulation 10 of the Housing Benefit Regulations'' substitute ''regulation 12 of the Housing Benefit Regulations or regulation 12 of the Housing Benefit (State Pension Credit) Regulations'';

(b) in paragraph (f) for "regulation 8(2A) of the Housing Benefit Regulations" substitute "regulation 11(3) of the Housing Benefit Regulations or regulation 11(2) of the Housing Benefit (State Pension Credit) Regulations";

(c) in paragraph (g) for "section 46(11) substitute "section 46(5)"";

(d) after paragraph (m) add–

"(n) a reduction in the amount of benefit due to recovery of an overpayment under Part 13 of the Housing Benefit Regulations or Part 12 of the Housing Benefit (State Pension Credit) Regulations, or recovery of excess benefit under Part 11 of the Council Tax Benefit Regulations 2006 or Part 10 of the Council Tax Benefit (Persons who have attained the qualifying age for state pension credit) Regulations 2006.".

Substitution of regulation 5
3. For regulation 5 of the Regulations (period for, or in respect of which, discretionary housing payments may be made) substitute–

"Period for, or in respect of which, discretionary housing payments may be made
5.–(1) Subject to paragraph (2), a relevant authority may restrict the period for or in respect of which discretionary housing payments may be made to such period as it considers appropriate in the particular circumstances of a case.

(2) A relevant authority may make discretionary housing payments to a person only in respect of a period during which that person is or was entitled to housing benefit or council tax benefit or to both.".

The Income-related Benefits (Subsidy to Authorities) Amendment (No.2) Order 2008
(SI 2008 No.695)

Made	*10th March 2008*
Laid before Parliament	*11th March 2008*
Coming into force	*1st April 2008*

The Secretary of State for Work and Pensions makes the following Order in exercise of the powers conferred by sections 140B, 140F(2) and 189(1), (4), (5) and (7) of the Social Security Administration Act 1992
In accordance with section 189(8) of the Social Security Administration Act 1992 the Secretary of State has sought the consent of the Treasury.
In accordance with section 176(1) of that Act the Secretary of State has consulted with organisations appearing to him to be representative of the authorities concerned.

Citation, commencement, interpretation and extent
1.–(1) This Order may be cited as the Income-related Benefits (Subsidy to Authorities) Amendment (No. 2) Order 2008 and shall come into force 1st April 2008.

(2) In this Order, "the 1998 Order" means the Income-related Benefits (Subsidy to Authorities) Order 1998.

(3) This Order extends to England and Wales.

Amendment of the 1998 Order
2. Schedule 4A to the 1998 Order (Rent rebate limitation deductions (Housing Revenue Account dwellings)) is amended in accordance with the Schedule to this Order.

THE SCHEDULE
AMENDMENTS TO SCHEDULE 4A TO THE 1998 ORDER

1. In paragraph 2 of Schedule 4A to the 1998 Order (England – liability to deduction), for sub-paragraphs (6) and (7) substitute–

"(6)   The RPI figure for the period beginning with September 2001 and ending with September of the year prior to the relevant year is 1.2124.

(7)   The annual factor for 2008-09 is 0.3.".

2.   For Part 3 substitute–

"PART 3
WEEKLY RENT LIMITS FOR PURPOSES OF PART 2: AUTHORITIES IN ENGLAND
TABLE
RELEVANT YEAR 2008-09

Authority	Weekly rent limit	Authority	Weekly rent limit
Adur	£70.12	Crawley	£75.46
Alnwick	£54.63	Croydon	£85.22
Arun	£73.85	Dacorum	£78.06
Ashfield	£51.41	Darlington	£54.83
Ashford	£70.61	Dartford	£69.61
Babergh	£67.42	Daventry	£66.26
Barking and Dagenham	£68.78	Derby	£59.51
Barnet	£81.49	Doncaster	£54.48
Barnsley	£54.95	Dover	£68.10
Barrow in Furness	£59.74	Dudley	£62.81
Basildon	£65.50	Durham	£55.09
Bassetlaw	£55.79	Ealing	£83.58
Berwick upon Tweed	£52.50	Easington	£52.36
Birmingham	£62.91	East Devon	£61.09
Blaby	£57.70	East Riding	£58.64
Blackpool	£53.71	Eastbourne	£60.62
Blyth Valley	£50.18	Ellesmere Port and Neston	£58.96
Bolsover	£58.09	Enfield	£78.35
Bolton	£55.42	Epping Forest	£74.97
Bournemouth	£64.34	Exeter	£57.44
Bracknell Forest	£76.67	Fareham	£69.15
Braintree	£69.74	Fenland	£63.88
Brent	£87.94	Gateshead	£56.71
Brentwood	£73.57	Gedling	£56.13
Bridgnorth	£63.48	Gloucester	£62.24
Brighton and Hove	£66.72	Gosport	£66.31
Bristol	£61.43	Gravesham	£69.76
Broxtowe	£55.61	Great Yarmouth	£56.22
Bury	£59.44	Greenwich	£77.02
Cambridge	£74.73	Guildford	£82.92
Camden	£92.04	Hackney	£79.90
Cannock Chase	£59.09	Hammersmith and Fulham	£87.19
Canterbury	£69.39	Harborough	£62.68
Caradon	£56.46	Haringey	£82.71
Carrick	£54.78	Harlow	£69.25
Castle Morpeth	£54.36	Harrogate	£64.14
Castle Point	£71.94	Harrow	£89.25
Charnwood	£56.00	Havering	£71.94
Cheltenham	£64.44	High Peak	£57.23
Chesterfield	£58.50	Hillingdon	£88.24
Chester-le-Street	£54.45	Hinckley and Bosworth	£58.95
Chorley	£51.34	Hounslow	£79.89
City of London	£83.88	Ipswich	£61.54
City of York	£61.37	Islington	£88.42
Colchester	£67.04	Kensington and Chelsea	£98.23
Corby	£58.09	Kettering	£61.17

Authority	Weekly rent limit	Authority	Weekly rent limit
Kings Lynn and West Norfolk	£61.11	Sandwell	£64.20
Kingston upon Hull	£56.13	Sedgefield	£53.84
Kingston upon Thames	£88.75	Sedgemoor	£62.19
Kirklees	£55.45	Selby	£60.57
Lambeth	£82.12	Sheffield	£53.41
Lancaster	£58.96	Shepway	£65.14
Leeds	£55.64	Slough	£80.32
Leicester	£56.73	Solihull	£63.27
Lewes	£69.01	South Bedfordshire	£74.36
Lewisham	£73.33	South Cambridgeshire	£76.72
Lincoln	£51.34	South Derbyshire	£60.13
Liverpool	£60.40	South Holland	£56.78
Luton	£65.39	South Kesteven	£58.24
Manchester	£61.84	South Lakeland	£66.16
Mansfield	£55.84	South Northants	£73.02
Medway Towns	£63.61	South Tyneside	£55.03
Melton	£57.32	Southampton	£64.28
Merton	£81.58	Southend-on-Sea	£67.11
Mid Devon	£61.12	Southwark	£80.34
Mid Suffolk	£63.59	St Albans	£82.47
Milton Keynes	£63.46	Stevenage	£75.31
Mole Valley	£79.56	Stockport	£56.04
New Forest	£75.65	Stockton on Tees	£59.59
Newark and Sherwood	£58.83	Stoke-on-Trent	£55.82
Newcastle upon Tyne	£56.65	Stroud	£64.53
Newham	£72.75	Sutton	£78.58
North Cornwall	£57.83	Swindon	£61.86
North East Derbyshire	£58.42	Tamworth	£62.14
North Kesteven	£57.31	Tandridge	£73.60
North Shropshire	£60.65	Taunton Deane	£62.34
North Tyneside	£56.07	Tendring	£63.83
North Warwickshire	£64.24	Thanet	£64.63
North West Leicestershire	£58.95	Three Rivers	£77.88
Northampton	£62.26	Thurrock	£64.99
Norwich	£60.02	Torridge	£55.91
Nottingham	£56.43	Tower Hamlets	£80.85
Nuneaton and Bedworth	£58.64	Uttlesford	£75.94
Oadby and Wigston	£58.89	Waltham Forest	£75.38
Oldham	£55.12	Wandsworth	£94.15
Oswestry	£60.05	Wansbeck	£50.39
Oxford City	£77.85	Warrington	£58.65
Plymouth	£51.63	Warwick	£69.73
Poole	£65.86	Watford	£80.05
Portsmouth	£64.68	Waveney	£60.19
Reading	£82.49	Waverley	£82.29
Redbridge	£85.02	Wealden	£64.86
Redditch	£59.77	Wear Valley	£54.82
Ribble Valley	£56.15	Wellingborough	£60.12
Richmondshire	£60.13	Welwyn Hatfield	£77.82
Rochdale	£56.00	West Lancashire	£58.33
Rochford	£68.20	Westminster	£96.08
Rotherham	£54.87	Wigan	£57.65
Rugby	£64.11	Winchester	£76.24
Runnymede	£83.65	Woking	£82.10
Rutland	£63.52	Wokingham	£83.06
Salford	£59.74	Wolverhampton	£59.82
Salisbury	£71.30	Wycombe	£81.88''

3.   In paragraph 4 (Wales – liability to deduction) in the definition of Q (average weekly rent for a dwelling for the authority for the relevant year), after ''(see paragraph 2(3))'' add ''and (5)''.

4.   For Part 5 substitute–

"PART 5
AMOUNTS FOR PURPOSES OF PART 4, PARAGRAPH 4: AUTHORITIES IN WALES
TABLE
RELEVANT YEAR 2008-09

Authority	(1) Specified Amount "O"	(2) Guideline rent increase
Blaenau Gwent	50.17	2.04
Caerphilly	56.78	3.05
Cardiff	63.45	3.06
Carmarthenshire	53.63	3.26
Ceredigion	56.56	2.77
Conwy	56.53	3.87
Denbighshire	51.93	2.98
Flintshire	54.68	3.60
Gwynedd	54.34	3.46
Isle of Anglesey	52.22	2.74
Merthyr Tydfil	50.21	2.50
Monmouthshire	-	-
Neath Port Talbot	51.83	2.58
Newport	58.46	3.33
Pembrokeshire	53.69	3.39
Powys	56.47	2.77
Rhondda, Cynon, Taff	-	-
Swansea	54.74	3.05
Torfaen	59.24	3.17
Vale of Glamorgan	60.66	2.97
Wrexham	52.68	3.75"

The Social Security (Miscellaneous Amendments) Regulations 2008

(SI 2008 No.698)

Made	*11th March 2008*
Laid before Parliament	*17th March 2008*
Coming into force in accordance with regulation 1	

The Secretary of State for Work and Pensions makes the following Regulations in the exercise of the powers conferred by–

– sections 123(1)(a), (d) and (e), 124(1)(d) and (e), 135(1), 136(3), (5)(a) to (c), 137(1) and (2)(d) and 175(1) to (4) of the Social Security Contributions and Benefits Act 1992,
– sections 5(1)(p), 189(1) and (3) to (5) of the Social Security Administration Act 1992,
– sections 4(5), 12(2), (4)(a) and (b), 35(1) and 36(1), (2) and (4) and paragraphs 1(2)(a) and 3(b) of Schedule 1 to the Jobseekers Act 1995,
– sections 2(3)(b) and (6), 17(1) and 19(1) of the State Pension Credit Act 2002.
The Social Security Advisory Committee has agreed that the proposals in respect of these Regulations should not be referred to it.
In respect of the provisions in these Regulations relating to housing benefit and council tax benefit, the Secretary of State has consulted the organisations appearing to him to be representative of the authorities concerned.

Citation, commencement and interpretation

1.–(1) These Regulations may be cited as the Social Security (Miscellaneous Amendments) Regulations 2008 and, subject to paragraphs (2) and (3), shall come into force on 14th April 2008.

(2) This regulation and regulations 2(6), (14)(b) and (15)(c), 4(11), (16)(a) and (17)(b), 6(3), (5)(a) and (6)(b) and 7(3), (5)(a) and (6)(b), in so far as they relate to a

particular beneficiary, shall come into force on the first day of the first benefit week to commence for that beneficiary on or after 7th April 2008.

(3) *Omitted*

(4) In paragraph (2), "benefit week" has the same meaning as in–

(a) *Omitted*

(b) *Omitted*

(c) regulation 2(1) of the Housing Benefit Regulations 2006(10), so far as it relates to regulations 6(3), (5)(a) and (6)(b);

(d) regulation 2(1) of the Council Tax Benefit Regulations 2006(11), so far as it relates to regulations 7(3), (5)(a) and (6)(b).

Amendment of the Housing Benefit Regulations 2006

6.–(1) The Housing Benefit Regulations 2006 are amended as follows.

(2) In regulation 2(1) (interpretation) omit the definition of "Intensive Activity Period for 50 plus".

(3) In regulation 37 (earnings of self-employed earners) after paragraph (2) add–

"(3) This paragraph applies to–

(a) royalties;

(b) sums paid periodically for or in respect of any copyright;

(c) payments in respect of any book registered under the Public Lending Right Scheme 1982.

(4) Where the claimant's earnings consist of any items to which paragraph (3) applies, those earnings shall be taken into account over a period equal to such number of weeks as is equal to the number obtained (and any fraction shall be treated as a corresponding fraction of a week) by dividing the earnings by the amount of housing benefit which would be payable had the payment not been made plus an amount equal to the total of the sums which would fall to be disregarded from the payment under Schedule 4 (sums to be disregarded in the calculation of earnings) as appropriate in the claimant's case.".

(4) In–

(a) regulation 42(7)(c)(iii) and (10)(b)(i) (notional income); and

(b) regulation 49(4)(b)(iii) (notional capital),

omit "or in the Intensive Activity Period for 50 plus".

(5) In Schedule 5 (sums to be disregarded in the calculation of income other than earnings)–

(a) after paragraph 28 insert–

"**28A.**–(1) Subject to sub-paragraph (2), any payment (or part of a payment) made by a local authority in accordance with section 23C of the Children Act 1989(67) or section 29 of the Children (Scotland) Act 1995(68) (local authorities' duty to promote welfare of children and powers to grant financial assistance to persons in, or formerly in, their care) to a person ("A") which A passes on to the claimant.

(2) Sub-paragraph (1) applies only where A–

(a) was formerly in the claimant's care, and

(b) is aged 18 or over, and

(c) continues to live with the claimant.";

(b) omit paragraphs 37 and 48;

(c) in paragraph 41 omit ", as the case may be,".

(6) In Schedule 6 (capital to be disregarded)–

(a) for paragraph 9(1)(b) substitute–

"(b) an income-related benefit under Part 7 of the Act;";

(b) after paragraph 19 insert–

"**19A.**–(1) Subject to sub-paragraph (2), any payment (or part of a payment) made by a local authority in accordance with section 23C of the Children Act 1989 or section 29 of the Children (Scotland) Act 1995 (local authorities' duty to promote welfare of children and powers to grant financial assistance to persons in, or formerly in, their care) to a person ("A") which A passes on to the claimant.

(2) Sub-paragraph (1) applies only where A–
(a) was formerly in the claimant's care, and
(b) is aged 18 or over, and
(c) continues to live with the claimant.";

(c) omit paragraph 29.

Amendment of the Council Tax Benefit Regulations 2006

7.–(1) The Council Tax Benefit Regulations 2006(69) are amended as follows.

(2) In regulation 2(1) (interpretation) omit the definitions of "Intensive Activity Period for 50 plus" and "Supplementary Benefit".

(3) In regulation 27 (earnings of self-employed earners) after paragraph (2) add–

"(3) This paragraph applies to–
(a) royalties;
(b) sums paid periodically for or in respect of any copyright;
(c) payments in respect of any book registered under the Public Lending Right Scheme 1982.

(4) Where the claimant's earnings consist of any items to which paragraph (3) applies, those earnings shall be taken into account over a period equal to such number of weeks as is equal to the number obtained (and any fraction shall be treated as a corresponding fraction of a week) by dividing the earnings by the amount of council tax benefit which would be payable had the payment not been made plus an amount equal to the total of the sums which would fall to be disregarded from the payment under Schedule 3 (sums to be disregarded in the calculation of earnings) as appropriate in the claimant's case.".

(4) In–
(a) regulation 32(7)(c)(iii) and (10)(b)(i) (notional income); and
(b) regulation 39(4)(b)(iii) (notional capital),
omit "or in the Intensive Activity Period for 50 plus".

(5) In Schedule 4 (sums to be disregarded in the calculation of income other than earnings)–
(a) after paragraph 29 insert–

"**29A.**–(1) Subject to sub-paragraph (2), any payment (or part of a payment) made by a local authority in accordance with section 23C of the Children Act 1989(70) or section 29 of the Children (Scotland) Act 1995(71) (local authorities' duty to promote welfare of children and powers to grant financial assistance to persons in, or formerly in, their care) to a person ("A") which A passes on to the claimant.

(2) Sub-paragraph (1) applies only where A–
(a) was formerly in the claimant's care, and
(b) is aged 18 or over, and
(c) continues to live with the claimant.";

(b) omit paragraphs 39 and 49;
(c) in paragraph 43 omit ", or as the case may be,".
(6) In Schedule 5 (capital to be disregarded)–
(a) for paragraph 9(1)(b) substitute–

"(b) an income-related benefit under Part 7 of the Act;";

(b) after paragraph 19 insert–

"**19A.**–(1) Subject to sub-paragraph (2), any payment (or part of a payment) made by a local authority in accordance with section 23C of the Children Act 1989 or section 29 of the Children (Scotland) Act 1995 (local authorities' duty to promote welfare of children and powers to grant financial assistance to persons in, or formerly in, their care) to a person ("A") which A passes on to the claimant.

    (2) Sub-paragraph (1) applies only where A–

    (a) was formerly in the claimant's care, and

    (b) is aged 18 or over, and

    (c) continues to live with the claimant.";

    (c) omit paragraphs 30 and 44.

The Welfare Reform Act 2007 (Commencement No.6 and Consequential Provisions) Order 2008
(SI 2008 No.787)

Made   *17th March 2008*

The Secretary of State for Work and Pensions makes the following Order in exercise of the powers conferred by sections 68 and 70(2) of the Welfare Reform Act 2007.

Citation and interpretation
    1.–(1) This Order may be cited as the Welfare Reform Act 2007 (Commencement No. 6 and Consequential Provisions) Order 2008.

    (2) In this Order "the Act" means the Welfare Reform Act 2007.

Commencement
    2.–(1) *Omitted*

    (2) 1st April 2008 is the day appointed for the coming into force of section 49 of the Act (loss of benefit for commission of benefit offences).

    (3) *Omitted*

Consequential provisions
    3.–(1) The following amendments have effect as from 1st April 2008 (in consequence of the coming into force on that day of section 49 of the Act).

    (2) *Omitted*

    (3) In the Social Security (Loss of Benefit) Regulations 2001, in regulation 2(2) (disqualification period), for "3 years" substitute "5 years".

The Social Security (Miscellaneous Amendments) (No.2) Regulations 2008
(SI 2008 No.1042)

Made   *7th April 2008*

Laid before Parliament   *11th April 2008*

Coming into force in accordance with regulation 1

The Secretary of State for Work and Pensions makes the following Regulations in exercise of the powers conferred by sections 123(1)(d) and (e), 135(1), 136(3) to (5), 136A(3), 137(1) and (2)(f), (h) and (i), 175(1), (3) and (4) of the Social Security Contributions and Benefits Act 1992, sections 5(1)(h) and (j), 6(1)(h) and (k), 75(1), (2) and (4), 134, 189(1) and (3) to (6) and 191 of the Social Security Administration Act 1992 and sections 10(6), 34(1) and (2), 79(1), (3) and (4) and 84 of the Social Security Act 1998.

The Social Security Advisory Committee has agreed that the proposals in respect of these Regulations should not be referred to it.

In accordance with section 176(1) of the Social Security Administration Act 1992, the Secretary of State has consulted with organisations which appear to him to be representative of the authorities concerned.

Citation, commencement and interpretation

1.–(1) These Regulations may be cited as the Social Security (Miscellaneous Amendments) (No.2) Regulations 2008.

(2) Subject to paragraph (3), these Regulations shall come into force on 19th May 2008.

(3) Regulations 3(12)(h) and 5(12)(d) shall come into force on 27th October 2008.

(4) In these Regulations–

"the Decisions and Appeals Regulations" means the Social Security and Child Support (Decisions and Appeals) Regulations 1999;

"the Housing Benefit Regulations" means the Housing Benefit Regulations 2006;

"the Housing Benefit (State Pension Credit) Regulations" means the Housing Benefit (Persons who have attained the qualifying age for state pension credit) Regulations 2006;

"the Council Tax Benefit Regulations" means the Council Tax Benefit Regulations 2006;

"the Council Tax Benefit (State Pension Credit) Regulations" means the Council Tax Benefit (Persons who have attained the qualifying age for state pension credit) Regulations 2006; and

"the Housing Benefit and Council Tax Benefit (Consequential Provisions) Regulations" means the Housing Benefit and Council Tax Benefit (Consequential Provisions) Regulations 2006.

Amendments to the Decisions and Appeals Regulations

2. *Omitted*

Amendments to the Housing Benefit Regulations

3.–(1) The Housing Benefit Regulations shall be amended as follows.

(2) In regulation 2(1) (interpretation)–

(a) in the definition of "concessionary payment", omit "or the Child Benefit Act 1975"; and

(b) omit the definition of "person on state pension credit".

(3) In regulation 7(8)(c)(ii) (circumstances in which a person is or is not to be treated as occupying a dwelling as his home) –

(a) for "Part 3", substitute "Part 8"; and

(b) omit "9,10,11,".

(4) In regulation 28 (treatment of child care charges)–

(a) for paragraph (11)(a), substitute "the claimant's applicable amount includes a disability premium on account of the other member's incapacity;";

(b) in paragraph (11)(b), omit "or a higher pensioner premium"; and

(c) in paragraph (11)(g), for "Department of Health and Social Services for Northern Ireland", substitute "Department of Health, Social Services and Public Safety in Northern Ireland".

(5) In regulation 42 (notional income), omit paragraphs (3) to (5).

(6) In regulation 53(1) (students – interpretation)–

(a) in the definition of "grant" for "paragraph 54", substitute "paragraph 51";

(b) for the definition of "sandwich course" substitute–

"sandwich course" has the meaning prescribed in regulation 2(9) of the Education (Student Support) Regulations 2008, regulation 4(2) of the

Education (Student Loans) (Scotland) Regulations 2007 or regulation 2(8) of the Education (Student Support) Regulations (Northern Ireland) 2007, as the case may be;''; and

(c) in the definition of ''student loan'' for ''Students' Allowances (Scotland) Regulations 1999'', substitute ''Students' Allowances (Scotland) Regulations 2007''.

(7) In regulation 56 (full-time students to be treated as not liable to make payments in respect of a dwelling)–

(a) in sub-paragraph (2)(c) omit ''pensioner premium for persons under 75 or, as the case may be, persons 75 or over, higher pensioner premium,'';

(b) for sub-paragraph (2)(i)(ii), substitute–

''(ii) an allowance or, as the case may be, bursary has been granted which includes a sum under paragraph (1)(d) of regulation 4 of the Students' Allowances (Scotland) Regulations 2007 or, as the case may be, under paragraph (1)(d) of regulation 4 of the Education Authority Bursaries (Scotland) Regulations 2007, in respect of expenses incurred; or'';

(c) in sub-paragraph (2)(i)(iv) for ''regulation 13 of the Education (Student Support) Regulations 2005'', substitute ''regulation 37 of the Education (Student Support) Regulations 2008'', and for ''regulation 13 of the Education (Student Support) Regulations (Northern Ireland) 2000'', substitute ''regulation 39 of the Education (Student Support) Regulations (Northern Ireland) 2007'';

(d) in sub-paragraph (2)(i)(v) for ''Student Awards Regulations (Northern Ireland) 1999'', substitute ''Students Awards Regulations (Northern Ireland) 2003''; and

(e) in paragraph (4), omit ''refers''.

(8) In regulation 63(2) (other amounts to be disregarded) for ''Students' Allowance (Scotland) Regulations 1999'', substitute ''Students' Allowances (Scotland) Regulations 2007''.

(9) In regulation 88(3)(d) (duty to notify changes of circumstances), after ''income support'' where it first occurs, insert ''or income-based jobseeker's allowance''.

(10) In Schedule 3 (applicable amounts)–

(a) in paragraph 3(3)(a) and (b), for ''sub-paragraph (a) of this paragraph'', substitute ''sub-paragraph (1)(a)'';

(b) in paragraph 3(4)(e), omit "9, 10, 11 or'';

(c) for paragraph 6, substitute–

''**6.** The following premiums, namely–
(a) a severe disability premium to which paragraph 14 applies;
(b) an enhanced disability premium to which paragraph 15 applies;
(c) a disabled child premium to which paragraph 16 applies; and
(d) a carer premium to which paragraph 17 applies,
may be applicable in addition to any other premium which may apply under this Schedule.'';

(d) omit paragraphs 9, 10 and 11;

(e) in paragraph 13 omit from the heading ''Higher Pensioner and Disability Premiums'' and substitute ''Disability Premium'';

(f) in paragraph 13(3), omit ''the higher pensioner premium or'';

(g) omit paragraph 13(4);

(h) in paragraph 13(8) for ''within the meaning of paragraph 11(5)'', substitute ''(a person to whom regulation 13A(1) of the Social Security (Incapacity for Work) (General) Regulations 1995 applies, and who again becomes incapable of work for the purposes of Part 12A of the Act)''; and

(i)   in paragraph 20, omit sub-paragraphs (2), (3) and (4).

(11)   In Schedule 4 (sums to be disregarded in the calculation of earnings)–

(a)   for paragraph 3(3)(a), substitute ''the claimant is a member of a couple and his applicable amount includes an amount by way of the disability premium under Schedule 3; and'';

(b)   omit paragraph 3(4) and (5);

(c)   in paragraph 9–

    (i)   for ''one of more employments'', substitute ''one or more employments''; and

    (ii)   for ''paragraph 6'', substitute ''paragraph 8'';

(d)   in paragraph 17(2)(b)(iv)(aa) omit ''a higher pensioner premium or'', ''11 or'' and ''respectively'';

(e)   in paragraph 17(2)(b)(iv)(bb) omit ''higher pensioner premium or''; and

(f)   in paragraph 17(3)(b) for ''regulation 28(1)(c)'', substitute ''regulation 27(1)(c)''.

(12)   In Schedule 5 (sums to be disregarded in the calculation of income other than earnings)–

(a)   for paragraph 15(b), substitute ''a war widow's pension or any corresponding pension payable to a widower or surviving civil partner;'';

(b)   omit paragraph 18;

(c)   in paragraph 25(1)(a) before ''with a scheme'', insert ''in accordance'';

(d)   in paragraph 44(1)(a) for ''or 12'' substitute ''or 11'' and after ''Regulations'', insert ''2003'';

(e)   in paragraph 44(1)(b) for ''3, 5 and 8'' substitute "5, 6 and 10'' and for ''National Health Service (Travelling Expenses and Remission of Charges) Regulations 1988'' substitute ''National Health Service (Travelling Expenses and Remission of Charges) (Wales) Regulations 2007'';

(f)   in paragraph 44(1)(c) for ''or 8'' substitute ''or 11'' and after ''(Scotland)'' insert ''(No. 2)'';

(g)   in paragraph 45 omit ''8,''; and

(h)   *Omitted*

(13)   In Schedule 6 (capital to be disregarded)–

(a)   in paragraph 16 for ''paragraph 11 of Schedule 4'', substitute ''paragraph 13 of Schedule 4'';

(b)   in paragraph 40(1)(a) for ''or 12'' substitute ''or 11'' and after ''Regulations'', insert ''2003'';

(c)   in paragraph 40(1)(b) for ''3, 5 or 8'' substitute "5, 6 or 10'' and for ''National Health Service (Travelling Expenses and Remission of Charges) Regulations 1988'' substitute ''National Health Service (Travelling Expenses and Remission of Charges) (Wales) Regulations 2007'';

(d)   in paragraph 40 (1)(c) for ''or 8'' substitute ''or 11'', and after ''(Scotland)'' insert ''(No. 2)'';

(e)   in paragraph 41 omit ''8,'';

(f)   in paragraph 43 after ''Disabled Persons (Employment) Act 1944'' omit ''or''; and

(g)   in paragraph 55(1)(b) for ''time'', substitute ''date''.

Amendments to the Housing Benefit (State Pension Credit) Regulations

4.–(1)   The Housing Benefit (State Pension Credit) Regulations shall be amended as follows.

(2)   In regulation 2 (interpretation)–

(a)   in the definition of ''concessionary payment'', for ''or the Social Security Act 1975'' substitute ''are charged''.

(b)   omit the definition of ''the former regulations'';

(c)   for the definition of "sandwich course", substitute—

"sandwich course" has the meaning prescribed in regulation 2(9) of the Education (Student Support) Regulations 2008, regulation 4(2) of the Education (Student Loans) (Scotland) Regulations 2007 or regulation 2(8) of the Education (Student Support) Regulations (Northern Ireland) 2007, as the case may be;".

(3)   In regulation 7(8)(c)(ii) (circumstances in which a person is or is not to be treated as occupying a dwelling as his home) for "Part 3", substitute "Part 8".

(4)   In regulation 22(5) (applicable amounts) for "Schedule 2A", substitute "Schedule 3".

(5)   In regulation 31(11)(f) (treatment of child care charges), for "sub-paragraph (c) or (d)", substitute "sub-paragraph (d) or (e)".

(6)   In regulation 67(4)(a)(ii) (evidence and information) for "London Bombings Charitable Relief Fund", substitute "London Bombings Relief Charitable Fund".

(7)   In regulation 83(4) (method of recovery) for "paragraphs 3 to 8", substitute "paragraphs 2 to 5 and 7".

(8)   In Schedule 5 (amounts to be disregarded in the calculation of income other than earnings)—

(a)   for paragraph 1(b), substitute "a war widow's pension or any corresponding pension payable to a widower or surviving civil partner;";

(b)   in paragraph 12(4) for "ordinary clothing and footwear", substitute "ordinary clothing or footwear".

(9)   In paragraph 22(2)(c) of Schedule 6 (capital to be disregarded generally) for "Schedule 5", substitute "Schedule 6".

(10)   In paragraph 9(1)(e) of Schedule 8 (matters to be included in decision notice) for "rate rebate", substitute "rent rebate".

Amendments to the Council Tax Benefit Regulations

5.–(1)   The Council Tax Benefit Regulations shall be amended as follows.

(2)   In regulation 2(1) (interpretation) omit the definition of "person on state pension credit".

(3)   In regulation 18 (treatment of child care charges)—

(a)   for paragraph (11)(a) substitute "the claimant's applicable amount includes a disability premium on account of the other member's incapacity";

(b)   in paragraph (11)(b), omit "or a higher pensioner premium"; and

(c)   in paragraph (11)(g), for "Department of Health and Social Services for Northern Ireland", substitute "Department of Health, Social Services and Public Safety in Northern Ireland".

(4)   In regulation 32(26) (notional income), omit paragraphs (3) to (5).

(5)   In regulation 43 (students – interpretation)—

(a)   for the definition of "sandwich course" substitute—

"sandwich course" has the meaning prescribed in regulation 2(9) of the Education (Student Support) Regulations 2008, regulation 4(2) of the Education (Student Loans) (Scotland) Regulations 2007(27) or regulation 2(8) of the Education (Student Support) Regulations (Northern Ireland) 2007(28), as the case may be;"; and

(b)   in the definition of "student loan" for "Students' Allowances (Scotland) Regulations 1999", substitute "Students' Allowances (Scotland) Regulations 2007(29)".

(6)   In regulation 50(2) (other amounts to be disregarded) for "Students' Allowance (Scotland) Regulations 1999", substitute "Students' Allowances (Scotland) Regulations 2007".

(7)   In regulation 70 (date of claim where claim sent or delivered to a gateway office) in sub-paragraph (1)(a)(ii) and sub-paragraph (1)(c)(iii) for "4 weeks", substitute "one month".

(8)   In regulation 71(1) (date of claim where claim sent or delivered to an office of a designated authority) for "4 weeks", substitute "one month".

(9)   In regulation 72(1) (evidence and information) for "4 weeks", substitute "one month".

(10)   In Schedule 1 (applicable amounts)–

(a)   in paragraph 3(4)(e), omit "9, 10, 11 or";

(b)   for paragraph 6, substitute–

"**6.**   The following premiums, namely–
(a)   a severe disability premium to which paragraph 14 applies;
(b)   an enhanced disability premium to which paragraph 15 applies;
(c)   a disabled child premium to which paragraph 16 applies; and
(d)   a carer premium to which paragraph 17 applies,
may be applicable in addition to any other premium which may apply under this Schedule.";

(c)   omit paragraphs 9, 10 and 11;

(d)   in paragraph 13 omit from the heading "Higher Pensioner and Disability Premiums" and substitute "Disability Premium";

(e)   in paragraph 13(3), omit "the higher pensioner premium or";

(f)   omit paragraph 13(4);

(g)   in paragraph 13(9) for "within the meaning of paragraph 11(5)", substitute "(a person to whom regulation 13A(1) of the Social Security (Incapacity for Work) (General) Regulations 1995 applies, and who again becomes incapable of work for the purposes of Part 12A of the Act)"; and

(h)   in paragraph 20–
(i)   omit sub-paragraphs (2), (3) and (4); and
(ii)   in sub-paragraph (5)(a), omit "or (b)".

(11)   In Schedule 3 (sums to be disregarded in the calculation of earnings)–

(a)   for paragraph 3(3)(a) substitute "the claimant is a member of a couple and his applicable amount includes an amount by way of the disability premium under Schedule 1; and";

(b)   omit paragraph 3(4) and (5);

(c)   in paragraph 9 for "one of more employments", substitute "one or more employments";

(d)   in paragraph 16(2)(b)(iv)(aa) omit "a higher pensioner premium or", "11 or" and "respectively";

(e)   in paragraph 16(2)(b)(iv)(bb) omit "higher pensioner premium or".

(12)   In Schedule 4 (sums to be disregarded in the calculation of income other than earnings)–

(a)   for paragraph 16(b), substitute "a war widow's pension or any corresponding pension payable to a widower or surviving civil partner;";

(b)   in paragraph 45–
(i)   for sub-paragraph (1)(a), substitute–

"(a) as respects England, under regulation 5, 6 or 11 of the National Health Service (Travel Expenses and Remission of Charges) Regulations 2003 (travelling expenses and health service supplies);";

(ii)   for sub-paragraph (1)(b), substitute–

"(b)   as respects Wales, under regulation 5, 6 or 10 of the National Health Service (Travelling Expenses and Remission of Charges) (Wales) Regulations 2007 (travelling expenses and health service supplies);"; and

(iii)   after sub-paragraph (1)(b), insert–

"(c)   as respects Scotland, under regulation 3, 5 or 11 of the National Health Service (Travelling Expenses and Remission of Charges) (Scotland) (No.2) Regulations 2003 (travelling expenses and health service supplies);";

(c)   in paragraph 46 omit "8,";
(d)   *Omitted*
(e)   omit paragraph 64.
(13)   In Schedule 5 (capital to be disregarded)–
(a)   in paragraph 40(1)(a) for "or 12" substitute "or 11" and after "Regulations", insert "2003";
(b)   in paragraph 40(1)(b) for "3, 5 or 8" substitute "5, 6 or 10" and for "National Health Service (Travelling Expenses and Remission of Charges) Regulations 1988" substitute "National Health Service (Travelling Expenses and Remission of Charges) (Wales) Regulations 2007";
(c)   in paragraph 40 (1)(c) for "or 8" substitute "or 11", and after "(Scotland)" insert "(No. 2)";
(d)   in paragraph 41 omit "8,";
(e)   in paragraph 43 after "Disabled Persons (Employment) Act 1944" omit "or"; and
(f)   in paragraph 57(1)(b) for "time", substitute "date".

Amendments to the Council Tax Benefit (State Pension Credit) Regulations
6.–(1)   The Council Tax Benefit (State Pension Credit) Regulations shall be amended as follows.
(2)   In regulation 2 (interpretation) for the definition of "sandwich course", substitute–

"sandwich course" has the meaning prescribed in regulation 2(9) of the Education (Student Support) Regulations 2008, regulation 4(2) of the Education (Student Loans)(Scotland) Regulations 2007 or regulation 2(8) of the Education (Student Support) Regulations (Northern Ireland) 2007, as the case may be;".

(3)   In regulation 21(11)(f) (treatment of child care charges) for "sub-paragraph (c) or (d)", substitute "sub-paragraph (d) or (e)".
(4)   After regulation 53(12) (time and manner in which claims are to be made) insert–

"(12A)   Paragraph (12) applies in the case of a person who has attained, or whose partner has attained, the age of 59 years and 35 weeks.".

(5)   In Schedule 3 (amounts to be disregarded in the calculation of income other than earnings)–
(a)   for paragraph 1(b), substitute "a war widow's pension or any corresponding pension payable to a widower or surviving civil partner;";
(b)   in paragraph 12(2)(a) and (4) for "ordinary clothing and footwear", substitute "ordinary clothing or footwear"; and
(c)   after paragraph 24, insert–

"**25.**   Where the claimant, or the person who was the partner of the claimant on 31st March 2003, was entitled on that date to income support or an income-based jobseeker's allowance but ceased to be so entitled on or before 5th April 2003 by virtue only of regulation 13 of the Housing Benefit (General) Amendment (No 3) Regulations 1999 as in force at that date, the whole of his income.".

(6)   After paragraph 26 of Schedule 4 (capital to be disregarded), insert–

"**26A.**–(1)   Subject to sub-paragraph (2), where a claimant satisfies the conditions in section 131(3) and (6) of the Act (entitlement to alternative maximum council tax benefit), the whole of his capital.

(2)   Sub-paragraph (1) does not apply, where in addition to satisfying the conditions in section 131(3) and (6) of the Act the claimant also satisfies the conditions in section 131(4) and (5) of the Act (entitlement to the maximum council tax benefit).".

Amendments to the Housing Benefit and Council Tax Benefit (Consequential Provisions) Regulations

7.–(1)   The Housing Benefit and Council Tax Benefit (Consequential Provisions) Regulations shall be amended as follows.

(2)   In paragraph 3(1) of Schedule 3 (transitional and savings provisions) for "paragraph 13(1)(a)(ii) of Schedule 2 to the 1987 Regulations", substitute "paragraph 12(1)(a)(ii) of Schedule 2 to the 1987 Regulations".

(3)   In paragraph 5(2) of Schedule 3 (transitional and savings provisions), in the paragraph inserted as paragraph (4)(b) of regulation 13 of both of the Housing Benefit Regulations and the Housing Benefit (State Pension Credit) Regulations, for that paragraph (4)(b) substitute–

"(b)   is incapable of work for the purpose of Part 12A of the Act; or "

(4)   In paragraph 9(3)(a)(ii) of Schedule 3 (transitional and savings provisions – care homes), in the paragraph inserted as paragraph (1A)(b) of regulation 9 of the Housing Benefit (State Pension Credit) Regulations for "regulation 83(4)", substitute "regulation 64(5)".

(5)   In paragraph 3(4) of Schedule 4 (transitory modifications), in the paragraph inserted as paragraph 37 of Schedule 4 to the Council Tax Benefit Regulations for "regulation 11A", substitute "regulation 10A".